Water Frontier

WORLD SOCIAL CHANGE

Series Editor: Mark Selden

First Globalization: The Eurasian Exchange, 1500–1800
Geoffrey C. Gunn

Istanbul: Between the Global and the Local
Edited by Caglar Keyder

Origins of the Modern World: A Global and Ecological Narrative
Robert B. Marks

Leaving China: Media, Mobility, and Transnational Imagination
Wanning Sun

Through the Prism of Slavery: Labor, Capital, and World Economy
Dale W. Tomich

Water Frontier

Commerce and the Chinese in the Lower Mekong Region, 1750–1880

EDITED BY NOLA COOKE AND LI TANA

SINGAPORE

and

ROWMAN & LITTLEFIELD PUBLISHERS, INC.
Lanham • Boulder • New York • Toronto • Oxford

ROWMAN & LITTLEFIELD PUBLISHERS, INC.

Published in the United States of America
by Rowman & Littlefield Publishers, Inc.
A wholly owned subsidiary of The Rowman & Littlefield Publishing Group, Inc.
4501 Forbes Boulevard, Suite 200, Lanham, MD 20706
www.rowmanlittlefield.com

P.O. Box 317, Oxford OX2 9RU, UK

First published in Singapore in 2004 by
Singapore University Press
National University of Singapore Publishing
Yusof Ishak House
31 Lower Kent Ridge Road
Singapore 119078
www.nus.edu.sg/npu
ISBN 9971-69-310-0 (cloth)
ISBN 9971-69-311-9 (pbk)
For distribution in Asia, Australia, and New Zealand

British Library Cataloguing in Publication Information Available

Library of Congress Cataloging-in-Publication Data

Water frontier : commerce and the Chinese in the Lower Mekong Region, 1750-1880 /
    edited by Nola Cooke and Li Tana.
        p.   cm. — (World social change)
    Includes bibliographical references and index.
    ISBN 0-7425-3082-5 (cloth : alk. paper) — ISBN 0-7425-3083-3 (pbk. : alk. paper)
    1. Indochina—Commerce—History—18th century. 2. Indochina—Commerce—
History—19th century. 3. Mekong River Region—Commerce—History—18th century.
4. Mekong River Region—Commerce—History—19th century. 5. China, Southeast—
Commerce—History—18th century. 6. China, Southeast—Commerce—History—19th
century. 7. Chinese—Indochina—History—18th century. 8. Chinese—Indochina—
History—19th century. I. Cooke, Nola. II. Li, Tana. III. Series.
    HF3790.8.Z5W38   2004
    381'.089'9510597—dc22
                                                                    2004008028
Printed in the United States of America

♾™ The paper used in this publication meets the minimum requirements of American
National Standard for Information Sciences—Permanence of Paper for Printed Library
Materials, ANSI/NISO Z39.48-1992.

This book is dedicated to Professor Chen Chingho,
the pioneering scholar of this field

Contents

List of Figures and Tables   ix

Preface   xi

1.   The Water Frontier: An Introduction   1
   Li Tana

**Part I: Permeable Frontiers: Chinese Trade and
Traders in the Region**

2.   Chinese Trade and Southeast Asian Economic Expansion
   in the Later Eighteenth and Early Nineteenth Centuries:
   An Overview   21
   Anthony Reid

3.   Eighteenth-Century Chinese Pioneers on the
   Water Frontier of Indochina   35
   Yumio Sakurai

4.   The Junk Trade between South China and
   Nguyen Vietnam in the Late Eighteenth and Early
   Nineteenth Centuries   53
   James Kong Chin

Part II: Commercial Eddies and Flows

5. The Late-Eighteenth- and Early-Nineteenth-Century
   Mekong Delta in the Regional Trade System   71
   Li Tana

6. The Nguyen Dynasty's Policy toward Chinese
   on the Water Frontier in the First Half of the
   Nineteenth Century   85
   Choi Byung Wook

7. Siam and the Contest for Control of the Trans-Mekong
   Trading Networks from the Late Eighteenth to the
   Mid-Nineteenth Centuries   101
   Puangthong Rungswasdisab

8. Ships and Shipbuilding in the Mekong Delta, c. 1750–1840   119
   Li Tana

Part III: Beyond the Water Frontier

9. Water World: Chinese and Vietnamese on the Riverine
   Water Frontier, from Ca Mau to Tonle Sap (c. 1850–1884)   139
   Nola Cooke

10. The Internationalization of Chinese Revenue
    Farming Networks   159
    Carl A. Trocki

Appendix A: A "Coastal Route" from the Lower
Mekong Delta to Terengganu   175
   Geoff Wade

Appendix B: Glossary   191

Index   195

About the Contributors   201

Figures

Map 1   The South China Sea   18

Map 2   Delta and Upper Mekong to Laos   67

Map 3   Gulf of Siam and Road Networks in 1850   68

Map 4   The Six Southern Provinces in 1836   100

Map 5   The Mekong Delta   136

Map 6   The Bassac Area   157

Tables

Table 2.1 Junk Traffic of the South China Sea from
               Home Ports in Siam, Guangdong, and Fujian   29

Table 2.2 Arrivals in Singapore of Square-Rigged (SRV)
               and Asian Vessels from Southeast Asia   30

Table 7.1 Battambang *Suai* Payment in Piculs of
               Cardamom, 1835–1847   111

Table 7.2 Pursat *Suai* Payment in Piculs of
               Cardamom, 1835–1856   111

Table 7.3 Value of Cardamom *Suai* from
            Battambang and Pursat, 1835–1854   112

Table 7.4 The Money Value of *Suai* from
            Northeast Siam and Laos, 1830–1855   113

Table 9.1 Approximate Population in Four
            Selected Provinces, c. 1883   141

Preface

Precolonial Chinese migration to southern Vietnam has been misunderstood and even mythologized for much of the twentieth century by a historiography that consistently privileged a state-centered and national perspective of Vietnamese dynastic, colonial, and postcolonial history. Over the last decade or more, the flaws in such an approach to Chinese contacts with and migration into southern Vietnam and, indeed, Southeast Asia generally, have become increasingly clear in the work of scholars like Wang Gungwu, Denys Lombard, Claudine Salmon, Anthony Reid, Carl Trocki, and (in regard to southern Vietnam especially) in the pioneering studies of the late Professor Chen Chingho, to whom this book is dedicated. We seek to contribute to this scholarly current by advancing a new approach to considering the shared history of Chinese settlement and interaction in southern Indochina and its surrounding areas. In this book we propose a nationally neutral concept that sets aside modern state boundaries to reconsider the far more open and fluid situation of the eighteenth and early nineteenth centuries from which those modern states emerged.

Our focus is principally on the lower Mekong region, an area stretching from modern south Vietnam into eastern Cambodia and southwest Thailand. For most of the eighteenth to mid-nineteenth centuries this area was a single trading zone woven together by the regular itineraries of thousands of large and small junk traders, mostly Chinese but also Malay, Cham, and Vietnamese. These overlapping itineraries in turn formed a regional component of wider trade networks that linked southern China to mainland and insular Southeast Asia. We call this area a "Water Frontier" because it was, at the time, a sparsely settled coastal and riverine frontier region of mixed ethnicities and often uncertain settlements in which waterborne trade and commerce, carried out in a long string of small ports, formed an essential component of local life. Indeed, it can be argued that the whole coastal region from the Mekong Delta in modern Vietnam to the sultanates and later British colonies of the Malay Peninsula formed a single economic region, an extended Water Frontier knit together by the commercial activities of Chinese and other merchants and small traders. In time this larger Water Frontier, organized around the Saigon–Singapore–Bangkok triangle, would come to act as the anchor for one end of an emerging Pan-Pacific network of Chinese commercial interests.

Based on a selection of earlier conference contributions and subsequently written chapters, this book seeks to take the first soundings and to assemble the first evidence that will establish the existence of the Water Frontier historically, and by so doing begin to expand or reposition our still limited understanding of the interactions of traders from south China and local peoples in the region generally, and in particular in the area of modern south Vietnam. It focuses mainly on matters of commerce and political economy, among the least explored fields in Vietnamese historiography to date. This fresh angle of observation has immediately uncovered abundant primary materials, many of them as yet scarcely touched, as they were redundant to the process of constructing national histories for nation-building purposes. Yet the Water Frontier region was the economic foundation of the two new powerful mainland kingdoms that arose in the later eighteenth century, Chakkri Siam and Nguyen Vietnam. To choose only narrowly nationalistic interpretations of this era is to discard as superfluous many of the most important historical sources and, for instance, to fail to understand the dynamics that created these two dynasties and their economic capitals, Bangkok and Saigon.

The concept of a "Water Frontier" here, a fluid transnational and multi-ethnic economic zone, allows us to perceive and talk about the lower Mekong as a single region. It is thus crucial to a clearer and more historically nuanced understanding of the time and place and of the multiple roles played here by Chinese sojourners, settlers, and junk traders in interaction with a kaleidoscope of local peoples. As this book shows, a Water Frontier perspective reveals the regional significance of individual events within an appropriately wider context. It decenters modern dominant cultures and ethnicities from a past era when they were hardly hegemonic. It underlines the existence of a multiethnic, open frontier society within which newcomers or outsiders, important among them various Chinese groups and individuals, often made major contributions to local economic, political, and cultural life that would later be domesticated and exploited to their own benefit by the powerful new states that came to dominate the Water Frontier region during the nineteenth century.

We are very conscious of the debt of gratitude we owe to several scholars who have helped to formulate aspects of the Water Frontier concept. Our thanks go in particular to Anthony Reid, Carl Trocki, Yumio Sakurai, and Paul Kratoska, participants in a 1999 workshop organized by Li Tana and entitled "Commercial Vietnam: Trade and the Chinese in the Nineteenth Century." That workshop gave birth to the idea that a much larger region than simply modern south Vietnam was implicated in our subject matter and, after the workshop ended, we wrestled together with the fundamental problem of how to talk about this wider area without inappropriately importing later national usages. The term "Water Frontier" arose from this fertile discussion. It took much longer, of course, to flesh out the concept and to carry out the additional research that breathed life into it, a process in which Carl Trocki played an indispensable role.

We would also like to acknowledge the long-suffering forbearance of our contributors, who patiently endured an extended and frustrating delay in the appearance of this book due to the persistent illness of one of the editors. We are greatly indebted, too, to Mark Selden for his assistance, encouragement, and critical commentaries during the process of preparing the manuscript for publication. Others who offered comments and suggestions on various drafts include David Marr, Victor Lieberman, and Christopher Goscha, whose contributions we deeply appreciate. Our thanks also go to Kay Dancey and Caroline O'Sullivan who assisted with maps and formatting.

We also wish to express our gratitude to the Australian Research Council, whose funding made possible the workshop in Ho Chi Minh City at which the Water Frontier concept was first mooted, and whose continued support has ensured its later development.

Finally, we would like to pay tribute to the goodwill and encouragement of our respective families, and especially to Bill and Lihong, without which this long drawn-out project might never have been completed.

1

The Water Frontier: An Introduction

Li Tana

> Thus restored in its global nature, and in a deliberately non-classical perspective, the history of Southeast Asia can reasonably escape the "polarized" history to which it is too often confined . . . and profit from a new approach which takes into account synchronisms and networks.
>
> —Denys Lombard[1]

The land we call the Water Frontier remained largely underwater or in the swamp not three centuries ago. A glance at a map of Southeast Asia between the thirteenth and the early eighteenth centuries reveals no major political center along the hundreds of miles of coastline from Champa in the north past the Mekong Delta around to the Gulf of Thailand and south to Nakon Sithammarat on the Malay Peninsula.[2] The Khmer name of "Can"[3] and Vietnamese of "Bien" or "Cuong" used in place-names in the lower Mekong Delta region all refer to frontier or border. In the late eighteenth century, however, on this once deserted coast, long regarded as a backwater, there emerged the two prominent political and economic centers of mainland Southeast Asia—Bangkok and Saigon— along with a string of bustling minor ports to flank them. South Chinese junk traders and a host of other itinerant merchants serviced all these ports. By the early twentieth century, rice, tin, rubber, and cash crop production had made this Water Frontier region Southeast Asia's most vigorous center of growth, both in terms of population and productivity.[4]

The history of the emergence of this significant area became obscured when the region was sliced into pieces and fitted into respective national histories. This national view placed each country at the center of the story while the South

1

China Sea, the heart of the region, was largely ignored as the "empty center of Southeast Asia."[5] Yet, as the eminent French scholar, the late Denys Lombard, has persuasively argued, during the last two millennia at least, south China and the lands surrounding the South China Sea were so interwoven by overlapping trading networks and cultural interactions as to form an ensemble that can fruitfully be compared to the Mediterranean of Fernand Braudel.[6] As Lombard concluded, "wanting to understand Southeast Asia without integrating a good part of southern China into one's thinking is like wanting to give an account of the Mediterranean world by abstracting Turkey, the Levant, Palestine and Egypt."[7]

Seeing the South China Sea as another Mediterranean means we must naturally take into account a number of surrounding shores at the same time, in this book we focus on the Water Frontier and southern China. This is not to impose a global vision onto complex historical reality but rather to seek to restore shared experiences and a shared history of the connected shores of the South China Sea, and to "rethink" the linked elements of this geographical ensemble simultaneously. Though sharing Lombard's vision, the goal of this book is more limited: it is to begin to reconstruct the lost history of one part of this South China Sea ensemble, the Water Frontier area, by highlighting its commercial integrity and importance in the eighteenth and nineteenth centuries.

As the following chapters reveal, this fresh angle of observation has been illuminated by newly available primary materials, much of which have scarcely been touched before. This is particularly useful, given the well-known poverty of primary materials for precolonial history across this region. These treasures have been overlooked because they were treated as extraneous remnants when different national histories were tailored out of the original historical fabric of the late eighteenth and early nineteenth centuries. These accounts formed a large and essential part of the history of these states and the region, but proved unusable when the neat modern dresses that would clothe the past of the new nation-states were fashioned.

The Water Frontier was a different world from that of these dynasties and successor nation-states. It was notable for the absence of the "relatively unconflicted acceptance of royal rule"[8] so typical of contemporary Malay *negeri* or Thai *muongs*. As Sakurai shows here, the extraordinarily weak and divided Khmer kingdom in this region provided a political environment in which vital elements of the Water Frontier could develop, the most important one being the free movement of peoples and commodities. Indeed, one of the characteristics shared by the whole coastal region between the Mekong Delta estuaries and the Malay Peninsula in the later eighteenth and early nineteenth centuries was this frequent movement of people and exchanges of commodities and cultural practices among Viets, Siamese, Mon-Khmer, and Malays, with Chinese settlers, sojourners, and junk traders forming the common thread weaving them all together. The ebb and flow of peoples, goods, and ideas will be the main focus of this book, the *Water Frontier*.

Water Frontier—A Major Arena of the Time

The period between the mid-eighteenth and nineteenth centuries, as Reid shows here and elsewhere, was an era of dynamic commercial expansion between the earlier "age of commerce,"and the colonial high noon from 1870 to 1940.[9] For mainland Southeast Asia in particular, it was also a time of vigorous state formation, characterized by strong commercial and demographic growth.[10] The modern Siamese and Vietnamese states basically attained their current territorial limits through the dynamism of this time.

The major sources of this mainland dynamism no doubt derived in no small measure from their coastal regions.[11] The principal external impetus for this dynamism came from south China, whose junk traders, as Chin's chapter shows, became the conduit through which China's burgeoning population accessed consumer goods from the "South Seas" (*Nanyang*). Trade with Southeast Asia increased so rapidly that customs revenue between 1724 and 1750 rose threefold in Fujian and almost fivefold in Guangdong.[12] The impact of the China trade is underlined by the fact that the number of Chinese junks visiting Cochinchina increased fourfold between 1750 and 1820.[13] This in turn boosted royal income remarkably. The total state revenue of the Nguyen ruler between 1746–1752 averaged 380,700 *quan*;[14] but by 1800 revenue from overseas trade in Saigon alone was 489,790 *quan*.[15] The same story unfolded in Siam. Between 1740 and 1820 the Siamese crown's income from maritime trade rose from a fourth or a third to well over half.[16] Changes taking place in southern China, how these distant people ate, dressed, and housed themselves, had so direct an impact on patterns of trade and production in Southeast Asia that the number of Chinese junks shuttling between China and Southeast Asia rightly marked this era as a "Chinese century" in Southeast Asia.[17]

Also in this period British country traders made their impact. Escaping the monopolistic Dutch grasp, they actively traded in the Malay Peninsula, making Terengganu and Riau, for instance, their dissemination point for opium and firearms in the 1760s.[18] The establishment of Penang enhanced the scope of commerce in the region, and when Singapore was founded in 1819, it soon became the acme of free trade and the hallmark of prosperity of the day. This whole story is usually evaluated from within the frame of nineteenth-century colonialism and presented as the start of an ineluctable process of colonizing and capitalizing a region whose future was then determined in London, Paris, and Amsterdam. But the establishment of Penang, and Singapore can be viewed quite differently, as a continuation of the active regional trading system of the eighteenth century rather than as a sudden foreign intrusion in the nineteenth century. An examination of the trade volumes demonstrates that the major participants of the trade at the British settlements of Melaka, Penang, and Singapore in the early nineteenth century were from the ports of Southeast Asia's last autonomous areas, while their trade to European-controlled Java and the Philippines was considerably minor.[19] Instead, "by far the most considerable branch of [Singapore's] traffic [was] with Siam, and next . . . with the port of Saigun,"[20] as

John Crawfurd observed in the early 1820s. The Saigon-Bangkok-Singapore triangle that Crawfurd described was the natural extension and product of a century-long movement of peoples and their economic exchanges.

Expanded cash revenues and more regular maritime contacts increased access to firearms, gunpowder, and strategic metals, and a large quantity of Western firearms flowed into the Water Frontier. This influx of wealth and weapons no doubt fueled the wave of piracy that characterized the coasts of Indochina from the Gulf of Tonkin to the mouth of the Chaophraya in the eighteenth century. Dian Murray has written extensively on the role of the south China pirates in the Vietnamese civil wars[21] and Sakurai has documented the importance of Teochiu pirates in the conflicts between Taksin and Mac Tien Tu in the late eighteenth century. This was accentuated by the civil war that erupted in southern Vietnam after the Tay Son rebellion (1772–1802) overthrew the ruling Nguyen house, leaving one precarious descendant, Nguyen Anh, to try to restore his family's fortunes. In Siam, too, the 1767 Burmese destruction of Ayutthaya led to years of conflict as the part-Teochiu general Taksin seized the vacant throne, only to be deposed in 1782 by the part-Cantonese Chakkri family. Trading profits from the Mekong Delta alone allowed missionary Bishop Pigneaux in 1787 to buy "several cargoes of arms and ammunitions" from Pondichery and Mauritius for the embattled last prince of the Nguyen family, Nguyen Anh.[22] The Nguyen leaders equally sent Chinese, French, and English officers to buy artillery from Goa, Melaka, Penang, Macao, and later, Singapore (see below). Backed with trading income Nguyen Anh was able to afford a huge munitions order in 1791 of 10,000 muskets, 2,000 cannons, and 2,000 shells.[23] This list was not unthinkable if we compare it to the one thousand muskets from India gifted to the king of Siam by Hunter, a British country trader, in the early 1820s.[24] Hunter was also the merchant who sold a steam warship to the Nguyen court for 50,000 Spanish dollars in 1844, plus 200 guns, mortars, and iron.[25]

It was also in this period that French mercenary officers trained Vietnamese troops in rifle drill, rolling fire, bayonet charges, and even handling and making grenades.[26] The European impact was evident in field artillery, infantry drill, fortifications, and construction of European square-rigged vessels. Apart from the elephant corps, no major Viet military tradition was left untouched. In such a way almost all the major players in the field of the late-eighteenth-century Southeast Asia participated in the state formation of the Water Frontier.[27]

Western weapons and technology flowing into the Water Frontier area went through a process of adaptation and assimilation that often changed their original form and infused them with local meanings. It is striking to note, for example, that the Saigon citadel as well as thirty-one other citadels constructed in early-nineteenth-century Vietnam were built "à la Vauban," rather than according to any Chinese or Vietnamese model. Moreover, after the building of the Saigon citadel, many citadels were designed according to the latest innovations in the art of fortifications developed in Europe.[28] Yet for all their fundamentally European design, these citadels met the standards of native geomancy and were topped with Chinese style pavilions, so that the Saigon citadel was called *"thanh bat quai"* ("a town built after the Chinese Eight Diagrams") and was described as shaped like a lotus, which has a strong Vietnamese connotation.[29]

This era was indeed a remarkable phase of experimentation with modernity. Different flows of energy came in, mixed, and blended with various indigenous elements of the Water Frontier, and reemerged in different local forms. It was based on these points of contact and accumulated energies that Taksin launched attack from the Water Frontier port of Chantaburi, and his Chakkri successors were able to consolidate Thai political power throughout the trans-Mekong region. Harnessing the same essential forces enabled Nguyen Anh to win central and northern Vietnam from bases in Phu Quoc, Hatien, and Saigon. The dynamic frontier turned out to be the principal base for launching attacks and ultimately controlling long-established areas.

The mid-eighteenth century also saw a peak of Chinese migration into Southeast Asia. The Chinese who came at that time readily moved between the territories of the present nations of mainland Southeast Asia, as well as between the mainland and island Southeast Asia. Since the strength of Chinese commerce lay in its networks, it is important to consider the role the Chinese played when they took the whole of the *Nanyang* as their arena rather than individual countries within it. While much of this crucial experience would be lost in the new frameworks of nationalist historiography, it is noteworthy that the early colonial Europeans sought to exploit these preexisting networks to help drive their new states. In many respects, early colonial activities reinforced or expanded upon preexisting Chinese achievements, particularly in southern Vietnam but above all in the Straits Settlements.

Fluid Population and Empty Labels of Ethnicity

It is important at this point to raise the question of what is a Chinese? It is clear that those we now call the "Chinese" were several groups rather than one. Indeed, their differences lay behind the deadly struggles between the Cantonese Mac family of Hatien, and Taksin and his Teochiu followers at the late-eighteenth-century Water Frontier.[30] It was this division that lay behind the eventual Siamese control of Chantaburi, as well as Vietnamese rule over Hatien. One might argue that people of the same ethnic origin fight each other everywhere, but rarely has dialect created so clear a division in both political sphere and business networks, and provided the basis for such large scale, bloody fighting among the "Chinese" throughout colonial Southeast Asia. Surely for those who made their living at the Water Frontier and beyond, there were categories much more compelling and powerful than "Chinese." The Fujianese who spoke southern Fujian or Minnan dialect were yet another story. They were earlier arrivals in southern Vietnam in general and formed the bulk of the rich merchants. They married extensively with the Viet elite and produced figures like

Trinh Hoai Duc (1765–1825),[31] a senior minister, and Tran Tien Thanh (1814–1884), the regent of the Nguyen dynasty in 1883.[32] Such men shared little with the relatively poor Hainanese and Hakkas. They were, as Trocki shows, even less comfortable with the rival Cantonese mercantile cliques of Saigon and Hong Kong in the nineteenth century. This rough sketch suggests the necessity to cut across the superficial body we label the "Chinese," to see them in section, to understand different interest groups whose networks and internal distinctions encompassed ethnicities or even subethnicities.

Charting the linguistic jungle of ethnicity in this Water Frontier region is as difficult as it is fun. The modern Vietnamese word for "Chinese," *Hoa*, was specifically used to differentiate Viet people from non-Viets in early-nineteenth-century official documents, while *Tang* and later *Qing* were used for "Chinese."[33] Similarly *Han*, the term for majority "Chinese" worldwide, was another term for *Hoa* but again referring to Viet people.[34] What *Minh Huong* means could also be confusing: originally applied to Minh émigrés who were registered in special associations, by the mid-nineteenth century came to refer specifically to the offspring of Sino-Viet or Sino-Khmer intermarriage.[35]

Contrary to the conceptual polarity between "Chinese" and "indigenous" that saw Chinese and local elements as inherently dissimilar, like oil that can only float on water, in the eighteenth century and in these places "Chinese" and "indigenous" were much more like milk and water that easily dissolve into one another. Because of this, in the late eighteenth century especially, but not only then, south Chinese people directly participated in shaping the politics and cultures that were later redefined as authentically "Vietnamese" or "Siamese." One example is the term *baba*. Because of their immediate associations with power and wealth in the British and Dutch colonies, the idea of the *Baba* Chinese came to signify success and high status, thus *baba* became an honorific when addressing people. Women vendors in Saigon, for instance, called people *baba* when they solicited customers.[36] There was a street called *Pho Baba* (Baba Street) in late-nineteenth-century Saigon, where most wealthy overseas Chinese stayed when in Saigon.[37]

In 1851, when King Mongkut decided to reform Siamese dress to conform more closely to "civilized standards," adopting *baba* dress was one important component of the reform. He reasoned as follows:[38]

> "People who wear no upper garments seem naked . . . But since Siam is a civilized country and understands civilized ways, we should not cling to the ancient ways of our forefathers, who were forest people. Let everyone, therefore, wear upper garments when coming to royal audience." . . . A new upper garment . . . was thus introduced, which was similar to the upper garments worn by the *baabaa*, who were peoples of Chinese descent in Batavia. The wearing of this garment from that time became customary.

Baba costume also became popular in the Vietnamese Water Frontier around the mid-nineteenth century, with the most common garment of southern men and women, the *ao baba*, derived from it.[39] First fashionable among rich men, then women, in Saigon, the style gradually spread throughout the whole Mekong Delta area. It ended up as the "classic" of "traditional" and "authentic" Vietnamese national dress by the twentieth century.[40]

Turning to the "indigenous peoples" we face similar problems if we assume ethnicity principally on the basis of the people described being the subjects of a particular "national" kingdom.[41] The "Khmers" who traded cattle with the Mekong Delta were partly immigrants from the Malay Archipelago and partly descendants of Chams.[42] The "Siamese" active in the eighteenth-century Mekong Delta and recorded in the nineteenth-century Hue chronicles discussed below, could well be Lao, Khmer, or Mon, just as the recorded "Malay" villages in Hatien might include both Malay and Chams. When it comes to ethnicity, Siamese sources of this period can also be confusing: when referring to "Indian" residents in Phnom Penh, they mean Chams.[43] A defining understanding of ethnicity in the context of the Water Frontier, therefore, is that all labels should be taken as tentative, fluid, even temporary.

Such a historical angle instantly challenges the conventional view that placed Viets and Vietnamese culture at the center of the Water Frontier as early as three hundred years ago. A careful reading of the contemporary sources shows that the Viets did not reach their current dominant position until long after they appeared in the Mekong Delta. There are many examples. In 1787 when Nguyen Anh came back from exile in Bangkok and was desperately trying to recruit soldiers, he could only gather about three hundred people, presumably Viets. A Khmer member of Nguyen Anh's entourage,[44] however, was able to recruit a few thousand "barbarians" from Khmer-held Tra Vinh and Ben Tre. This army's camp then became known as "*don binh Xiem*" (Siamese troop garrison),[45] with the Vietnamese word "*Xiem*" (Siamese) here most likely a nonderogatory collective term for the non-Viet peoples here at the time.[46] In those difficult early years after his return from Bangkok, this largely non-Viet army might have been Nguyen Anh's main force. In fact, the proportion of Nguyen Anh's non-Viet soldiers was still so high in 1793 that he issued an edict forbidding the markets where his troops were stationed from selling alcohol, because "the *Tang* [Chinese], Western[47] and Siamese soldiers are intrepid, rough and hard to control when drunk."[48]

Laotians, long regarded as people with no access to the ocean, were once active in the My Tho area.[49] They may also have been present in a remote corner of the Mekong Delta, in modern Bac Lieu Province. This case suggests the complex intermingling of the peoples in the region and indicates a very different map of ethnicities from that of modern times. Unlike most Vietnamese place names, Bac Lieu has no meaning in Vietnamese, but, according to a local historian, instead derived from Teochiu Chinese pronunciation of a Khmer name, Po Leo, meaning "Lao Hill." In his view, the place had been a camp of Lao soldiers before the Teochiu Chinese arrived.[50]

Long before Viet people had become the dominant group in the Mekong Delta, they had begun to spread along the Water Frontier coast. They were much more mobile than was previously believed and made critical contributions to the establishment of ports or townships far from the national boundaries of modern Vietnam.[51] A Cochinchinese quarter existed in mid-seventeenth-century Ayutthaya,[52] while Chantaburi, the base from which Taksin staged the restoration of the Siamese kingdom in the 1760s, was predominately Viet and Chinese at the time.[53] Many Chams, after losing their country to Nguyen Vietnam, also became wanderers through the Water Frontier. The famous Thai silk industry, for instance, owed its existence to Cham weavers who migrated from Cochinchina and Cambodia between the reigns of Rama I and Rama III. Assigned to produce silk for the court, the resulting "Thai silk" gained worldwide fame.[54] As these examples suggest, the story of different ethnic groups participating in each other's formative stages or helping create other people's "national heritage" on the Water Frontier is yet to be fully explored.

Fluidity is a remarkable characteristic of all the peoples discussed above. The frontier nature of the Water Frontier made life uncertain and potentially violent. Warfare was almost endemic here in the eighteenth and early nineteenth centuries: violent struggles repeatedly broke out between Vietnamese, Khmer and Siamese armies, civil wars erupted between the Nguyen and the Tay Son or between royal Khmer rivals, and in the nineteenth century nearly two decades of conflict darkened relations between the Nguyen and the Chakkri dynasties in the 1830s and 1840. When the Siamese sacked Hatien in 1771, its population scattered or died; when the Tay Son sacked Bien Hoa in 1776, almost all Chinese fled. Wharfs might be built but abandoned soon after to war and chaos;[55] workers might be gathered for mining and iron manufacturing only to be so scattered when the ore was exhausted that even the memory of such bustling enterprises was lost.[56] This fluidity determined the nature and volume of production in certain localities.[57] The repeated shaping and reshaping of local communities is one of the most remarkable characteristics of the Water Frontier.

Economic Exchange and Markets

The eighteenth century saw a significant change in Southeast Asian trade from luxuries to bulk goods,[58] with commercial rice trade the cornerstone of the change. This development fostered a suitable climate for the rise of the Water Frontier, since this region at the time was never primarily a zone of subsistence agriculture. Although both the Mekong Delta and the Menam Chaophraya basin were best known for their rice by the mid-eighteenth century, rice production in both areas had relied on regional trade networks right from the start because both areas had to buy the draft animals required for commercial farming from other, more distant, ethnic groups. The main difference between the Chaophraya basin and the Mekong Delta is that northeastern Thailand supplied about 60 percent of its water buffalo and 40 percent of its cattle needs,[59] while the Central Highlands in contemporary Vietnam never played this crucial role for the Mekong Delta. From the late seventeenth to the mid-twentieth centuries, Cambodia was its major source of buffalo and cattle. Saigon's former name Ben Nghe, or "ferry for young buffalo," hints at this economic link between Vietnamese and Khmers in the eighteenth century.[60] But many of the cattle that ended up in the eighteenth-century Mekong Delta undoubtedly came from much further, as draft animals were "one of the significant goods [exported] from northeastern Siam to Cambodia."[61] If large numbers of cattle were crucial for the mass production of rice, this regional exchange system, which is discussed in more detail in a chapter by Li, was essential for large-scale commercial cultivation of rice that characterized the Mekong Delta area by the later eighteenth century.

The Water Frontier was also deeply involved with the south China junk trade. Newly discovered European records, for example, show that in the 1760s the coast between the Mekong Delta (Bassac branch), Cancao (Hatien) and Cambodia was a major focus of the Canton junk trade.[62] Of the thirty-seven Canton junks sailing annually between Canton and Southeast Asia, 85 to 90 percent traded in ports here.[63] There must have been a considerable degree of integration of sub-regional markets, as data suggests that in 1761 a huge volume of sappanwood and tin were exported from Cochinchina, an area that produced neither commodity, but only a small quantity from Siam, the chief producer of both.[64] Undoubtedly the many small Chinese junks based in the Water Frontier shuttled between the different collecting centers and transported the goods to the main emporia for export by cargo junks to China. It was mainly through these merchants that Nguyen Anh was able to purchase essential strategic items like pig iron, wrought iron, tin, and sulfur.[65] The Chinese junk trade grew even more between the three ports of Singapore, Bangkok, and Saigon from the 1820s on. As Reid has shown, Chinese trade in Bangkok rose more than tenfold by the 1820s and that of Saigon about fivefold.[66] The most spectacular growth of Saigon's rice trade was from 1841 to 1845, interestingly, straight after the death of Minh Mang who, as Choi's chapter discusses, had tried to prohibit Chinese settlers from engaging in maritime rice trading. Rice exports increased about tenfold during this short span of time and in 1848 doubled again.[67] Trade between Singapore, Bangkok, and Saigon at this time linked mainland and insular Southeast Asia to an unprecedented extent.

The Water Frontier was equally well interconnected by internal trade routes and market exchanges. The Khmer names of Rach Gia ("White Wax Market") and Sa Dec ("Iron Market")[68] suggest a long history of exchanges in the region. Many species of plants were introduced to southern Vietnam through the waterways of the Bassac area. Durian and mangostine, for example, arrived by this route towards the end of the eighteenth century, as did a type of banana originally called Siamese (*chuoi Xiem*), but later domesticated as My Tho bananas (*chuoi My Tho*).[69] Such economic exchanges were so integral to Mekong Delta life that it was natural for Nguyen Anh to reward his army in 1800 with tea from China and tobacco from Siam,[70] suggesting that the economies of the Mekong Delta, Cambodia, and Siam were more closely linked than was previously believed. In the minor ports dotting the Water Frontier, the seasonal flow of water, geographical distance, and trade items, not national boundaries, dictated when and with whom to trade. Even in the late nineteenth century Ca Mau "smuggled" tobacco from Cambodia rather than buy it legally from Go Vap, the tobacco producing area near Saigon,[71] since transport costs were much cheaper. Likewise, rice brought from the Chaophraya basin of Siam to Cancao (Hatien) cost much less than rice from the Mekong Delta. In fact, exchanges between these areas were so vital and frequent that the rice price inflation in Nguyen Vietnam in 1803,[72] caused by the government's uncontrolled coin casting, immediately brought price inflation in Siam in 1803–1804, forcing Rama I to prohibit rice exports.[73]

These extensive regional exchanges were critical to Nguyen Anh's ultimate victory in the three-decade civil war. The Nguyen chronicles record that weapons were bought from Goa, Melaka, Penang, and Macao.[74] Combat elephants were bought in Phnom Penh and Battambang.[75] Large quantities of iron came from Siam. In an edict of 1797, Anh ordered all junks from Siam to bring between 10,000 and 30,000 *can* of pig iron and quantities of saltpeter to exchange for silk and cotton fabrics.[76] The main force in transporting strategic items was again the Chinese, who had to bring each time from 40,000 to 100,000 *can* (24 to 60 tonnes) of pig iron, wrought iron, tin, and sulfur to buy rice from the Mekong Delta tax free.[77] In 1802, when a Vietnamese delegation went to Bangkok to thank the Siamese for assisting Nguyen Anh, the Bangkok chronicle listed the strategic items they had provided: "guns, gunpowder and shot, pig iron, cast iron, lead, tin, flint stone, and sappanwood, some of these were given to him outright, some he was allowed to purchase."[78] This enormous shopping list shows the scope and scale of resources exchanged at this corner of the Water Frontier, as well as the vast potential of the Mekong Delta to sustain such economic exchange. It is equally astonishing, from a historian's point of view, that such a regional dimension has been overlooked for so long, a dimension which must have been crucial to the outcome of thirty years of Vietnamese civil war. The war, which was never truly "civil," was ultimately a contest of long-term strength based on each side's ability to control their natural and human resources, a contest in which the winner Nguyen Anh was firmly backed by the regional trade system of the Water Frontier. It has become increasingly clear that it was the combined strength of the Water Frontier that made possible the rise of three major political actors (Taksin, Rama I, and Nguyen Anh/Gia Long) in late-eighteenth-century mainland Southeast Asia.

From Water Frontier to State Integration

Commercial expansion accelerated competition between the new mainland powers. As Puangthong's chapter reveals, Nguyen Vietnam and Chakkri Siam fought fiercely in the 1830s and 1840s to control the trading routes, networks, and resources of the Water Frontier hinterland. The first post-Ayutthayan kings had successfully consolidated Thai political power throughout the trans-Mekong region and Siam soon dominated the major commercial centers of Vientiane, Champassak, Battambang, and Phnom Penh. If the Minh Mang reign (1820–1841) saw Vietnamese win an upper hand in the trading zone from the middle Mekong basin to its coastal delta, by the mid-nineteenth century tribute and tax were flowing to Bangkok from northeast Siam, the Lao principalities, and northwest Cambodia, rather than southeast to Saigon. Political control generated more trade. For instance, the Siamese sugar industry that supplied a lucrative nineteenth-century export trade relied largely on Khmer producers who had been forcibly resettled to Nakhon Chaisi, Chachoengsao, and Ratchaburi in the late eighteenth century.[79]

By the early nineteenth century, the hands of states were anything but invisible along the Water Frontier, a region that for much of the eighteenth century had seemed free of major state-centered dynamics. Ironically this situation resulted in part from the success of the two major Water Frontier cities, Saigon and Bangkok. Though initially founded on the frequent exchanges between minor ports of the Water Frontier and coastal southern China, once they emerged as political and economic centers the two tended to dominate and ultimately take over the trade previously shared among the minor ports. The rise of Saigon marginalized Bien Hoa, My Tho, Bassac, and Hatien, while Bangkok attracted most of the cargoes formerly exchanged in and exported from Chantaburi, Rayong, Ligor, and Pattani. The resulting cycle of declining trade seriously undermined the capability of minor Water Frontier ports, disposing them to accept economic and political orders previously unknown.

As state-sponsored security increased, other changes followed. When Taksin, Rama I, and Nguyen Anh had been forced to move from their respective central regions to the southern frontier, the new political forces had been created that generated unprecedented vigor there. In particular, production for overseas trade was organized to a previously unheard of extent, both in terms of quantity and variety. Thanks to this economic dynamism, both Siam and Vietnam expanded in territory, population, and productive capacity to unprecedented levels. The lure of new land in the south, whose security was backed by the firmly established political centers of Saigon and Bangkok, continually attracted Thai and Viet immigrants from longer-settled areas. By the late nineteenth century, these immigrants from the ethnic majority would permanently change the character of the region, displacing or swamping existing Khmer, Chinese, Malay, Cham, and Lao inhabitants and transforming them into the "minorities."

If Nguyen Anh, Taksin, and Rama I had drawn on frontier energies for their initial success, each had also directed those energies as soon as possible back to the center, to the conquest of established states where human and natural resources had long been regulated and taxed, and where the established cultural base of the majority provided comfort and confidence. Yet the same impulse had very different consequences because Taksin and Rama I were newcomers to power while Nguyen Anh had fought, as the last Nguyen representative, to restore his family's heritage.[80] Thus the new Chakkri dynasty felt free to establish itself in Bangkok, a move south that discouraged Burmese attacks while it expedited commerce by cutting out several days of river travel compared to Ayutthaya. Bangkok thus became both the political and economic capital of Siam, while Nguyen Anh returned to Hue, the capital of his forebears and great symbol of Restoration victory that was strategically located at the geographic center of his new enlarged kingdom.[81]

This move split the economic and political capitals of the Nguyen kingdom and left the Nguyen emperors permanently torn between the desire for overseas trade on the Water Frontier and wariness of the political threats it engendered. The frequent turning on and off of a red light toward overseas trade during the first half of the nineteenth century can be largely traced back to this split, as is evident in a close reading of the Nguyen chronicles. A more immediate factor worsened the situation. Aware that the Mekong Delta economy was more closely integrated with the Water Frontier region than with central and northern Vietnam, Minh Mang set out to make the Nguyen economy one unit organized around its less advanced agricultural sectors. Overseas trade, the vital element that had sustained Nguyen Anh over his Tay Son enemies, thus came to be viewed as a force undermining state integration. This tension ultimately led to the Le Van Khoi rebellion between 1833 and 1835, followed by an outflow of population from the Mekong Delta to Cambodia, Siam, the Malay Peninsula, and the Philippines. Suppressing this rebellion cost considerable resources and manpower and led ultimately to the strengthening of the political incorporation of the south.

Yet, thanks to its overlapping commercial networks, elements of the Water Frontier still persisted in some places and evolved in new forms in others during the early colonial period. As Cooke's chapter shows, a riverine Water Frontier persisted into the late nineteenth century in formerly underdeveloped areas with similar characteristics, while Trocki's chapter indicates one way in which the wider Water Frontier region developed into a significant link in emerging colonial trade complexes between Saigon, Singapore, and Canton–Hong Kong. These chapters, like the rest of the book, raise as many questions as they answer. But this is part of the value of a book that does not claim to be a definitive account but seeks rather to offer a new angle of observation and to inspire a new set of questions for historical analysis.

Notes

My thanks go to Mark Selden for his guidance on the framework and to Nola Cooke for numerous suggestions and comments. Many thanks also to Carl Trocki for his ongoing participation in forming the major ideas of this chapter and to Chris Goscha, Victor Lieberman, and David Marr for help with earlier drafts.

    1. Denys Lombard, "Une autre 'Mediterranée' dans l'Asie du sud-est," *Hérodote*, 88 (1998): 92.

2. See *Southeast Asia in the Early Modern Era*, ed. Anthony Reid (Ithaca and London: Cornell University Press, 1993), map 1, 4.

3. Tam Hoan, "Tim hieu chu 'can' trong dia danh Can Duoc" [Understanding the Word "Can" in the Place-Name of Can Duoc], in *Can Duoc dat va nguoi* [The Land and People of Can Duoc] (Long An: So van hoa va thong tin Long An, 1988), 326–32.

4. Fujianese migration illustrates the trend. In 1912–1913, half of those who left from Amoy (Xiamen) and 81 percent from Swator (Shantou) went to southern Vietnam, Thailand, the Malay Peninsula, and Singapore. See *Qiao hui liu tong zhi yan jiu* [A Study on Chinese Remittances] (Taipei: Zhonghua xue shu yuan Nanyang yan jiu suo; Jing xiao zhe Wen shi zhe chu ban she, 1984), 17–19.

5. Carl Trocki, "Chinese Pioneering in Eighteenth-Century Southeast Asia," in *The Last Stand of Asian Autonomies*, ed. Anthony Reid (London: Macmillan Press, 1997), 86.

6. Fernand Braudel, *The Mediterranean and the Mediterranean World in the Age of Philip II*, 2 vols. (New York: Harper & Row, 1975).

7. Other eminent scholars have also explored a similar concept, but without Lombard's emphasis on and argument about the integral role of south China in Southeast Asia. For instance, see Oliver Wolters, *History, Culture, and Region in Southeast Asian Perspectives* (Singapore: Institute of Southeast Asian Studies, 1982); or Anthony Reid, *Southeast Asia in the Age of Commerce, 1450–1680* (New Haven: Yale University Press, 1988).

8. For Malay *negeri* and Thai *muong*, see *A Comparative Study of Thirty City-State Cultures*, ed. Mogens Herman Hansen (Copenhagen: The Royal Danish Academy of Sciences and Letters, 2000), especially Anthony Reid, "Negeri, the Culture of Malay-Speaking City-States of the Fifteenth and Sixteenth Centuries," 418; and Richard A. O'Connor, "A Regional Explanation of the Tai *Muang* as a City-State," 334.

9. Anthony Reid, "A New Phase of Commercial Expansion in Southeast Asia, 1760–1850," in *The Last Stand of Asian Autonomies*, ed. Anthony Reid (London and New York: Macmillan Press, 1997), 57–82.

10. Victor Lieberman, "Local Integration and Eurasian Analogies: Structuring Southeast Asian History, c.1350–1830," *Modern Asian Studies* 27, no. 3 (1993): 475–540.

11. For Burma see *The Maritime Frontier of Burma: Exploring Political, Cultural and Commercial Interaction in the Indian World, 1200–1800*, ed. Jos Gommans and Jacques Leider (Leiden: KITLV Press, 2002).

12. Reid, "Commercial Expansion," 71.

13. Li Tana, "Rice Trade in the Eighteenth- and Nineteenth-Century Mekong Delta and Its Implications," in *Thailand and Her Neighbors (II): Laos, Vietnam and Cambodia*, ed. Thanet Aphornsuvan (Bangkok: Thammasat University Press, 1995), 198–214.

14. Le Quy Don, *Phu Bien Tap Luc* [Miscellaneous Border Records (seized in 1775–76)] (Saigon: Phu Quoc Vu Khanh Dac Trach Van Hoa, 1973), 36b–37a.

15. *Dai Nam Thuc Luc Chinh Bien, De Nhat Ky* [Preliminary Compilation of the Chronicles of Greater Vietnam, First Reign] [hereafter *DNTL*] (Tokyo: The Oriental Institute, Keio University, 1968), vol. 12, 500.

16. Victor Lieberman, "Mainland–Archipelagic Parallels and Contrasts," in *The Last Stand of Asian Autonomies*, ed. Anthony Reid (London and New York: Macmillan Press, 1997), 35.

17. Anthony Reid, "Introduction," in *The Last Stand of Asian Autonomies*, ed. Anthony Reid (London and New York: Macmillan Press, 1997), 11–14.

18. Barbara Andaya, *To Live as Brothers: Southeast Sumatra in the Seventeenth and Eighteenth Centuries* (Honolulu: University of Hawaii Press, 1993), 222.

19. Anthony Reid, "Commercial Expansion," in *The Last Stand of Asian Autonomies*, 63–68.

20. John Crawfurd, *Journal of an Embassy to the Courts of Siam and Cochin China*, reprint (Kuala Lumpur: Oxford University Press, 1987), 542.

21. Dian H. Murray, *Pirates of the South China Coast, 1790–1810* (Stanford: Stanford University Press, 1987).

22. Frédéric Mantienne, "Military Technology Transfers from Europe to Lower Mainland Southeast Asia, c.16th–19th Centuries," (paper presented at the annual conference of the Association of Asian Studies, March 2002).

23. *DNTL* I, vol. 5, 372.

24. "An Early British Merchant in Bangkok," *The Siam Society: Selected Articles from the Siam Society Journal* VIII (1959): 233.

25. William Bradley, *Siam Then* (Pasadena, Calif.: William Carey Library, 1981), 38. The Nguyen chronicles said it cost 280,000 *quan*. *DNTL* III, vol. 40, 5,275; and "An Early British Merchant."

26. Mantienne, "Military Technology Transfers," 3–5.

27. "The envoy of San Hoat (Songkhla) Kapitan Dien Hoa sent weapons in 1790. When he returned to his country the emperor sent his king one gold umbrella and 10,000 *can* of rice." *DNTL* I, vol. 4, 358.

28. Mantienne, "Military Technology Transfers," 3–5.

29. Trinh Hoai Duc, "Gia dinh thong chi: thanh tri chi," annotated by Chen Chingho, *Nanyang xuebao*, [Journal of the South Seas Society] 12, no. 24 (Dec. 1956): 7.

30. Chen Chingho, "Mac Thien Tu and Phrayataksin: A Survey on Their Political Stand, Conflicts and Background," *Proceedings of the Seventh IAHA Conference* (Bangkok: Chulalongkorn University Press, 1979), vol. 2, 1534–1575.

31. Trinh Hoai Duc, "Thanh tri chi," 22.

32. Chen Chingho, *A Brief Study of the Family Register of the Trans, a Ming Refugee Family in Minh Huong Xa, Thua Thien (Central Vietnam)* (Hong Kong: New Asia Research Institute, Chinese University of Hong Kong, 1964), 83–93.

33. This usage is readily found in the Nguyen chronicles from the early nineteenth century onward, as there appeared an urgent need to define Vietnamese when there were numerous Khmers around. For instance, this comment on Bassac in the *Gia Dinh Thong Chi*: "*Hoa dan, Tang* [Chinese] and Khmers are mixed here." Trinh Hoai Duc, *Gia Dinh thong chi: Thanh tri chi*, in *Lingnan zhi guai deng shi liao san zhong* (Three Primary Sources of Linh Nam trich quai, Gia dinh thong chi and Hatien tran dipe tran Mac thi gia pha), ed. Dai Kelai and Yang Baoyun (Zhengzhou: Zhongzhou guji Press, 1991), 100.

34. Examples abound: for instance, a 1791 edict that forbade "Han" people from exploiting the land of "Phien" (Khmer in this context]) did not apply to the "Tang" (Chinese). *DNTL* I, vol. 5, 375.

35. See also *Dictionary of Overseas Chinese*, ed. Zhou Nan Jing (Beijing: Peking University Press, 1993), 494–95.

36. "*Chong you yuenan ji*" [Revisiting Vietnam, 1893], in *Chen Sing Tang wen ji* [Collected Works of Chen Sing Tang], ed. Ye Zhong Ling (Singapore: Singapore Society of Asian Studies), 1994, 39. *Chinese Repository* 6, no. 7 (1837): 151.

37. Claudine Salmon and Ta Trong Hiep, "De Batavia à Saigon: Notes de voyage d'un merchand chinois (1890)," *Archipel* 47 (1994): 188.

38. Mongkut also urged royal officials not to be like "Lawas and the Laos who are forest dwellers of an uncivilized country and do not use clothing." *The Dynastic Chronicles Bangkok Era, the Fourth Reign (AD 1851–1868)*, trans. Chadin Flood (Tokyo: Centre for East Asian Cultural Studies, 1965), vol. 1, 5–6.

39. Phan Thi Yen Tuyet, *Nha o, trang phuc, an uong cua cac dan toc vung Dong bang Song Cuu Long* [Styles of Housing, Dress, and Foods among the Peoples in the Mekong Delta Area] (Hanoi: Khoa hoc xa hoi, 1993), 62–63.

40. The same style was called "pajamas" by American soldiers during the Vietnam War. Interestingly, in the 1920s *baba* fever was replaced by a *towka* craze, when Teochiu Chinese became rich and influential in Siam. In Saigon, everyone loved to be called *towka*, even women who sold vegetables. Vuong Hong Sen, *Saigon nam xua* [The Olden Days of Saigon] (Ho Chi Minh City: n. d.), 161.

41. For an illuminating discussion on ethnicity in Vietnam, see K. W. Taylor, "On Being Muonged", *Asian Ethnicity*, 2, no. 1 (March 2001): 25–34.

42. David Chandler, "Cambodia before the French: Politics in a Tributary Kingdom, 1794–1848," Ph.D. dissertation, University of Michigan, 1973, 31. An army of Khmer King Chan in 1820, which was led by a Muslim, included Chinese, Chams, and Malays, but no Khmer. See David Chandler, "An Anti-Vietnamese Rebellion: Rebellion in Early Nineteenth-Century Cambodia: Pre-colonial Imperialism and a Pre-Nationalist Response", *Journal of Southeast Asian Studies* 6, no.1 (March 1975): 21.

43. See the chapter by Puangthong Rungswasdisab in this book.

44. This Khmer officer, Nguyen Van Tuan, had been a court slave before he followed Nguyen Anh to Siam. *Dai Nam Chinh Bien Liet Truyen, So Tap* [First Collection of the Primary Compilation of Biographies of Imperial Vietnam], vol. 28, 307–8 (Tokyo: Keio Institute of Linguistic Studies, 1962).

45. *DNTL* I, vol. 3, 334.

46. "To restrict the scope of this examination to specifically 'Thai' activities is to beg questions of ethnic identification and composition in the formative years of Siam's history." David Wyatt, *Studies in Thai History* (Bangkok: Silkworm Books, 1994), 23.

47. They were mainly French although an English captain served Nguyen Anh from 1793 to 1800. He was sent to buy weapons in Goa in 1793 and helped train the Nguyen navy. *DNTL* I, vol. 6, 398; vol. 12, 495.

48. *DNTL* I, vol. 6, 390. There is much evidence for the Siamese in Nguyen Anh's army. For example, in 1782 a Siamese general offered his forces, bringing over 200 Siamese soldiers on a dozen ships. *DNTL*, I, vol. 2, 322.

49. In 1731, for example, a Lao rebel army, led by a sojourning Lao prince from Vientiane called Sotot, was defeated by a Chinese army near My Tho. Trinh Hoai Duc, *Gia Dinh thong chi: Thanh tri chi*, 209. Sotot was said to be associated with some Laotians from Phra Nakorn who had migrated from Vientiane to Cambodia in 1705. Chen Chingho, "The Migration of the Cheng Partisans to South Vietnam" (part 2), *Hsin Ya Hsueh Pao*, no. 2 (August 1968): 473, 477. According to A. Leclère, *Histoire du Cambodge,* reprint (New York: AMS Press, 1975), 375, Sotot was a Lao refugee settled in Preah Saut (Ba Phnom). Claiming prophetic powers, he boasted he would sweep the Vietnamese from the south and thus had many followers.

50. Huynh Minh, *Bac Lieu xua va nay*, reprint (n. p., Calif: Bach Viet, 1994), 15.

51. Christopher E. Goscha, *Thailand and the Southeast Asian Networks of the Vietnamese Revolution* (Richmond: Curzon, 1999), 14–21.

52. Anthony Reid, *Southeast Asia in the Age of Commerce, 1450–1680*, vol. 2, 81 (New Haven and London: Yale University Press, 1993).

53. Nguyen Dinh Dau, *Che do cong dien cong tho trong lich su khan hoang lap ap on Nam ky luc tinh* [The Communal Land Holding System in the History of Opening Up the Six Provinces of Southern Vietnam] (Ho Chi Minh City: Youth Press of Ho Chi Minh City, 1999), 38–39.

54. Cholthira Satyawadhna, "Ban Khrua Community: The Cham in Bangok Metropolis," *Tai Culture*, V, no. 2 (Dec. 2000): 197. Thanks to Philip King for bringing this to my attention.

55. See my chapter on shipbuilding in this book.

56. Tha Chanuang, a 1830s iron manufacturing site in northern Siam only operated for a few decades and had been forgotten locally by the 1900s. See Arnold Wright, ed., *Twentieth Century Impressions of Siam* (London, 1910).

57. Burmese raids between 1784 and 1824 caused the population of Phuket to fall four- or fivefold to 6000, so tin output crashed from 500 tons annually to 20 tons. See G. E. Gerini, *Old Phuket: Historical Retrospect of Junkceylon Island* (Bangkok: The Siam Society, 1986), 98.

58. Victor Lieberman, "Local Integration and Eurasian Analogies: Structuring Southeast Asian History, c.1350–1830," *Modern Asian Studies*, 27, no. 3 (1993): 491.

59. Fukui Hayao, *Food and Population in the Northeast Thai Village* (Honolulu: University of Hawaii Press, 1993), 21. My gratitude goes to Professor Fukui for calling my attention to this important aspect for the Mekong delta, when he asked me about the source of local draft animals when I visited his project team investigating the dry areas of Southeast Asia. It had not occurred to me earlier.

60. See chapter 6 in this book.

61. Puangthong Rungswadisab, "War and Trade: Siamese Interventions in Cambodia, 1767–1851," Ph.D. thesis, University of Wollongong, 1995, 77.

62. Paul Van Dyke, "The Canton–Vietnam Junk Trade in the 1760s and 1770s: Some Preliminary Observations from the Dutch, Danish, and Swedish Records," paper for the International Workshop "Commercial Vietnam: Trade and the Chinese in the Nineteenth Century South", Ho Chi Minh City, December 1999. For more detailed discussion on this trade see Li Tana, "The Late Eighteenth Century Mekong Delta and the World of the Water Frontier," in *Viet Nam: Borderless Histories*, ed. Nhung Tuyet Tran and Anthony Reid, (Center for Southeast Asian Studies, University of Wisconsin-Madison), forthcoming.

63. Van Dyke, "Canton–Vietnam Junk Trade," chart 5.

64. Van Dyke, "Canton–Vietnam Junk Trade," 13.

65. *DNTL* I, vol. 4, 350.

66. Reid, "Introduction," 12.

67. Li Tana, "Vietnam's Overseas Trade in the Nineteenth Century: The Singapore Connection" (paper for the International Conference on Vietnamese Studies, 14–17 July 1998, Hanoi).

68. See Nola Cooke's chapter in this book for Rach Gia. For Sa Dec, see Bui Duc Tinh, *Luoc khao nguon goc dia danh Nam Bo* (HCM: Nha xuat ban Van Nghe, 1999), 39.

69. Son Nam, *Dong bang*, 70.

70. *DNTL* I, 211.

71. Son Nam, *Dong bang*, 38.

72. *DNTL* I, vol. 20, 325.

73. Junko Koizumi, "Some Observations on the Economic Administration of King Rama I," paper presented at the 13th IAHA conference, Tokyo, 1994, 12–13.

74. *DNTL* I, vol. 3, 340 for 1788; vol. 6, 398 for 1793; vol. 7, 412 for 1795; vol. 10, 462 for 1798, vol. 14, 535 for 1801.

75. *DNTL* I, vol. 8, 432.

76. *DNTL* I, vol. 9, 448.

77. *DNTL* I, vol. 4, 350. When the Nguyen realm badly needed rice in 1802 it bought 500 *kwien* (2,080 ton) from Siam, plus levied 1,000 *kwien* (4,160 ton) of rice from

Cambodia. *DNTL* I, vol. 16, 562. For the Siamese *kwien*, see Hong Lysa, *Thailand in the Nineteenth Century: Evolution of the Economy and Society* (Singapore: ISEAS, 1984), ix.

78. *Bangkok Era, the First Reign*, vol. 1, 256. Elephants should be added to this list, mainly from Cambodia. In the two years 1812 and 1813 Cambodia "presented" Gia Long with 127 elephants. Alexander Woodside, *Vietnam and the Chinese Model* (Cambridge, Mass.: Council on East Asian Studies, Harvard University, 1988), 252.

79. Puangthong, "War and Trade," 144–46.

80. Nola Cooke, "The Myth of the Restoration," in *Last Stand of Asian Autonomies,* 269–95.

81. Keith Taylor comments that the decision to rule from Hue "deprived [Anh's] successors of the perspective that had enabled his success and left Nam Bo vulnerable to other powers." K. W. Taylor, "Surface Orientations in Vietnam: Beyond Histories of Nation and Region," *Journal of Asian Studies*, 57, no. 4 (Nov. 1998): 949–78.

© Cartography ANU 03-071a

Suzhou

Ningbo

Fuzhou
FUJIAN
Xiamen
Zhanglin

YUNNAN

GUANGXI
GUANGDONG
Guangzhou
Macao
Hong Kong

Hanoi

Luang
Prabang

Leizhou
Gulf of
Tongking
Qiong Shan
Hainan

Chiang
Mai
Vientiane

Hue
Hoi An

Ayutthaya   Korat
Bangkok
Tonle Sap
Battambang   Lake

Pnom
Penh
Bien Hoa
Hatien
Saigon
My Tho

Ligor

Songkhla
Pattani

Penang
→TERENGGANU

0   100

SINGAPORE
km

Map 1: The South China Sea

I

PERMEABLE FRONTIERS: CHINESE TRADE AND TRADERS IN THE REGION

2

Chinese Trade and Southeast Asian Economic Expansion in the Later Eighteenth and Early Nineteenth Centuries: An Overview

Anthony Reid

Hardly more than thirty years ago it was still possible to dismiss the precolonial economic history of Southeast Asia as one of self-sufficient villages insulated from the broader cycles of world trade.

> After 1870 . . . all the barriers that had previously prevented European exploitation of interiors were rapidly broken down. Thus traditional systems of economic life which for centuries had resisted the European impact, and in which subsistence agriculture, cottage industries and barter were dominating features, disappeared with startling suddenness, to be succeeded by new conditions under which crops, financed by money advances, were grown for a world market.[1]

This static view of the Southeast Asian economies before 1870 was prolonged by the weakness of economic history in the decades following the end of the colonial system, and the inclination of scholars both inside and outside Southeast Asia to emphasize the autonomy of national histories in reaction to the excesses of colonial historiography. In general Southeast Asian data remains underrepresented in the new writing attempting to make sense of the global economy in the longer term. "It is remarkable," notes Janet Abu-Lughod, "that a region that for so long occupied the position of cross-waterway of the world should have had so little to say for itself."[2] Much more research of the type exemplified by this book is needed, but at last there is now some data. It begins to be possible to discern some of the broader rhythms of Southeast Asian economic life, which often show surprising similarities with those in other parts of the world.[3]

Relatively few long-term indices have been assembled for Southeast Asia or its constituents before 1820. What we do have so far is some time series about population, shipping, exports, and imports. The most helpful for estimating cycles of the commercial economy are the series assembled for four key exports—cloves, pepper, coffee, and sugar—over four centuries. These show that the revenue to Southeast Asians from the four long-distance export items went through a sustained period of growth between 1530 and 1630, and a major slump in 1650–1670 followed by a long stagnation until the 1780s. From the 1780s onward for almost a century there was a second and even stronger sustained period of growth during which these four exports grew by an average of over 4.5 percent per year. Far from being an export-led capitalist revolution, the colonial period after 1870 marked a sharp slowdown of export growth, turning negative for these four commodities in the 1890s for the first time since the 1770s.[4] The turnaround at the end of the eighteenth century deserves particular attention, since it occurred at a time of crisis in Europe, which has usually been considered the engine of global trade at that period. The crises that marked mainland Southeast Asia in the second half of the eighteenth century (1752–1788) came a little earlier than those in Europe and appear to have led to a period of renewed strength and stability just as Europe was undergoing the crisis of the French revolutionary wars. The three new dynasties that emerged from the crises in Burma, Siam, and Vietnam gained much of their economic strength from their proximity to a booming China, though something too from the global commercial strength of Britain. Although the export data mentioned above were derived primarily from the archipelagoes of Southeast Asia, in what follows I will focus more on the commodities of greater importance to mainland Southeast Asia.

The Chinese Century

During the long reign of the Qianlong emperor (1736–1795), China's population and economy had expanded as the country enjoyed the last period of peace and relative prosperity before its modern decline. Late in that reign, China conducted a series of energetic if not particularly successful interventions in the succession crises of its southern neighbors, followed by exceptionally cordial relations with the courts of Burma, Siam, and Vietnam after 1788. Vietnam and Siam sent tribute missions to Beijing almost every year from 1788 to 1830, which in turn provided excellent opportunities for expanded trade. In the early 1820s, John Crawfurd noted that the annual mission enabled the Siamese court "every year to send two large junks of . . . between nine hundred and one thousand tons each, to Canton, which, at the expense of a few trifling presents, are exempted from the payment of all duties."[5]

The Chinese population as a whole grew rapidly in this period, from about 150 million in 1700 to 400 million in 1850. Despite improvements in agriculture, with new varieties and extensive double-cropping of rice in the south, the pressure of this burgeoning population on the land became profound in many areas. In another of the great migrations Chinese history has witnessed, many left the crowded Yangzi valley for still-open frontiers in the south. In one of these, Yunnan, the population grew at more than 3 percent per annum in the period 1790–1805, and the whole population expanded from 3.1 million in 1777 to 6.3 million in 1825.[6] Both by land into Burma, Laos, and northern Vietnam and by sea from Guangdong and Fujian to the remainder of the region, the frontier of Chinese enterprise moved further south in the same period.

The last of the many imperial bans on private Chinese trade and travel abroad, that of the Kangxi emperor in 1717, had been revoked in 1727, legitimating and encouraging the overseas junk trade. Sojourning abroad continued to be condemned, but the wealthy Batavia trader Chen Ilao may have been the last to be punished for this offense in 1749. In 1754 the Chinese authorities declared for the first time that any Chinese with valid reasons would be entitled to return home and have his property protected.[7] The effect of this relaxation was quickly evident in the outflow of traders, miners, planters, shipbuilders, mariners and adventurers of all kinds. Crawfurd estimated that seven thousand Chinese a year were migrating to Siam alone around the time of his 1822 mission.[8]

The next half-century saw colonies of Chinese miners established in the northern border provinces of Vietnam, western Borneo, Phuket, Kelantan, and Bangka. Chinese planters established new export industries of pepper in Brunei, Cambodia, and Chantaburi, gambier in Riau-Johor, sugar in Siam and Vietnam. Most of these economic pioneers produced or traded for the China market. Hence a great expansion occurred in the junk trade to such ports as Hatien, Saigon, Terengganu, Riau, Brunei, and Sulu. The greatest of all Chinese ports outside China, however, was Bangkok, which probably replaced Batavia at the end of the eighteenth century as the busiest port between Calcutta and Canton.

The Nguyen dynasty of southern Vietnam and the Chakkri dynasty of Siam were particularly adept at using Chinese migrants to extend their frontiers and their revenue base. Around 1700 the Cantonese adventurer Mac Cuu established a port-state at Hatien, which was initially tributary to Cambodia and very mixed in population and culture. From 1708 it was an autonomous enclave under the Nguyen of Dang Trong (Cochin-China). Its second ruler Mac Thien Tu (1735–1771) brought in a number of Chinese literati and began to emulate the manners of a Chinese court. Although the population remained very mixed, with Malays and Khmers prominent in the army, increasing numbers of Cantonese immigrants took up pepper cultivation like their rivals the Teochiu of Chantaburi. By the middle of the eighteenth century, the Chinese population of southern Vietnam was probably in excess of thirty thousand.[9]

The effective use of Chinese migrants was also the primary factor that enabled Siam to recover quickly from the Burmese conquest of 1769 and allowed its new capital to rise to unprecedented importance as the economic hub of mainland Southeast Asia. In 1771 the renascent Siamese regime under the half-Chinese king Taksin conquered Hatien, which had been a formidable trading rival at the end of the Ayutthaya period. Taksin was in turn driven out of Hatien by a Nguyen army, one of the southern dynasty's last successes before being itself engulfed by the thirty-year Tay Son rebellion (1772–1802). As has recently been pointed out, the rise of Chinese port-polities in the Gulf of Siam, which had been facilitated by the first collapse of Ayutthaya in 1569, "was halted by the two big states that emerged at the end of the eighteenth century: the Siam of Thonburi and Bangkok and the Vietnam of the Tay Son and Nguyen rulers."[10]

Chinese on the Mining Frontier

The growth of China's economy in the eighteenth century and the decreasing supplies of copper and silver available from a Japan now deliberately discouraging most direct foreign trade stimulated a mining boom around the mineral-rich southern frontiers of China. Both through deliberate government recruitment and the attraction of labor opportunities, miners migrated in large numbers into Yunnan, where there were reported to be 500,000 miners by 1800. The desire for further mining sites was not halted by any notional boundary of Chinese imperial control. The hills in the north of what are today Burma, Laos, and Vietnam held similar resources of copper, lead, iron, and silver as those of Yunnan. Chinese miners became far more numerous on all these frontiers in the eighteenth century, making deals as necessary with local or state power-holders. Probably the most valuable example was the huge Bawdwin silver mine in the Shan area tributary to Burma, largely manned by Chinese.

In the northern border area of Le/Trinh Dai Viet, or northern Vietnam, notably in what is today Thai-Nguyen Province, there was a vast eighteenth-century expansion of copper and silver mining. Although a Trinh decree of 1717 had attempted to limit the number of Chinese miners to 100, 200, or 300 according to the size of the mine, by midcentury there were upwards of 20,000 Cantonese at the Tong-tinh copper mining complex alone. By the 1760s, with large tracts of agricultural land earlier devastated by famine and peasant taxes contributing little to the government's coffers, the Trinh state was reportedly drawing half its revenue from levies on these northern mines. Control of the mining enterprises (usually governed collectively through a form of *kongsi*) became increasingly difficult, however, so the court vainly attempted in 1767 to expel the Chinese from northern Vietnam. Though turbulence continued on this difficult frontier, the output of two of the largest copper mines throughout the second half of the century was thought to have averaged 280 and 220 tons respectively per annum, making this one of the largest copper complexes of Asia.[11]

Further south, the production of tin on the Malay Peninsula and the islands to its south remained modest until the systematic exploitation of tin discoveries on Bangka by Chinese miners in the middle of the eighteenth century. The tin of

Bangka had been discovered around 1710, but production by traditional Southeast Asian methods was modest until about 1750 when a local Chinese began importing Chinese contract workers from Guangdong. Their sophisticated sluicing techniques lifted production rapidly so that Bangka deliveries to the Dutch Company averaged 1562 tons a year in the 1760s, probably more than all of Southeast Asia had produced thirty years earlier.[12] European ships alone sold an average of 2162 tons a year of Southeast Asian tin (chiefly from Bangka) in Canton in 1771–1774.[13] Presuming that an equal amount was being imported to China by Chinese vessels or taken by Indian and Southeast Asian consumers, Southeast Asia's tin production must have exceeded Cornwall's to become the main world source by the 1770s.

Chinese mining gradually wrought the same transformation on the rich peninsular tin fields as it had in Bangka, though with many initial setbacks from the lack of security. Chinese had been involved in leasing the mine fields of Phuket (Junk Ceylon) from the Siamese king early in the eighteenth century and were smelting there while Malays and Thais dug for the tin. Ambitious Malay rulers periodically introduced Chinese to boost the existing production elsewhere in the peninsula. The sultan of Perak adopted a Dutch suggestion in the 1770s that he emulate the favorable Bangka experience by employing Chinese miners, and the ruler of Selangor followed suit around 1815. In Sungei Ujung (now Negri Sembilan) there were said to be nearly a thousand Chinese working in 1828 when a massacre of them caused an exodus.[14]

In the early nineteenth century the uneasy cooperation between Malay rulers, Chinese smelters, and a mixture of Malay and Chinese miners began to open up the forested peninsula and attract a variety of migrants to it. By 1835 the whole peninsula was estimated to produce 2050 tons a year, and around 1850 3750 tons a year, by then roughly matching the Bangka production.[15]

Gold was another of the items that attracted Chinese miners in the mid-eighteenth century to the eastern Malay Peninsula but more particularly to West Borneo. An average of sixty thousand Chinese miners were at work in the goldfields north of the Kapuas River in West Borneo from the mid-eighteenth to the mid-nineteenth centuries. Their organizations provide the best-known example of the *kongsi*, a ritual brotherhood in which capital and labor were shared in acknowledged portions. The sultans of Pontianak and Sambas had originally invited the Chinese to mine the upstream areas, profiting by selling them rice and supplies at inflated monopoly prices. But gradually the *kongsis* became autonomous by forming their own relations with interior Dayaks (including marriage), farming the surrounding land, and smuggling their gold out by channels not controlled by the rulers. As Dutch power advanced in the nineteenth century, most of the *kongsis* made their peace with it through a system of indirect rule, but the strongest Montrado *kongsi* remained defiant until conquered in the 1850s.

Agricultural Exports

One of the factors that drew global trade eastward in the eighteenth century was the English infatuation with tea, which became generalized around the middle of the eighteenth century. Large-scale trade grew along with direct English and Dutch access to Chinese ports after 1727. Much of the new English interest in Southeast Asian trade arose from the need to find trade goods salable in Canton in exchange for this tea. Pepper, gambier, cotton, and rice each played a role here.

Having been the cash crop par excellence that had brought Southeast Asia into the world economy in the sixteenth and seventeenth centuries, pepper had fallen victim to the system of monopolies and forced deliveries of the English and Dutch Companies. Southeast Asian exports had reached a peak of 6,500 tons a year in the 1670s, but were still somewhat less than that in the 1780s.[16] The entrepreneurs who turned this situation around in a newly freed market thereafter were Chinese, American, and Acehnese.

The Chinese began growing pepper themselves on a large scale in the mid-eighteenth century at centers outside the Dutch and English orbits. The Brunei Chinese were said to be able to produce 1200 tons a year in "good times" around the period 1760–1790.[17] From the 1740s there was a growing community of Chinese gambier and pepper growers also in the Riau Archipelago south of Singapore, while other small communities mingled with Malay growers at Terengganu and other ports on the eastern coast of the Malay Peninsula. The Teochiu agriculturalists in the southeast corner of Siam around Chantaburi appear also to have begun planting pepper in the late eighteenth century. Here and in the adjacent coastal area of Cambodia, production increased in the early nineteenth century entirely for the China market.[18]

The Chinese developed much more intensive pepper-growing methods than had been the Southeast Asian practice, with high applications of labor and fertilizer. Nevertheless, the most spectacular expansion of pepper growing occurred along the west coast of Aceh, in northern Sumatra, where Acehnese growers and American buyers combined in the late 1780s to create a new plantation area. From about 800 tons in 1795, its production reached a record 9,000 tons in 1824, representing about half of the world's supply.[19]

Gambier, an astringent obtained from the gum of a Sumatran shrub (*Uncaria gambir* or terra Japonica), had long been collected from wild plants and occasionally added to the betel chew. In the eighteenth century, however, both demand and supply took off. The demand came initially from Java, where addition of gambier to the quid of betel became virtually universal, and almost 700 tons of the valuable little blocks of gum were annually imported by the 1770s.[20] Chinese also discovered in the eighteenth century (or learned from Malays) that gambier was a valuable astringent for tanning leather. In the late 1730s the rulers of Riau contracted with Chinese traders to bring out Chinese laborers, on the usual indebted basis, to grow gambier in association with pepper. The industry spread to Singapore as soon as the city was founded in 1819 and thereafter to adjacent Johor on the mainland where the finances of the state were largely built by contracting land to Chinese gambier and pepper growers. In the early decades of the nineteenth century much of the thick forest and mangrove of the islands south of Singapore and the Johor coast was cleared for the first time to make way for gambier and pepper and to provide fuel for the gambier cooking pots.[21]

Since the thirteenth century or earlier, cotton had been exported from the dryer parts of Southeast Asia in which it flourished to other parts of the region and to China. Burma, Vietnam, Luzon, and Java were particularly noted in Chinese texts as sources for cotton. The great expansion of Chinese demand in the eighteenth century, however, caused an expansion of production and export from all these Southeast Asian centers. Chinese imports of cotton by sea expanded markedly, from 1375 tons in 1768 to 2866 in 1774.[22] The largest expansion seems to have been in the dry areas of upper Burma, where raw cotton was collected in the market of Sagaing, turned into yarn, and sold to Chinese traders from Yunnan and elsewhere. By the 1820s the overland traders were reckoned to be taking out over 6000 tons of cotton a year.[23]

Another agricultural commodity that began to play a major role in international trade in the eighteenth century was rice. The stimulus was once again the demand of southern China, where population pressure and the easing of trade restrictions gradually opened a large market. The desire for rice from Siam and Luzon was one of the factors that forced the liberalization of the China trade in the 1720s and 1730s. Imports were encouraged in midcentury by halving customs duties on ships carrying at least 10,000 *picul* (600 tons) of rice.[24] Siam was the principal beneficiary of this policy at first, but in the latter part of the eighteenth century rice exports to southern China became a major factor also for the economies of southern Vietnam and Luzon.

Li Tana has shown that a substantial rice surplus was first mobilized in the area around modern Saigon in the middle of the eighteenth century, as a mixed population of Chinese and Vietnamese gradually established Vietnamese control over this turbulent Khmer frontier.[25] From the Burmese invasions of Siam until 1780 there are no reports of Siamese rice reaching China, and the gap may have been filled by southern Vietnamese (and Luzon) rice. When the Tay Son rebellion (1772) cut the rice lifeline from Saigon to Hue, the rice surplus of the Mekong Delta became available for overseas trade. This resource was the principal economic asset of Nguyen Anh, the unifier of Vietnam and founder of its Nguyen dynasty (1802), who used rice exports to China and elsewhere to purchase his arms. Though not itself of high value, rice was often a key to open new markets for more profitable luxury items. Nguyen Anh exported it to Siam and south China in times of famine, building a network of support through this means. After 1840 Singapore became the main destination of the Saigon area rice, with a peak of Spanish $300,000 worth of rice being exported in 1855.

Nevertheless, the biggest single rice exporter may have been the Philippines, where the central Luzon plain was one of the first areas to fully commercialize the production of rice. Although poorly monitored because they avoided Manila in favor of small, uncontrolled ports in northern Luzon, Philippine rice exports to China were thought to amount to 60,000 tons in 1850, worth upward of two million Spanish dollars.[26] We should therefore regard first Ayutthaya and later independent Vietnam and Luzon as the pioneers of large-scale rice exports, on whose success the later colonially supervised exploitation of the Mekong, Irrawaddy, and Chaophraya Deltas was built.

A Shipping Boom

The greatly increased exports to China discussed above were made possible by the increasingly relaxed attitude of Qing authorities to external trade and a major expansion in shipping capacity. Crawfurd in the early 1820s estimated that there were about 140 sizable junks totaling 35,000 tons engaged in the trade between Siam and various southern Chinese ports, with two-thirds of the tonnage being based in Siam.[27] This represents about a tenfold rise over the situation a century earlier when the numbers fluctuated between three or four in some years and as many as twenty in others.[28] Most of this enormous increase in the Siam–China trade had occurred in the first forty years of the Bangkok dynasty, for the new Chakkri dynasty of Siam had shown itself highly flexible in exploiting the China trade for its own financial ends.

Table 2.1, summarizing John Crawfurd's data, shows the pattern of the junk trade in the early part of the nineteenth century, before the establishment of Singapore brought about a major reorientation. This table combines the China-based trade to Southeast Asian ports, the Siam-based trade to China (listed as Siam below) and the Siam-based trade to the main Southeast Asian destinations.

Crawfurd's data reveals the extent to which Saigon had already come to dominate Vietnamese foreign trade despite still being in a multiethnic frontier context. He notes that Bangkok-based Chinese junks also visited Hoi An and Hue, "but by far [traded] to the greatest extent" with Saigon.[29] Though fewer in number, the tonnage of even China-based junks trading to Saigon considerably exceeded that to northern Vietnam. At the time of Crawfurd's visit to Saigon in 1822 it had a flourishing Chinese population of three to four thousand, and the Cantonese temple was "the handsomest building of the sort that I have anywhere seen."[30] Crawfurd unfortunately does not provide details of the Saigon-based Chinese shipping as he does for the Bangkok-based, though it was certainly much less. Chinese manned all the Saigon junks except for the royal vessels that Minh Mang sent to Singapore and Batavia in the 1820s. Crawfurd does give some detail of one of the larger Saigon-based Chinese junks to visit Singapore in 1822. This was a vessel of 240 tons, bigger than most Chinese ships, and built at a cost of four thousand dollars in "the river of Kamboja." Her three officers and thirty-two men were well paid by English standards and had made the crossing from Pulo Condore to the Malaya coast in three days.[31]

A useful time series based on the Melaka harbormaster's records provides one quantitative demonstration that the increase in Chinese shipping in Southeast Asian waters documented by Crawfurd was already beginning in the late

Table 2.1: Junk Traffic of the South China Sea from Home Ports in Siam, Guangdong, and Fujian

Route to	Siam		Guangdong		Fujian		Total	
	No.	Tons	No.	Tons	No.	Tons	No.	Tons
Nth Vietnam			24	3,100	14	2,000	38	5,100
Central VN			28	4,050	20	3,750	48	7,800
—Saigon	45	6,300	22	3,625	7	2,875	74	12,800
Siam*	81	24,560	56	10,155	2	375	139	35,090
Riau-Lingga	44	6,160	1	500	2	1,600	47	8,260
Kelantan					1	800	1	800
Terengganu					1	800	1	800
Brunei			3	1,500			3	1,500
Sambas			2	1,000			2	1,000
Pontianak			3	1,500			3	1,500
Mampawa			2	1,000			2	1,000
Banjarmasin			1	600			1	600
Java			4	2,000	3	3,300	7	5,300
Makasar					2	1,000	2	1,000
Ambon					1	500	1	500
Sulu					2	1,600	2	1,600
Manila					4-5	2,000	4	2,000
Total	about 200#	unknown	146	29,030	59-60	20,600	375	86,650

Source: Anthony Reid, "The Unthreatening Alternative: Chinese Shipping in Southeast Asia, 1567–1842", *Review of Indonesian and Malaysian Affairs* 27 (1993): 27; and John Crawfurd, *Journal of an Embassy to the Courts of Siam and Cochin China*, reprint (Kuala Lumpur: Oxford University Press, 1967), 414–415.

* Crawfurd's estimate of Siam-based junks sailing to peninsular and archipelagic ports of the south. They cannot be distributed among ports.
# Crawfurd's overall estimate of Siam-based Chinese shipping sailing to all ports.

eighteenth century. The total number of ship arrivals in the port of Melaka rose nearly threefold between 1761 and 1785, from 188 to 539. Classifying by the ethnicity of ships' captains, the two big winners in the period were Chinese (from 55 to 170) and Malays (54 to 242). If we further break down the ships calling in Melaka under Chinese captains on the basis of their home port, it transpires that some other ports were growing even faster than Melaka as bases for Chinese shipping. Chinese ships based in Melaka increased their calls from 30 in 1761 to 106 in 1785; but those based in Riau grew from 1 to 12 and in Siak from 0 to 22.[32] Chinese ships from Hatien also made the trip to Melaka, with 2 arriving in 1761 and 5 in 1770, not long before the city's fall to Taksin. Thereafter it is "Cochin-China" (probably referring to Saigon) which features as the main Indochina port for Melaka, four ships reported arriving from thence in 1775 and three in 1780.[33]

After Singapore's foundation in 1819 the numbers of ships calling quickly surpassed anything Melaka or any other Southeast Asian port had experienced. By 1822 there were already a hundred European ships and a thousand Asian ones clearing the port,[34] roughly double Melaka's trade at its 1785 height. The expansion of shipping in the region in the following years can be gauged from table 2.2, covering the arrivals in Singapore of vessels from various places.

Table 2.2: Arrivals in Singapore of Square-Rigged (SRV) and Asian Vessels from Southeast Asia

Arrived from:	1829–1830		1835–1836		1841–1842		1847–1848	
	SRV	Asian	SRV	Asian	SRV	Asian	SRV	Asian
Siam	12	31	9	23	15	28	21	28
"Cochin-China"	3	49	4	35	1	52	1	162
Sumatra	1	276	14	339	10	497	22	445
Java	59	62	78	56	110	75	93	55
Celebes	0	61	0	87	0	88	0	76
Borneo	0	176	13	193	18	95	45	151
Bali & nearby	0	36	0	73	7	123	29	90
Riau	1	346	3	264	3	308	4	314
Manila	14	-	27	-	27	-	16	-
Nearby Is.	-	214	-	160	-	251	-	207
E Malay Pen.	-	114	-	70	-	252	10	515
W Malay Pen.	-	205	-	59	-	69	-	57
Penang/Melaka	92	124	110	68	108	560	151	303
Total SE Asia	182	1694	258	1427	299	2398	392	2403
Tonnage		33576		49277		58564		82989
	36282		33183		46792		67726	
Av. ton/ship	184	21	191	23	196	20	212	28

Calculated from Wong Lin Ken, "The Trade of Singapore, 1819–69," *Journal of the Malayan Branch of the Royal Asiatic Society* 33, no. 4 (1950): 278–90

The rapid increase in the tonnage of shipping centered on Singapore in less than twenty years is a good measure of the rise in Southeast Asia's commercial tempo. The table shows that "Cochin-China," probably referring primarily to Vietnam's southern port of Saigon, was the largest Southeast Asian partner of Singapore for the Chinese junk trade (Sumatra and Riau sending chiefly small Malay vessels), and that its trade rose threefold in this period in step with a more general expansion of the trade of independent states.

The trade of Singapore with Siam, Cambodia, and Vietnam (still called Cochin-China by the British) is of particular interest because of the "hermit kingdom" stereotype that those countries unjustly enjoyed among Europeans. The Vietnamese kingdoms and Siam had not opted out of foreign trade at the end of the seventeenth century, but rather entrusted it almost entirely to Chinese merchants because of their justifiable suspicions of armed European ships.[35] The expansion of Chinese commerce we have described in the latter part of the eighteenth century made it possible for these kingdoms also to interact more intensively with their neighbors. Thonburi and Bangkok were particularly successful in attracting Chinese shipping from their foundation in 1767 (Taksin) and 1782 (Rama I), respectively. Crawfurd reckoned that it cost Chinese shipbuilders only half as much to build their vessels here as it did in Fujian and substantially less than in Guangdong.[36] Under the pro-Chinese early Bangkok dynasty these shippers also enjoyed a trade regime more benign and predictable than was available in Canton or Amoy. Bangkok assumed around the turn of the century the role of principal Chinese redistributive center that Manila and Batavia had played in 1680–1740 and Singapore would do after about 1825. From his observations in the early 1820s, Crawfurd declared it the largest independent port in Asia after Canton.[37]

This Siam-based trade was already reaching Malacca Straits entrepôts before the fall of Ayutthaya, with as many as ten Siamese junks entering Palembang in the year 1758–1759,[38] though only two identified as Siamese reached Batavia in the midcentury years 1750 and 1752.[39] It was quick to recover from the Burmese conquest, since there were already eleven junks a year bringing Siamese fish and rice to Batavia in the late 1770s and a couple visiting Dutch Melaka to pick up Indian cloth, opium, and European goods, if the situation in 1785 was typical.[40] British Penang began to attract the Bangkok Chinese shippers in 1817, but Singapore was far better placed and in the 1820s already had become the most important Southeast Asian port for Siam, as well as its rival. The size of junks on the Bangkok–Singapore run rose quickly: from an average of 127 tons in 1829–1830 to an average of 252 tons in 1841–1842. Table 2.2 disguises what is in fact a consistent upward trend in terms of the tonnage of junks, with 7,500 tons arriving from Siam in 1829–1830 to 12,400 in 1841–1842. The value of the trade roughly doubled in the same period, with Siamese sugar, salt, rice, and lac, with some Chinese manufactures being exchanged for British and Indian cloth, opium, and manufactures.[41]

The Nguyen rulers who unified Vietnam in the early nineteenth century, despite their reputation for "real or pretended contempt of foreign traffic in gen-

eral," as Crawfurd's instructions phrased it,[42] showed great interest in the establishment of Singapore as an international port. Although their export economy
had been oriented towards China, Saigon-based Chinese vessels such as the one
described above were among the first to visit Singapore when it was opened for
business in 1819. There was profit to be made in exchanging Vietnamese rice in
Singapore for opium. This was presumably the main business of the surprisingly
large number of Vietnamese/Chinese junks of about one hundred tons, known as
"topes" in Singapore, which made the voyage in the 1840s and 1850s. Although
some of this must have been smuggling in Vietnamese official eyes, since importing opium had been forbidden, Emperor Minh Mang also embarked on a
significant royal trade with Singapore after receiving the report of a mission he
sent there in 1825. The emperor, however, discouraged private trade by prohibit-
ing Vietnam-based vessels from carrying guns. The topes therefore became the
principal targets of pirates in the Gulf of Siam. The emperor himself conducted a
substantial monopoly trade exporting silk, tea, rhinoceros horn, sugar, and rice
and importing cloth for his military uniforms, tin for his bullets, firearms, and
opium. Overall the trade of Vietnam with Singapore expanded very rapidly,
from a value of about 150,000 Spanish dollars in the 1820s to an average of
around 600,000 Spanish dollars in the late 1840s—a level then similar to Siam's
trade.[43]

Conclusion: Vietnam and the Region

As the long history of the Chams demonstrated, the coast of what is now southern Vietnam is extremely well situated for commerce, in terms of both its harbors and its proximity to the main routes of maritime trade between China and
the rest of the world. On the other hand, the long, indented coast and mountainous terrain makes the region difficult to unify by land and prone to piracy by
sea. The history of the region since becoming part of the Vietnamese world may
be seen as a long contest between a maritime geographical heritage and the imperatives of political control.

The end of the eighteenth century and the beginning of the nineteenth
marked a major increase in the tempo of commerce throughout Southeast Asia,
largely influenced (especially in the mainland) by the economic growth of
China. The Water Frontier of southern Indochina was a major element in this
moment of dynamic Southeast Asian growth and provided the resources for the
establishment under the Nguyen of the first unified government over this whole
long coastline. In this as in many other respects, a broader regional perspective
can assist us in understanding the economic dynamics of this frontier.

Notes

1. D. G. E. Hall, *A History of South East Asia*, 3rd ed. (Basingstoke: Macmillan, 1968), 781.

2. Janet Abu-Lughod, *Before European Hegemony. The World-System A.D. 1250–1350* (New York: Oxford University Press, 1989), 296–97.

3. Victor Lieberman, "Transcending East–West Dichotomies," in *Beyond Binary Histories: Re-imagining Eurasia to c.1830*, ed. Victor Lieberman (Ann Arbor: University of Michigan Press, 1999), 82–90; Anthony Reid, "The Seventeenth Century Crisis in Southeast Asia," *Modern Asian Studies* 24 (1990): iv.

4. Bulbeck et al., *Southeast Asian Exports since the Fourteenth Century: Cloves, Pepper, Coffee and Sugar* (Singapore: Institute of Southeast Asian Studies, 1998), 10–15.

5. John Crawfurd, *Journal of an Embassy to the Courts of Siam and Cochin China*, reprint (Kuala Lumpur: Oxford University Press, 1967), 409.

6. James Lee, "The Legacy of Immigration in Southwest China, 1250–1850," *Annales de demographie historique* (1982): 294–95.

7. Ng Chin Keong, "The Case of Chen I-lao: Maritime Trade and Overseas Chinese in Ch'ing Policies," in *Emporia, Commodities and Entrepreneurs in Asian Maritime Trade, c. 1400–1750*, ed. Roderich Ptak and Dietmar Rothermunde (Stuttgart: Franz Steiner, 1991), 373–400.

8. Crawfurd, *Journal*, 412.

9. Li Tana, "The Chinese in Vietnam," in *The Encyclopaedia of the Chinese Overseas* (Singapore: Archipelago Press and Landmark Books, 1998), 228–33; Chen Chingho, "Mac Thien Tu and Phraya Taksin: A Survey of Their Political Stand, Conflicts, and Background," in *Proceedings of the 7th IAHA Conference* (Bangkok: Chulalongkorn University Press, 1979), 1534–1575; Yumio Sakurai and Takako Kitagawa, "Hatien or Banteay Meas in the Time of the Fall of Ayutthaya," in *From Japan to Arabia: Ayutthaya's Maritime Relations with Asia*, ed. Kennon Breazeale (Bangkok: The Foundation for the Promotion of Social Sciences and Humanities Textbooks Project, 1999), 150–220.

10. Sakurai and Kitagawa, "Hatien or Banteay Meas," 150–220, 207.

11. Alexander Woodside, "The Relationship between Political Theory and Economic Growth in Vietnam, 1750–1840," in *The Last Stand of Asian Autonomies: Responses to Modernity in the Diverse States of Southeast Asia and Korea, 1750–1900*, ed. Anthony Reid (London: Macmillan 1997), 259–60; Nguyen Thanh-Nha, *Tableau économique du Vietnam aux XVIIe et XVIIIe siècles* (Paris: Cujas, 1970), 86–90.

12. Mary Somers Heidhues, *Bangka Tin and Mentok Pepper: Chinese Settlement on an Indonesian Island* (Singapore: Institute of Southeast Asian Studies, 1992), 2–9.

13. H. B. Morse, *The Chronicles of the East India Company Trading to China*, 5 vols., reprint (Taipei: Ch'eng-Wen Publishing Company, 1966) vol. 5, 155, 170, 191.

14. Wong Lin Ken, *The Malayan Tin Industry to 1914* (Tucson: University of Arizona Press, 1965), 17–20; Somers Heidhues, *Bangka Tin*, 10.

15. Wong, *The Malayan Tin Industry*, 12, 20.

16. Bulbeck et al., *Southeast Asian Exports*, 86.

17. Tan Peck Leng, "A History of Chinese Settlement in Brunei," in *Essays on Modern Brunei History* (Bandar Seri Begawan: Universiti Brunei Darrusalam Department of History, 1992), 110–12.

18. William Skinner, *Chinese Society in Thailand: An Analytical History* (Ithaca: Cornell University Press, 1957), 46, 84; Crawfurd, *Journal*, 413.

19. James Gould, "Sumatra—America's Pepperpot, 1784–1873," *Essex Institute Historical Collections* XCII (1956): 100–19, 344–45.

20. Gerrit Knaap, *Shallow Waters, Rising Tide: Shipping and Trade in Java around 1775* (Leiden: KITLV Press, 1996), 97.

21. Carl Trocki, *Prince of Pirates: the Temenggongs and the Development of Johor and Singapore, 1784–1885* (Singapore: Oxford University Press), 18–20.

22. Morse, *East India Company Trading to China*, Vol. 5, 139, 155, 170, 191.

23. I owe this data to Teruko Saito (Tokyo University of Foreign Studies).

24. Jennifer Cushman, *Fields from the Sea* (Ithaca: Cornell SE Asia Program, 1993), 89–92; Sarasin Viraphol, *Tribute and Profit: Sino–Siamese Trade 1652–1853* (Cambridge, Mass.: Harvard University Press, 1977), 55–57.

25. Li Tana, "Rice Trade in the 18th and 19th Century Mekong Delta and Its Implications," in *Thailand and Her Neighbours (II): Laos, Vietnam and Cambodia*, ed. Thanet Aphornsuvan (Bangkok: Thammasat University Core University Proceedings, 1994), 198–214.

26. Robert MacMicking, *Recollections of Manilla and the Philippines during 1848, 1849 and 1850* (London, 1851; reprinted Manila: Filipiniana Book Guild, 1967), 169.

27. Crawfurd, *Journal*, 410.

28. Viraphol, *Tribute and Profit*, 55, 72; Anthony Reid, *Southeast Asia in the Age of Commerce*. vol II: *Expansion and Crisis* (New Haven: Yale University Press, 1993), 308.

29. Crawfurd, *Journal*, 414.

30. Crawfurd, *Journal*, 414.

31. Crawfurd, *Journal*, 49–51.

32. Anthony Reid and Radin Fernando,"Shipping of Melaka and Singapore as an Index of Growth, 1760–1840," *South Asia* 19 (1996): 66–75.

33. Reid and Fernando,"Shipping of Melaka," 67.

34. Wong Lin Ken, "The Trade of Singapore, 1819–69," *Journal of the Malayan Branch of the Royal Asiatic Society* 33, no. 4 (1960): 133–34.

35. Anthony Reid, "The Unthreatening Alternative: Chinese Shipping in Southeast Asia, 1567–1842," *Review of Indonesian and Malaysian Affairs* 27 (1993): 13–32.

36. Crawfurd, *Journal*, 49.

37. Crawfurd, *Journal*, 49, 414–16.

38. Barbara Andaya, *To Live as Brothers: Southeast Sumatra in the Seventeenth and Eighteenth Centuries* (Honolulu: University of Hawaii Press, 1997), 205.

39. George Souza, *The Survival of Empire: Portuguese Trade and Society in China and the South China Sea, 1630–1754* (Cambridge: Cambridge University Press, 1986), 137.

40. Knaap, *Shallow Waters*, 52, 87; Reid and Fernando, "Shipping of Melaka": 78.

41. Wong, "Trade of Singapore," 134–43, 278.

42. Crawfurd, *Journal*, 590

43. Wong, "Trade of Singapore," 240–41.

3

Eighteenth-Century Chinese Pioneers on the Water Frontier of Indochina

Yumio Sakurai

The Water Frontier of Indochina

Geographically, the Water Frontier of the Indochina Peninsula comprised an area including the Tonle Sap River, the lower Mekong basins, the Dong Nai highlands and rivers, and the coastal regions along the South China Sea and Gulf of Thailand. The people who came to this region in the eighteenth century played an important historical role in early modern Southeast Asia. The area had once been a trading crossroad, but local peoples had largely abandoned it as an important commercial center long before Chinese immigrants later began to develop its potential. First the newcomers transformed the region into a major trading center between the Cambodian core region (from Phnom Penh to Lovek) and the sea, and between the Gulf of Thailand and the South China Sea. Then they helped develop it as an export-oriented rice bowl. Unlike the deltas of the Chaophraya ruled by Ayutthaya, the Irrawaddy under the Konbaung, or the Red River under Dai Viet, the Water Frontier of Indochina was politically free land distant from the rule of big states.[1] In the eighteenth century it rapidly became a Chinese "Promised Land," attracting Chinese immigrants ranging from adventurers like Mac Cuu,[2] who founded the Chinese port polity kingdom of Hatien,[3] through to adventurers, merchants, soldiers, and dreamy youths.

As used here, the concept of "Water Frontier" contains two main ideas. First, it locates a newly emerging center in maritime Southeast Asia and recognizes the role Chinese played in its development. It was the last large space open to Chinese adventurers in what Anthony Reid has called the "Chinese Century" in Southeast Asia.[4] Second, from the broader perspective of Chinese maritime activity in Southeast Asia, the Water Frontier refers to a transitional era between the markets and trade networks typical of the Age of Commerce and the mandala-style state structures of the seventeenth century, on the one hand, and, on the other, the newly emerging late-eighteenth-century maritime commerce that occurred as expansionary local states approached their late precolonial limits. These states included the Konbaung in Burma, the Tay Son in Vietnam, and Siam under Taksin. Dutch expansion in Java can also be considered an example of this movement in the archipelago. Maritime Chinese played a historical role as the vanguard of this change through the formation and operation of their original international networks. Newly developed local powers first followed these early Chinese networks, in order to establish the territory of their own precolonial states, before later abandoning the Chinese pioneers, as we see with Taksin in Thonburi, Mac Thien Tu in Hatien, and Tran Dai Dinh in Bien Hoa. The Water Frontier of Indochina was not, in the end, to become the frontier of maritime Chinese.

This chapter tries to describe the formation and decline of the Water Frontier of Indochina by treating it as a historical circle, that is, by describing it as a unit of geographical and historical space whose population shared similar historical experiences essentially caused by the same historical factors.[5] It begins with a brief look at the area's geographic foundations.

Historical Geography: Two Water Frontiers

In geographic terms, most of the Water Frontier area is low-lying flatland along the two great faults of the Mekong running from north to south and on the Tonle Sap from west to east. Both meet at Phnom Penh and expand southeast to form the Mekong Delta. On the borders of these lowlands are two basalt massifs, the Dong Nai highlands to the east and the Takeo plateau to the west. History reflected geography here, with the Water Frontier divided into western and eastern parts. The eastern part was the more compact and extended from the Dong Nai highlands to the main Mekong branch (the Tien Giang River) and the sea. The western part ran from the foothills of the Cardamon Mountains in Cambodia along the lower Mekong branch (the Hau Giang or Bassac River) and then south to the sea. The next sections introduce each part, beginning with the eastern Water Frontier.

The Eastern Water Frontier

The Highlands and Plateaus—Dong Nai and Tay Ninh
     The wide, gentle slopes of the Dong Nai highlands expand from the southern foot of the Da Lat range south to Cape Vung Tau and west to Kompong Cham in Cambodia. In the eighteenth century, its basalt-based red soil was cov-

ered by thick tropical vegetation, including equatorial trees with huge trunks that later settlers found were good for boat building.[6] Local tribal peoples (Stieng, Kohor, and others) grew dry-cropped rice, yam, and maize by shifting cultivation and collected forest products that were ultimately exported by sea.[7] Before the seventeenth century, there had been Khmer and Cham trading centers along the Dong Nai River, the main waterway to the sea, and along tributaries like the Saigon River. Modern Bien Hoa, in the area called Daung Nay in Khmer,[8] was the most important because it was the last inland port navigable by seagoing vessels. Below Bien Hoa, the site of modern Saigon or Prey Nokor, near the eastern foot of the highlands, was also long settled by Khmer people.[9]

West of the Dong Nai highlands, in present Binh Duong and Tay Ninh Provinces and across into Cambodia, runs the Tay Ninh plateau, an area of tropical savanna about ten to thirty meters above sea level. Numerous remains along the East Vam Co River in Tay Ninh Province indicate many earlier Khmer settlements here.[10] This area forms the eastern periphery of the Khmer agricultural plateau stretching from north of Tonle Sap Lake to the Kompong Cham region and within which Khmer-Indian rice cropping methods were traditionally used.[11] The rivet point of the network was Srei Santor on the opposite Mekong bank from Phnom Penh and an anti-Udong-Lovek center during the post-Angkor period.[12]

The Young Delta—Tan An, My Tho

The young Mekong Delta, covered with an alluvial soil layer, stretches west from modern Ho Chi Minh City through to My Tho, Vinh Long, and Can Tho and back up the two Mekong branches to Phnom Penh. In the eighteenth century it was a mosaic of narrow natural levees (about 2 meters high and 200–300 meters wide) and low swampy land. Few Angkor remains have been found in the Vietnamese portion. Indeed, the thirteenth-century Chinese text *Chenla fengtu ji* (The Customs of Cambodia) reported no rice fields at all along the Mekong until Kompong Chnang but only forests and small rivers.[13] Seventeenth-century Dutch and Japanese records reported no river ports along the young Mekong Delta, with merchants going to Phnom Penh to trade.[14] In the eighteenth century, however, this area would become the land frontier of Indochina for Vietnamese farmers.

Inland Back Swamp—Dong Thap Muoi

The inland Back Swamp probably formed from a shallow sea left behind by the expanding delta. The area dried into marshy lowlands that are generally deeply submerged in the flood season and strongly influenced by tidal movements. Around 500,000 hectares now, Dong Thap Muoi was twice that size in the eighteenth century.[15] Fresh swampy forests of melaleuca (*tram*) or mangrove trees cover the portion that surrounds the delta. The central Back Swamp, called Dong Thap Muoi, forms a huge inundated depression of strongly acidic soil. Until the 1970s, only primitive floating rice could be grown successfully here. A similar huge swampy floodplain also stretches along the Bassac River from

Chau Doc to the foot of Takeo plateau.

Despite its difficulties for agriculture, many ancient remains from Funan and pre-Angkor eras have been found along the West Vam Co River.[16] The Vam Co may once have connected with the main Mekong branch at the Dong Thap Muoi swamp, making it likely that these rivers formed the main route from Cambodia to the South China Sea. After the river junction silted up, the Khmer abandoned Dong Thap Muoi for about a thousand years.

Coastal Back Swamp—Can Gio and Ben Tre

South from Ho Chi Minh City to the tip of Ca Mau peninsula is a large coastal swamp belt between the Young Delta and a number of coastal, raised beach ridges. Before French colonization the area was a little populated jungle of mangrove and nippa forests, with mostly brackish tidal water and only occasional huts scattered on small beach ridges.

The Western Water Frontier

The Takeo Plateau

From Tonle Sap Lake a sandstone-based plateau extends south to the eastern foothills of the Cardamon Mountains and across to Kampot. Its lower flatlands are cultivated as rain-fed rice fields. Many Angkor remains exist in this area and several province (*sruk*) names from this plateau appear in traditional Khmer records.[17] Although important today because the highway connecting the international port of Kompong Som to Phnom Penh runs through it, according to Takako Kitagawa, post-Angkor kings and French colonialists alike paid little attention to this land access from the Cambodian core to the coast.[18]

The Coastal Ridge—Tra Vinh and Soc Trang

The Mekong coastal estuaries feature several raised beach ridges. Some of these beach ridges, like Ben Tre, Mo Cay, and Tra Vinh, show archeological evidence from Funan as well as significant Khmer constructions in the past. However, with the main exception of the Tra Vinh area (or Prea Trepeang in Khmer), from the late-eighteenth-century Khmer numbers here declined due to expanding Vietnamese control and settlement. By the early colonial period, only about 50,000 Khmer remained in Tra Vinh.[19]

Small Ridge and Wide Swamp—Ca Mau, Rach Gia, and Hatien

In the southern Ca Mau Peninsula, long raised beach ridges stretch from east to west behind a narrow belt of mangrove and nippa forest. The western coast of the peninsula, formed by alluvial soil from the Bassac (Hau Giang) River is fertile but strongly influenced by tidal movements. This was long an underpopulated area, covered in tidal mangrove swamps to the south and capable mainly of supporting only fishing villages. The name derives from the original Khmer Tuk Khmau, meaning "black water," a term that well describes its sulfate acidic water.[20]

Back from the coast, a wide marshy belt of melaleuca swamp stretches behind the beach ridges from Ca Mau to Hatien. Several Mekong tributaries reach their estuaries through these ridges. Along the west coast, from modern Rach Gia city to Hatien there stretches a series of narrow, raised beach ridges. Rach Gia itself stands on a complex of such ridges and higher land made from old alluvial soil that forms a natural levee of the Bassac River. The higher parts of this area contain several sites from the Funan and pre-Angkor periods.[21] Before the eighth century, this place may have been part of an international trading network linking the Indian Ocean and the South China Sea through the Malay Peninsula and the Gulf of Thailand. The area had been abandoned by the Angkor period, however, because the development of the Malacca Strait then connected the two seas directly. According to Michael Vickery, Portuguese navigators in the sixteenth century knew little of the Bassac River as a possible route to Phnom Penh[22] and only used the upper Mekong stream (Tien Giang). The seventeenth-century compilation, *Shunfeng xiangsong* (Sailing under Favorite Winds)[23] also says nothing of any ports on the west coast.

As this brief survey indicates, local peoples had abandoned much of the Indochina Water Frontier, except for certain coastal and plateau areas, well before the late-seventeenth-century proto–Water Frontier period. This means that when the first Chinese immigrants arrived there was little significant agriculture in the region and virtually no commerce, a situation that changed dramatically during the eighteenth-century. In that century, this "Promised Land," a Water Frontier for Chinese and Land Frontier for Vietnamese, would become the scene of a long struggle to decide its possession and exploitation.

Vietnamese Expansion in the Eastern Water Frontier

After the decline of the Age of Commerce, the first stage of the eastern Water Frontier began in 1679 when more than three thousand armed Chinese refugees arrived there after being sent south by the Nguyen lord to find refuge.[24] One group led by a Cantonese named Chen Shangchuan (Tran Thuong Xuyen) entered the Saigon River mouth at Can Gio and sailed to Ban Lam, an old fortified Khmer holding at present-day Bien Hoa city, where they opened markets and attracted Chinese junk traders. This was the first time that a well-organized group of Chinese established a commercial terminal in a Khmer river port in the Water Frontier region with the recognition of a Vietnamese government.[25] Meanwhile, another group led by Yang Yandi (Duong Ngan), a general commanding a Cantonese corps called *Long Men* (Dragon Gate), entered the Cua Xoai Lap estuary and settled at My Tho in 1679. There they opened land, established markets, and began to attract Chinese, Europeans, Japanese, and Malay traders, just as in Bien Hoa.

However, in this sector of the eastern Water Frontier the Chinese were not alone. Both Khmer and Vietnamese military and political forces were struggling to control the area through a recurrent civil war between different Khmer royal factions. According to Kitagawa, citing reports made to Japanese officials by seventeenth- and eighteenth-century Chinese traders, for much of the post-Angkor period two Khmer power bases existed, one at the fan top of the Water Frontier in the Srei Santor region and one centered on Udong-Lovek. The Chinese merchants called the Srei Santor power *shui wang* or "water king," and the Udong-Lovek dynasty *shan wang* or "mountain king." Both powers shared territories at Phnom Penh. The former was closely connected to the Vietnamese through the eastern Water Frontier, while the latter maintained a special relationship to Siam by land routes via Battambang and Khorat, and the western Water Frontier through Kampot and Peam Banteay Meas (later Hatien).[26] In the 1670s and 1680s, the capital of the "water king" and Vietnamese protégé Nac Non[27] was at Saigon, close to the Chinese in Bien Hoa. Kitagawa has also argued, from Cambodian chronicles and provincial details in the Cambodian Legal Code (*Kram Srok*) of 1693,[28] that the Udong government did not control the lower Mekong area by the late seventeenth century. Rather, coastal ridges here, like Ba Thac (present-day Soc Trang) and Koh Haong Peam Me So (present-day My Tho), were under the semi-independent rule of local Khmer chiefs called *Okna*.[29] The first Chinese pioneers had thus come to the most crowded corner of a largely empty land.

Inevitably, the new settlers were drawn into the local conflicts. In the early 1680s when the Vietnamese joined with the new second king, Ang Tan,[30] to fight his rival, Yang Yandi reportedly took advantage of the new war to invade Cambodia via the Mekong in 1682 with 70 ships and 3000 men. However, in 1688 he was assassinated by one of his followers, Huang Jin (Hoang Tan), who then moved the *Long Men* corps from My Tho to the junction of the My Tho and Vam Co Rivers in a bid to control Mekong shipping.[31] The move failed. The Vietnamese killed Huang Jin and sent the *Long Men* to Chen Shangchuan, who took them to fight in Cambodia for the Vietnamese.[32]

It is probable that behind the Vietnamese invasions of Cambodia in 1682 and 1688 was the leadership of the Chinese military group who used the conflict to try to win control of the Tien Giang commercial network from My Tho and Saigon right through to Phnom Penh. When that failed, they turned to piracy. In 1690, one Chinese trading ship reported to Japanese officials that Chen Shangchuan of Taiwan was pillaging merchant ships in the Cambodia river estuary and supporting the second king against the first. In 1699, more reports of piracy of ships trading in Cambodia were made in Nagasaki.[33] In one case, Chen Shangchuan was named as leader of the pirates to whom the ship's master had been forced to pay a share of his cargo as protection money.

It thus seems certain that by then Chen Shangchuan had unified the Chinese armed groups and taken over hegemony of the Tien Giang route, from Xoai Lap to Saigon and Bien Hoa, from the competing Dong Nai Chinese network. The first structured coastal and river network in the east Water Frontier thus emerged in the late seventeenth century due to the military power of Chinese originating from Canton. Even so, Chen Shangchuan still had to deal with Vietnamese power in the area.

The Vietnamese chronicle for this period, *Dai Nam Thuc Luc Tien Bien*, always described Chen Shangchuan as a subordinate of the Vietnamese armed forces. For example, in 1699 when he was based at Tran Bien (Bien Hoa), *Tien Bien* recorded that Chen Shangchuan invaded Cambodia under Vietnamese orders in 1699 and occupied Phnom Penh in 1700. But Chinese merchant reports at Nagasaki suggest a more complex relationship. According to two such reports in 1699, the Nguyen planned to invade Cambodia in 1698 and had prepared hundreds of war boats to take his troops there. As chief of the pirates based in the Cambodian estuaries, Chen Shangchuan had heard of the plan and sought Vietnamese appointment as a head of the fleet.[34] This story suggests a more autonomous position at the time than the nineteenth-century chronicle later described.

Before he died in Bien Hoa in 1715, Chen Shangchuan supported other Vietnamese incursions into Cambodia, as did his son and successor, Tran Dai Dinh. But in the early 1730s, Tran Dai Dinh lost the confidence of the Nguyen ruler following two rounds of fighting against Laotians in Cambodia. In 1731, Tran Dai Dinh had attacked Lao forces invading Cambodia and had forced the Cambodian king Neac Ta to flee to Son Pho (Pursat).[35] Then in 1732 he marched on some Lao bandits. But after a Vietnamese general sent a slanderous account of the campaign to the Nguyen ruler, the Chinese general was arrested and died shortly after in a Hue prison.[36]

If Vietnamese rulers exploited the *Long Men* corps at this time, they had also begun to consolidate their own power by expanding administratively into the Young Delta in the 1690s, especially after the death of the Vietnamese protégé Ang Nan in 1691. In 1698 the Vietnamese presence was formalized by establishing Gia Dinh Province in the Dong Nai region. As part of this expansion, they established one military government (Tran Bien) in close proximity to Chinese Bien Hoa and another (Phien Tran) in the second king's former capital, Saigon. At the same time, they organized Chinese settlers in Bien Hoa into the Thanh Ha commune and Chinese in Saigon into the Minh Huong commune.[37] Significantly, this was the first attempt by the Vietnamese government to organize Chinese merchant activity in the eastern Water Frontier region.

This early consolidation was expanded a generation later when, in 1732, Dinh Vien district was established along with a military government called Long Ho Camp. This was located at present-day Cai Be across the river from modern Vinh Long. As this site was an important river port, another part of the river and coastal network came under Vietnamese control. Twenty years later this expansion was further consolidated. In 1753, the Vietnamese government established the office of *Kinh Luoc Cao Man* (Royal Delegate [in charge of] Cambodia) at Ben Nghe (Saigon), commanding army corps in Binh Khanh (Khanh Hoa), Binh Thuan, Tran Bien (Bien Hoa), Phien Tran (Gia Dinh), and Long Ho (Cai Be). For the first time Saigon became the political and military center of the eastern Water Frontier. Then, when a large Vietnamese expedition against Cambodia in 1754 won more Cambodian land, the Vietnamese army controlled all the Tien

Giang trade route.

Soon after, in 1755, the Vietnamese set up a military base in the important Chinese trading center of My Tho. My Tho was a pivotal center from which Chinese commercial and Vietnamese military power could expand, not only along the main Mekong branch but also southwards to the Bassac or lower Mekong branch. The town had been attacked in 1747 by a Khmer leader called *Okna* Noren Tok,[38] who was said to be the Khmer governor of Khaet Bassak (present Soc Trang region), but in Kitagawa's view was probably an autonomous local chief.[39] Vietnamese intervention had saved the town, and the establishment of the military camp ensured its safety for some time to come. Vietnamese control did not immediately change the situation of local Chinese communities there, who enjoyed economic autonomy for nearly two more decades.[40]

Elsewhere in 1755, on the Tay Ninh plateau, a Khmer army attacked Vietnamese forces that were expelling many Chams from Vietnamese-controlled Thuan Thanh to Kompong Cham in Cambodia.[41] In revenge, the Vietnamese sacked Phnom Penh, killed some high Khmer officials and forced the king, Ang Ton, to flee to the western Water Frontier Chinese state of Hatien. There he offered to cede two provinces, Tam Don and Xuy Lap, to its Minh Huong ruler, Mac Thien Tu, if he could broker a peace.[42] By 1755, Vietnamese power stretched across an area reaching from the Tay Ninh plateau to the Mekong in the west, and the whole eastern half of the Young Delta, with the Nguyen administrative frame reaching the east bank of the main Mekong branch.

Two years later, the Vietnamese court showed the first sign of its willingness to extend its power to the coastal region of the western Water Frontier when it demanded two Cambodian provinces (Tra Vinh and Ba Thac, currently Tra Vinh and Soc Trang areas) as reward for putting the new Cambodian king, Neac Nhuan, on the throne. When Neac Ton[43] returned with an escort from Hatien, he also ceded Tam Phong Long (perhaps present Long An) to the Nguyen. The Nguyen moved the Long Ho military government from Cai Be to Long Tan Bao (current Long Ho town) and also pushed further west by establishing Dong Khau Dao in Sa Dec, Tan Chau Dao at Cau Lao (or Cu Lao Gieng Island), and Chau Doc Dao near Meat Chrouk on the Bassac in 1757.[44]

In the late 1750s, for the first time, Vietnamese-administered territory entered the western Water Frontier where it directly encountered Mac Thien Tu's Chinese kingdom of Hatien or Banteay Meas. The discussion now moves to this western Water Frontier.

The Chinese Western Water Frontier along the Gulf of Siam

In the Age of Commerce, the trade significance of central Siam had increased due to the prosperity of maritime worlds from the Indian Ocean to the East China Sea. Several ports like Chantaburi were established along the southeast

Siamese coast to service this international trade. Although Chinese traded here, the most significant maritime commercial network in the seventeenth-century Gulf of Siam probably belonged to Malay and Bugis merchants. Most of the islands in the gulf have Malay names from that era;[45] and in 1687 a French missionary named Tachard reported that the governor of Chantaburi was a Malay Muslim who controlled a fleet of galleys.[46] Although important in the Gulf of Siam, the Malay-Bugis people apparently played little role further east along the coast. Here the best-known trading center was an old river port known as Banteay Meas to the Khmer, Kang Kou to the Chinese, and Ponteamas to Europeans.[47]

Several other ports existed or were developed in the eighteenth-century western Water Frontier, like Rach Gia, Hon Dat, and Kampot, but none had a navigable link to the Bassac River. Only Banteay Meas, and Hatien at the mouth of the same river, had access to a seasonal route to the lower Mekong branch near Chau Doc by following its own river and then crossing a low-lying area that flooded deeply in the wet season. Alexander Hamilton, who visited the river port of Ponteamas (Banteay Meas) on the eastern rim of the Gulf of Siam in 1720, reported that it was connected to the city of Cambodia (that is, Phnom Penh) by a narrow, deep river that was navigable in the winter.[48]

This asset would make Banteay Meas/Hatien a significant local political and commercial power in the eighteenth century. As mentioned above, the coastal ridges of the western Water Frontier had not been important commercially in the previous centuries. But when Chinese fleets began to take control of Mekong navigation in the late seventeenth century, the Cambodian core region needed to find another route to the sea. Increasingly, in the eighteenth century, attention moved to the western Water Frontier as the place to establish a new network connecting the Cambodia hinterland with the Gulf of Siam. This is the background to the rise of the Chinese kingdom of Hatien founded by Mac Cuu. The growth of the Mac family's semi-independent power in the eighteenth century allowed free trade to flourish in Hatien, far from the royal monopolies of Cambodia, and encouraged the town to become the main seaport of central Cambodia right up to the early nineteenth century.[49]

Banteay Meas appeared in the 1693 *Kram Srok* as only a minor province.[50] According to Vietnamese documents, at some time between 1687 and 1695 Mac Cuu, a Chinese adventurer born in Leizhou in Canton, migrated there under the patronage of the Cambodian king. He was chief of the Chinese community with the Khmer title of *Okna*. Local Khmers, however, continued to be administered by a Khmer governor, called *Okna* Reachea Setthi, until Taksin's expedition of 1771 overthrew the local system of government. It thus seems that Banteay Meas/Hatien had a dual political structure in the eighteenth century, just as in Bien Hoa and My Tho power was shared between Chinese and Vietnamese.

However, this power structure began to evolve in the early eighteenth century as Mac Cuu was confronted with the newly rising movement of Vietnamese power into the Young Delta. In 1708, Mac Cuu sent his first tribute mission to the Nguyen court and, according to *Tien Bien*, was appointed *Tong Binh* (or

general commanding a regional corps) of Hatien Protectorate in return.[51] This is
the same title as that of Chen Shangchuan, who was called *Tong Binh* of *Long
Mon* (*Long Men* in Chinese) corps, suggesting that in 1708 Hue similarly recognized Mac Cuu and his Chinese followers as a local military clique.

Mac Cuu died in 1735 after Hatien had fully recovered from earlier attacks
by Siam, whose court understood its strategic location gave access to the Cambodian core. His eighteen-year-old son, Mac Thien Tu, informed the Nguyen
court of his father's death and in 1736 was appointed *Do Doc* (governor general)
and given three ships with the dragon mark. He was also exempted from ship
tax, allowed to mint coins, to establish civil and military offices, and to organize
an army. It was a difficult time, however. By 1732 Vietnamese power had already reached Cai Be in the Young Delta; but more immediately perilous was
the attack on Hatien by Khmer leader Nac Bon in 1739. Though no Cambodian
chronicle recorded the Nac Bon affair, Mac Thien Tu's victory was highly significant since it allowed Hatien to enjoy full independence from Cambodia
thereafter.

Generally speaking, from about the middle of the eighteenth century the
states of mainland Southeast Asia began a lengthy process of struggle with each
other that ended by forming the outer frames of their respective territories. This
process also occurred in the Water Frontier. In the western Water Frontier, the
effectively independent power of Hatien directly faced Vietnamese expansion
from the Tien Giang to the Hau Giang in 1757, when vanguard units of the
Vietnamese army were stationed at Chau Doc and Long Xuyen.[52] Mac Thien Tu
responded by offering the Vietnamese court the five provinces that the Cambodian king Nac Ton had ceded to him.[53] Although the Nguyen accepted, they also
allowed him to continue ruling those five provinces as before. This suggests that
the Nguyen at the time were less concerned with the western Water Frontier area
but instead ambitious to control the Tien Giang route to Cambodia. Mac Thien
Tu also established two divisions (*dao*) to the east of Hatien, Kien Giang at
Rach Gia and Long Xuyen at Ca Mau (or modern Kien Giang and Ca Mau Provinces).[54] By the late 1750s, therefore, Hatien was not simply a union of port
towns but a state with its own hinterland throughout all the western Water Frontier, including Kampot. In this regard, the 1757 affair should be seen as settling
the borders between two powers, the Nguyen realm and Mac Hatien, as well as
between Vietnamese and Chinese Water Frontiers, or between the east and west
Water Frontiers.

As a local ruler, Mac Thien Tu showed different faces to different powers
and peoples. In a 1742 letter to the Japanese shogun, for example, he called himself Reachea Krong Kampucea Tiptei (king of Cambodia)[55] and later Neak
Somdec Preah Sotat or Sotoat, who was identified in 1756 in a Cambodian
chronicle as an adoptive father of the Cambodian king Nak Ton. The Siamese
chronicle in 1767, however, called Mac Thien Tu both Ong Chien Chun (Chinese general) and *Phraya* Ratchea Setthi, thus confusing him with the Khmer
governor of Banteay Meas.[56] To the Vietnamese, Mac Thien Tu was Tong Binh
of Hatien, a military title suggesting armed force was an important component

of his political power in Vietnamese eyes. All this confusion over names and titles suggests the dual political structure established in Mac Cuu's time still continued, with a Khmer *Okna* administering Khmer peasants and a Chinese "governor general" ruling the Chinese, Vietnamese, Malay speakers, and various others living in Hatien town.[57]

Like Hatien itself, the Mac army was drawn from several different ethnic groups. Apart from Cantonese and Vietnamese, it also contained Malay-Bugis soldiers. The *Gia Dinh Thanh Thong Chi* recorded that one of their number, a general, died protecting Mac Thien Tu in Chau Doc in 1771.[58] A Cambodian chronicle also recorded that in 1757 the Khmer governor of Banteay Meas donated his Khmer soldiers, called *pol*, to the Hatien army. In times of trouble this powerful local army could also call on Vietnamese support. After the 1757 settlement with the Nguyen, Mac Thien Tu used his military might to expand his territory. That same year Mac forces joined Nac Ton to march on the Cambodia core through Kampot, Banteay Meas, and Takeo, whose governors followed them to Udong.[59] Later, after the Burmese destroyed Ayutthaya in 1767, Mac Thien Tu also used his powerful navy to coerce several important islands on the sea route to the Gulf of Siam, among them Koh Kong, Koh Kut, and Koh Khram. Although Hatien was originally based on port-polities in the western Water Frontier, in the changed conditions after the fall of Ayutthaya, Mac Thien Tu tried to expand his state in the same way as did its other newly forming rivals. But this expansionary strategy attracted the response of other maritime powers in the western Water Frontier, ultimately to Hatien's cost.

From the late seventeenth century onward, many Teochiu Chinese had settled along the southeast coast of Siam, establishing important trading centers at Chantaburi and Trat.[60] The expansion of Cantonese marine power in Hatien threatened the profit of their trading networks and generated a violent response. The first Teochiu counterattack occurred in 1767. The second, in 1769, was led by Tran Thai, who tried to attack Hatien from nearby Bach Ma hill. The Hatien army defeated both attackers, but the latter fled to Chantaburi where he enlisted the support of the new Siamese king, the half-Teochiu general Taksin.

At this point, Taksin can be understood as representing the interests of Teochiu Chinese in southeastern Siam and the gulf. After Ayutthya fell in 1767, he had moved to Phatthaya and Rayon to organize support among Teochiu Chinese. Indeed, Taksin's early military strategy basically amounted to the unification of Teochiu powers in the Gulf of Siam. He appointed a Chinese named Chiam, who was chief of the Chinese junk fleet in Trat, as the new vice-governor of Trat with the title of *Phraya* Phipit (Tran Lien or Tran Chieu Khoa in Vietnamese documents). The new vice-governor and his fleet formed the core of the Teochiu armed groups that opposed Hatien Cantonese expansion further west into the gulf.

At the high point of this conflict, Hatien attacked Chantaburi in 1769 but was defeated by Taksin's troops under Tran Lien's command. The battle for Chantaburi marked the watershed of Hatien's expansionary efforts. Less than two years later, in 1771, Taksin and Tran Lien landed at Kampong Som and

Kampot, then besieged and sacked Hatien. When Hatien fell, Taksin marched to Udong via the Banteay River and the Bassac following in part the same route by which Mac Thien Tu had fled the defeat of his army. Tran Lien remained in control at Hatien until the Vietnamese forced his retreat to Kampot in 1773. Only then did both main ports of the western Water Frontier, Hatien and Kampot, pass from the rule of Taksin and Teochiu power.

Mac Thien Tu never returned to Hatien, not even after the Siamese army left in 1773. The historic role of Hatien as a trading emporium between the South China Sea and the gulf thereafter declined. Economic circumstances were changing and the main focus of trade was moving towards exports from the Young Delta. Rice exports from the Mekong Delta became highly developed in the early nineteenth century.[61] Water Frontier ports like Saigon, with access to this export trade, flourished in the new conditions, but many others with no connections to the Young Delta slowly declined, especially those on the western Water Frontier. The Mac family tried to set up a new central base in Tran Giang (present Can Tho) on the Hau Giang. Perhaps they chose this place for the same reason that Taksin later abandoned Hatien—to be successful in the new emerging conditions, Taksin needed to shift his power base from port emporia to areas of export production, that is, from the gulf to the Chaophraya Delta (Thonburi-Bangkok) and from Teochiu Chinese to Sino-Thai families. But the Mac were too late. The rice cropping areas of the Mekong Delta were already under Vietnamese rule and most local farmers were Vietnamese. In Can Tho, the Mac could only be subordinate to Vietnamese power. In other words, the fall of Hatien in 1771 can be regarded as the last stand of the autonomous western Water Frontier.

The End of the Chinese Water Frontier of Indochina

Even before the Siamese withdrew from a sacked and ruined Hatien, events further north were unfolding that would push the whole Water Frontier into long, bloody warfare for at least the next twenty years. In 1772 the Tay Son rebellion erupted in central Vietnam, a revolt that ended two hundred years of Nguyen rule and sent the last Nguyen king fleeing for his life to the Mekong Delta in 1776. Mac Thien Tu tried to assist him, but the famous Tay Son general Nguyen Hue followed and sacked the Saigon area before catching and killing the last Nguyen ruler and several of his male relatives in Ca Mau. Mac Thien Tu was exiled to Thonburi where Taksin, still aiming to monopolize Gulf of Siam commerce, later slaughtered him and much of his family on a false charge in 1780.

However, the removal of the Mac did not end Chinese involvement in the bloody wars and political infighting that now consumed eastern and western sections of the Water Frontier. In the eastern sector, a surviving Nguyen prince, Nguyen Phuc Anh (later Gia Long), rallied his forces in 1777 and began to fight back. A key component of his military coalition was a large Chinese unit under a former Tay Son supporter, Ly Tai. Nguyen remnants had enough difficulty surviving in the eastern sector without dreaming of organizing effective rule over the western sector after the fall of Hatien. Instead, competing local forces fought to control the area for several years. For instance, in 1776 the Cambodian king Ramaracea exploited the situation to try to regain control of Soc Trang, Tra Vinh, and Rach Gia from the Vietnamese.[62] But factional disputes within the Khmer court persisted, and Nguyen forces were once more drawn into Cambodian affairs. In 1779 two Nguyen generals marched on Udong, and in 1780 one of them, Do Thanh Nhan, attacked a Khmer chief in Tra Vinh for not remaining loyal to the Nguyen after the Tay Son expedition of 1780.[63] Local Khmer chiefs were also setting themselves up in various strong points in the western Water Frontier, forcing the Nguyen to deal with them at the same time that the Tay Son were turning increasing attention on the loyalist Nguyen remnants in the south.

In 1783 Saigon fell to the Tay Son and many of its Chinese residents were massacred. Nguyen Anh fled to My Tho, then to Phu Quoc Island from where he marched on Hatien. There he defeated the Chinese governor Chen Xing (Tran Hung) and drove out his armed Chinese supporters before receiving assistance from former Hatien soldiers and a Siamese fleet formerly in Taksin's service.[64] As this incident suggests, there was no effective central power in the coastal regions of the western Water Frontier either, where control shifted between whichever of the local powers, whether Chinese, Thai, Vietnamese, and Khmer, was superior at the time.

After Taksin was overthrown in 1782 and replaced by the Chakkri general as Rama I, and despite the long-standing hostility between the earlier Vietnamese and Thai states, Nguyen Anh went to Bangkok to seek assistance from the new Siamese king. Even before Nguyen Anh's arrival, Rama I had shown a special interest in the western Water Frontier region by sending two military corps to Udong and from there down the Tien Giang Mekong branch causing the Tay Son to build a fort at Sa Dec.[65] Then later a Siamese admiral occupying Hatien marched to Ca Mau to meet Nguyen Anh.[66] After Anh's arrival at Bangkok in 1784, Rama I sent his army to the western Water Frontier to support Anh's restoration. Anh also appointed the second son of Mac Thien Tu, Mac Tu Sinh, who had been brought up among Siamese, as governor of Hatien administering all the western Water Frontier, while a Siamese army occupied Hatien, Can Tho, Soc Trang, and Sa Dec. They only left after their 1785 defeat by the Tay Son in My Tho. This suggests that from 1784 until their retreat in 1785, the whole western Water Frontier was under strong Siamese influence.[67] Even after the main army left, several thousand Siamese or Khmer soldiers remained in Tra Vinh. In 1787 Nguyen Anh organized them into the *Xiem Binh Don* (Siamese soldiers' post), which remained until 1810.[68]

Even after Nguyen Anh recaptured Saigon in 1787, Siamese political power still had a big influence there. For instance, Nguyen Anh appointed a Viet-Siamese, Mac Tu Sinh, as governor of Hatien after Rama I's appointee died. After his death in 1787, a Siamese general named Ngo Ma[69] was appointed as acting governor of Hatien before a grandson of Mac Thien Tu, Mac Tu Binh, was sent from Bangkok to govern Long Xuyen (modern Ca Mau). When he died shortly thereafter, Siam sent a son of Mac Thien Tu, Mac Tu Diem, who had been raised among ordinary Siamese, to be governor of Hatien in 1799. After Mac Tu Diem was sent back to Siam in 1807, Gia Long appointed his nephew, Mac Cong Du, as acting governor of Hatien.[70] On Cong Du's retirement in 1829, emperor Minh Mang allowed another grandson of Mac Thien Tu, Cong Tai, to succeed to the position. A few years later, however, when the south rebelled against Minh Mang's tightening control, Cong Du and two male relatives joined the rebels. The sole survivor of the three was later captured and sent back to Siam. All this suggests that between the late eighteenth and the early nineteenth centuries, Mac descendants had become so "Siamized" that they could embody in one person both the Chinese governor of Hatien and the Reachea Setthi of Banteay Meas.

Other parts of the western Water Frontier were also slow to come under close Vietnamese control, in particular the Long Xuyen (Ca Mau) and Ba Thac (Soc Trang) regions. As late as 1790 the Khmer chief in charge of Ba Thac was able to collect taxes from local Chinese.[71] It was not until 1791 that Nguyen Anh was able to appoint local officials here, and even then he chose to appoint a Khmer as *Okna la* to control the Khmer peasants and a Chinese as *Tong Phu* to control the Chinese community, a strategy as old as the Water Frontier itself.[72]

Conclusion

In 1802 Nguyen Anh finally defeated the Tay Son and established the Nguyen dynasty. His victory ultimately meant the end of the Water Frontier as a separate region, even though it would be his son, Minh Mang, who finally took the necessary steps in the 1820s and 1830s to integrate the area into the Vietnamese state. Tra Vinh and Ba Thac (Soc Trang), like other parts of the far south, were organized into Vietnamese administrative units and placed within the newly centralized provincial system of the early 1830s. As part of this integration, Khmer cultural autonomy was attacked on several fronts.[73] The insurrections of the early 1840s that followed this aggressive policy of assimilation brought together Chinese and Khmer for one last time in a joint effort to defeat Vietnamese power. Although the Khmer ultimately won back core areas seized by the Vietnamese in the later 1830s, the Chinese were forced to submit to a much reduced and restricted role in the Vietnamese south. At the same time, due to the construction of several strategic canals, the Tien Giang and Saigon via My Tho emerged as the main route for the rice trade of the eastern Water Frontier. By contrast, the network of the western Water Frontier that connected with the Gulf of Siam played a small role in South China Sea trade. The era of the Chinese Water Frontier, the "Promised Land" of eighteenth-century Indochina, was finished, along with the transitional commercial and political structures that had sustained Chinese pioneering polities in the region. In its place was opening the time of overseas Chinese under modern colonialism.

Notes

I want to thank Nola Cooke for her assistance with the text of this chapter.

1. Victor Lieberman, "Mainland–Archipelagic Parallels and Contrasts, c. 1750–1850," in *The Last Stand of Asian Autonomies, Responses to Modernity in the Diverse States of Southeast Asia and Korea, 1750–1900*, ed. Anthony Reid (London: Macmillan and St. Martin's Press, 1997), 30–31.

2. Chen Chingho, "He Hsien Chen Hsieh Chen Mo Shih Chia Pu Chu Chi'ih" [Notes on the Family History of the Mac Governors General of Hatien], *Bulletin of the College of Arts, National Taiwan University*, 7 (1956): 83; and Fujiwara Riichro, *Tonan Ajia shi no Kenkyu* [A Study of the History of Southeast Asia] (Kyoto: Hozokan Shuppan, 1986), 210–35.

3. The reasons for describing Hatien as a "kingdom" are discussed below.

4. Anthony Reid, "Introduction," *Last Stand of Asian Autonomies*, 11–14.

5. For a more detailed discussion of the concept of a historical circle, see Yumio Sakurai, "Sosetsu" [Introduction] in *Genshi Tonan Ajia Sekai* [Proto-Historical World of Southeast Asia] *Tonan Ajia Shi* [History of Southeast Asia], ed. Tatsuro Yamamoto (Tokyo: Iwanami Shoten, 2001), vol. 1, 128.

6. Phan Dat Lien, *Ban Do Dat Viet Nam* [Soil Map of Viet Nam] (Hanoi: Hoi Khoa Hoc Dat Viet Nam, no date), sheet 1; and Vu Tu Lap, *Viet Nam, Geographic Data* (Hanoi: Foreign Language Publishing House, 1979), 232–33.

7. There were several Neolithic sites in the region. See Le Trung Kha, "Sai Gon thoi Tien Su" [Prehistoric Saigon] in *Dia Chi Van Hoa, Thanh Pho Ho Chi Minh* [Geography and Culture of Ho Chi Minh City], ed. Tran Van Giau (Ho Chi Minh City: NXBan Thanh Pho Ho Chi Minh, 1987), 13–77.

8. Vo Si Khai, "Dat Gia Dinh the ky 7 den the ky 16" [The Land of Gia Dinh from the 7th to 16th Centuries] in Giau, *Dia Chi Van Hoa*, 93–112.

9. Giau, *Dia Chi Van Hoa*, 94–99.

10. *Van Hoa va Cu Dan Dong Bang Song Cuu Long* [Culture and People of the Mekong Delta], ed. Nguyen Cong Binh, Le Xuan Diem, Mac Duong (Ho Chi Minh City: NXB Khoa Hoc Xa Hoi, 1990), 121.

11. For Indian-style rice cropping, see Takaya Yoshikazu, *Agricultural Development of a Tropical Delta. A Study of the Chaophraya Delta* (Honolulu: University of Hawaii Press, 1987), 260–61.

12. Takako Kitagawa, "Suio no Keifu–Srei Santor Ocho Shi" [History of the Water King—Dynastic History of Srei Santor], *Southeast Asian Studies* 38, no. 1 (2000): 5073; and Takako Kitagawa, "Posuto Ankoru" [Post Ankor] in *Tonanajia Kinsei Kokka Gun no Tenkai* [Development of Early Modern States of Southeast Asia], ed. Yumio Sakurai (Tokyo: Iwanami Shoten, 2001), vol. 4, 133–60.

13. Wada Hisanori, *Shinrou Fudoki (Chên La Fêng T'u Chi)* (Tokyo: Heibonsha, 1988), 227.

14. Takako Kitagawa, "Kanbojia Kairo no Kansei 1719 seiki, Mekong, Tonlesap Chiiki niokeru Network no Tanjo" [Formation of the Cambodian Corridor: The Birth of the Mekong and Tonle Sap Regional Network in the 17th–19th Centuries], unpublished doctoral thesis, the University of Tokyo, 1999, 235.

15. According to Etienne Aymonier, it covered one million hectares before any colonial drainage works occurred. *Le Cambodge. Tome 1. Le Royaume actuel* (Paris: Ernest Leroux, 1900), 138.

16. Nguyen Cong Binh, *Van Ho and Cu Dan*, 115.

17. Yumio Sakurai and Takako Kitagawa, "Hatien and Banteay Meas in the Time of the Fall of Ayutthaya," in *From Japan to Arabia, Ayutthaya's Maritime Relations with Asia*, ed. Kenon Breazeale (Bangkok: The Foundation for the Promotion of Social Science and Humanities Textbooks Project, 1999), 167.

18. The exception was King An Duong who constructed a road from Udong to Kampot in the mid-nineteenth century because the water route was controlled by Vietnam. Kitagawa, "Kanbojia Kairo," 364–75.

19. Aymonier, *Le Cambodge*, 141. Ohashi Hisatoshi, Truong Mealy, *Vetonamu no Naka no Kanbojia Minzoku* [Cambodian People in Viet Nam] (Tokyo: Kokon Shoin, 1999), 118. There were 354,000 Khmer by 1998.

20. Sakurai and Kitagawa, "Hatien and Banteay Meas," 191.

21. Nguyen Cong Binh et al., *Van Ho and Cu Dan*, 108.

22. Michael Vickery, "Cambodia after Angkor: The Chronicler Evidence for the Fourteenth to Sixteenth Centuries," Ph. D. dissertation, Yale University, 1977, 400–404.

23. *Liang Zhong Hai Tao Zhenjing* [Navigation Guide for Two Sea Routes] (Beijing: Zhong Hua Shu Ju, 1961), 81.

24. Trinh Hoai Duc, *Gia Dinh Thanh Thong Chi* (Saigon: Nha Van Hoa Phu Quoc Vu Khanh Dac Trach Van Hoa Xuat Ban, 1972), vol. 2, 12, or *Gia Dinh ThungChi, Histoire et Description de la Basse Cochinchine*, trans. G. Aubaret (Paris: Imprimerie impériale, 1863, republished Westmead, Hants.: Gregg International Publishers, 1969), 46. Also see *Dai Nam Thuc Luc* [Veritable Records of Dai Nam] (Tokyo: Keio Gikuku University, 1961), vol. 1, 82. Fujiwara, *Tonan Ajia shi*, 192–96 believed they were not from Taiwan but were former pirates from the Gulf of Guangchou.

25. According to Trinh Hoai Duc, Bien Hoa and nearby Ba Ria had been settled by Vietnamese from 1658, but they were probably only peasant migrants among the Khmer. *Gia Dinh Thanh Thong Chi*, vol. 2, 67, or Aubaret, *Gia Dinh Thung Chi*, 2.

26. Kitagawa, "Suio no Keifu," 65–70.

27. Ang Non in the Cambodian chronicles. Mak Phoen, *Chroniques Royales du Cambodge (de 1594 à 1677)* (Paris: Ecole Française d'Extrême Orient, 1981), 431; Kitagawa, "Suio no keifu," 65.

28. Kitagawa, "Kanbojia Kairo," 102–4.

29. Kitagawa, "Kanbojia Kairo," 260.

30. According to two ships from Cambodia in 1681, the second king of Cambodia fled to Chan In, which should be identified as "Tran Dinh," or a Vietnamese military camp. See also reports by the twenty-second ship from Quang Nam in 1675, the twentieth ship from Cambodia in 1679, and the fourth and fifth ships from Cambodia in 1681. Kitagawa, "Suio no Keifu," 66–69.

31. Reports by the fifth and nineteenth ships from Siam in 1682. Kitagawa, "Kanbojia kairo," 279.

32. According to two ships' reports from Cambodia in 1689 and one from Viet Nam, Huang Jin and the second king invaded Cambodia with 500 soldiers and 5 ships in 1688. They fought the first king's army but were later defeated by the Vietnamese. Kitagawa, "Suio no Keifu," 6.

33. Kitagawa, "Kambojia Kairo," 280.

34. Kitagawa, "Kanbojia Kairo," 280.

35. *Dai Nam Thuc Luc,* vol. 1, 128.

36. *Dai Nam Thuc Luc,* vol. 1, 129, 281.

37. *Gia Dinh Thanh Thong Chi*, vol. 2, 17, and Aubaret, *Gia Dinh Thung Chi*, 810.

38. According to one chronicle, he was called *Okna* Noren Tok, while another gives

the title as *Okna* Norenphut or *Okna* Noren Kok. Kitagawa, "Kanbojia Kairo," 240. The Nguyen chronicle says My Tho was attacked by a Khmer called Suu Lien Toc, who is surely the Noren Tok of the Khmer chronicles. *Dai Nam Thuc Luc*, vol. 1, 141.

39. As Khaet Bassak was not listed as a province in the 1693 compilation it could not have had a governor with a Cauvay Srok title. Kitagawa, "Kanbojia Kairo," 104. After then, there was no evidence that Udong expanded its influence into the eastern Water Frontier. The *Okna* in My Tho mentioned in the Vietnamese chronicle and Khmer VJ chronicle should be understood as independent from either Udong–Cambodia or Quang Nam–Vietnam although in a nominal tribute relation. Kitagawa, "Kanbojia Kairo," 246.

40. According to the Nguyen provincial gazetteer for Dinh Tuong Province, the Chinese established nine quarters in My Tho called Dai Pho ("Large Market"). They were allowed to organize themselves into *Ban* (semiautonomous Chinese communities) and to own plantations. *Dai Nam Nhat Thong Chi* [Imperial Gazetteer of Dai Nam], *Luc Tinh Nam Viet* [Six Southern Provinces], trans. Nguyen Tao (Saigon: Nha Van Hoa Phu Quoc Vu Khanh Dac Trach Van Hoa Tai Ban, 1973), vol. 2, 24. This situation lasted until the Siamese occupied Hatien in 1772, when My Tho came under the direct rule of Vietnamese officials. Phan Khoang, *Viet Su: Xu Dang Trong, 1558–1777* [Viet History: The Dang Trong Region, 1558–1777] (Saigon: Nha Sach Khai Tri, 1967), 434.

41. Sakurai and Kitagawa, "Hatien and Banteay Meas," 164.

42. Sakurai and Kitagawa, "Hatien and Banteay Meas," 165.

43. *Utei Reacea* Ang Tan in the Cambodian chronicles. Kitagawa, "Kanbojia Kairo," 242.

44. *Gia Dinh Thanh Thong Chi*, vol. 2, 25, or Aubaret, *Gia Dinh Thung Chi*, 16.

45. John Crawfurd, *Journal of an Embassy to the Courts of Siam and CochinChina*, (Kuala Lumpur: Oxford in Asia Reprint, 1967), 191–207.

46. Kitagawa, "Kanbojia Kairo," 150.

47. Chen Chingho, "He Hsien Chen Hsieh Chen Mo," 84, fn 3.

48. Kitagawa, "Kanbojia Kairo," 154. Probably the present Banteay River.

49. In the early nineteenth century, the *Hai Lu* [Maritime Record] states that the small state of Pen Ti (Ponteamas) mediated between Vietnam and Siam and traded in lead, tin, ivory, peacock feathers, kingfisher arrow feathers, and dry fish. These are all products of the Cambodian plateau. *Hai Lu* (Taipei: Kuang Wen Shu Chu, 1968), 1b.

50. Kitagawa, "Kanbojia Kairo," 102–3.

51. The date of appointment varies in different documents: Fujiwara, *Tonan Ajia shi*, 210–212.

52. Sakurai and Kitagawa, "Hatien and Banteay Meas," 170.

53. Sakurai and Kitagawa, "Hatien and Banteay Meas," 167. The five "provinces" were Phung Than, Can Bot, Chan Sam, Say Mat, and Linh Quynh. All except Cam Bot (Kampot) had belonged to Banteay Meas.

54. *Gia Dinh Thanh Thong Chi*, vol. 2, 130.

55. Noël Péri, "Essai sur les relations du Japon et de l'Indochine aux XVIe et XVIIIe Siècles," *Bulletin de l'Ecole Française d'Extrême Orient* 23 (1924): 131–32.

56. Sakurai and Kitagawa, "Hatien and Banteay Meas," 180.

57. Sakurai and Kitagawa, "Hatien and Banteay Meas," 169–70. In the early nineteenth century one Malay quarter remained in Hatien as well as six Chinese quarters and twenty-six Khmer villages. *Gia Dinh Thanh Thong Chi*, vol. 2, 179–81. Traditional Vietnamese sources use the term *She Po* for Malay or Muslim people. Although meaning "Javanese" in Chinese, its use in Vietnamese sources comes from "C'vea" in Khmer, meaning Malays and Muslim Chams.

58. *Gia Dinh Thanh Thong Chi*, vol. 2, 33–34.

59. Sakurai and Kitagawa, "Hatien and Banteay Meas," 170.

60. This account follows Chen Chingho, "Mac Thien Tu and Phraya Taksin. A Survey on Their Political Stand, Conflicts and Background," in *Proceedings of the Seventh IAHA Conference* (Bangkok: Chulalongkorn University, 1979), vol. 2, 1534–1575.

61. Fujiwara, *Tonan Ajia shi*, 283–285.

62. Kitagawa, "Kanbojia Kairo," 224.

63. *Dai Nam Thuc Luc*, vol. 2, 23–25.

64. *Dai Nam Thuc Luc*, vol. 2, 32.

65. Khin Sok, *Le Cambodge entre le Siam et le Vietnam (de 1775 à 1860)* (Paris: Ecole Française d' Extrêmeorient, 1991), 51.

66. *Dai Nam Thuc Luc*, vol. 2, 35–36.

67. *Dai Nam Thuc Luc*, vol. 2, 37–38.

68. *Dai Nam Thuc Luc*, vol. 2, 45; vol. 3, 190.

69. *Dai Nam Thuc Luc*, vol. 2, 48.

70. *Dai Nam Thuc Luc*, vol. 1, 279.

71. *Dai Nam Thuc Luc*, vol. 2, 58, 71.

72. *Dai Nam Thuc Luc*, vol. 2, 82.

73. Shimao Minoru, "Betonamu Genchoki no Kokka Togo to Nanki Chiho" [State Unification and South Vietnam during the Nguyen Dynasty in Vietnam], unpublished masters thesis, University of Tokyo, 1988, 100–105.

4

The Junk Trade between South China and Nguyen Vietnam in the Late Eighteenth and Early Nineteenth Centuries

James Kong Chin

It is widely known that Chinese merchants had long been active in the junk trade between China and the ports of mainland Southeast Asia in the early modern period. In particular, historians of China's maritime trade have produced a number of excellent research works focused on Sino-Siamese commercial relations.[1] While several others have examined aspects of late traditional Vietnamese economic history,[2] few have paid much attention to the role of maritime shipping from south China, at least in the late eighteenth and early nineteenth centuries, in forming an interregional trade system. While mapping the external features of this trade system dominated by the southern Chinese junks, I also want in this chapter briefly to explore China's maritime trade with southern Vietnam (Cochinchina) by examining several major emporia and ports scattered from the south China coast down to Mekong Delta.

The emporia of Cochinchina were widely recognized as important mainland Southeast Asian collection centers by merchants from south China. Located on one of the principal trade routes to Southeast Asia, the coast of Nguyen Vietnam was also fortunate to contain several well-endowed natural harbors or navigable rivers that encouraged coastal trade by foreign junks patronizing these emporia. However, it was a one-way trading system. Although many junks from different Chinese ports regularly traded each year with southern Vietnam, Vietnamese merchants were seldom seen at the principal ports of south China. This was not because such maritime Vietnamese merchants did not exist: in island Southeast

Asia, especially along the Malay Peninsula and in the Indonesian Archipelago, local Vietnamese traders actively engaged in commercial activities. Perhaps similar to other parts of Southeast Asia, a sort of tacit division of labor existed between the two merchant groups. Local authorities generally preferred foreign merchants in large junks, including from south China, to carry out long-distance maritime trade, leaving the short-distance coastal or inland river-borne trade for indigenous merchants. This was not always the case. One late-eighteenth-century Vietnamese source reported that small Chinese junks were also involved in short-distance trade, competing with native merchants.[3]

The trade routes and navigation patterns employed by Chinese junks were a noteworthy feature of the trading system. Though junks from south China generally preferred to take a direct route when sailing south to Cochinchina, they would often call first at some insignificant ports in Zhejiang, Zhanglin, Hainan Island, or Macao to change cargoes or to purchase new goods before heading for Cochinchina. They might even rebuild their junks to escape the strict control imposed by the Chinese court. Consequently, many junks that originally set out from southern Fujian and eastern Guangdong would register with Nguyen harbor officials as being from Suzhou, Ningbo, or Hainan. As a result, in practice trade routes and navigation patterns were often triangular or multiangled. This practice helps explain why, although a large number of small junks from Hainan Island frequented southern Vietnamese entrepôts each year in the late eighteenth and early nineteenth centuries, the local mercantile economy of Hainan did not become noticeably more developed, since most Southeast Asian imports were transshipped there to the major ports of mainland China. It was in this manner that southern Chinese merchants, Fujianese (Hokkien) merchants in particular, maintained a stable mercantile bond between China and Cochinchina through regular shipping toward and trading at the emporia of Nguyen Vietnam.

Emporia on the South China Coast

Emporia and ports on the south China coast open to foreign trade emerged quickly in the years after 1683, when the Qing court finally conquered Taiwan and lifted its ban on maritime trade. At least seven emporia and ports deserve attention in terms of China's junk trade with Cochinchina. They are Suzhou, Ningbo, Xiamen or Amoy, Zhanglin, Guangzhou, Hainan Island, and Macao. Of them, one was in Jiangnan Province, one in Zhejiang Province, one in south Fujian, and four came within the jurisdiction of Guangdong authorities under the Qing dynasty. I discuss them in turn below.

Xiamen

The rise of Xiamen or Amoy as one of the important emporia in modern China can be traced back to 1684, when the Qing court decided to give it the function of trading with the Philippine Islands and Ryukyu Islands.[4] As one of the four major ports in the Qing dynasty, Xiamen was officially granted the privilege of foreign trade by the Kangxi emperor and was initially responsible for issuing shipping licenses to, and collecting custom duties from, all the junks of south Fujian engaged in long-distance trade. However, it was only after 1727 when the Yongzheng emperor finally lifted the ban on maritime trade with Southeast Asia, that Xiamen's trade with Cochinchina entered a booming period. Hokkien-speaking junk traders from Xiamen visited all the main port-polities of Southeast Asia and East Asia, including Taiwan, Nagasaki, Batavia, Semarang, Singapore, Banjarmasin, Saigon, Siam, Johor, Ligor, Songkhla, Terengganu, Cebu, Annam, Manila, and Maluku. Of these ports in the Philippine Islands, Batavia and other places on the Malay Peninsula were the major destinations for Xiamen junks.

It is most noteworthy that unlike the port of Guangzhou (or Canton) that was frequently visited by foreign ships, Xiamen was basically a port used by private Chinese maritime shipping. In other words, at least in the period before the 1830s, there were more Chinese junks sailing from Xiamen than from Canton. Another point worth mentioning is that there was no distinct division between trading junks and fishing junks in south Fujian. As the Qing court only limited the number of masts and the volume of loads for ocean-going vessels,[5] a large number of junks operating with fishing licenses were actually involved in maritime trade. Moreover, those registered with the Xiamen customs as small junks with only two masts were often seen quietly rebuilding their junks and increasing their masts to three while on business overseas. According to a contemporary record, more than 1,000 ocean-going junks and trading junks, carrying from 6,000 to 10,000 piculs, could be found in Xiamen in 1796.[6] Of them, 100 to 200 specialized in trade with Southeast Asia. Apart from these large junks based in Xiamen, there were also a great number of medium and small-sized junks in lesser ports of south Fujian, such as Jinjiang, Huian, Nanan, Zhangpu, and Zhaoan.

As was generally known in south China from the seventeenth to the nineteenth centuries, the Hokkien junk, which was characterized by a green-painted junk-head, was larger than the redheaded junk of Zhanglin of eastern Guangdong.[7] On the other hand, there was no difference between east Guangdong and south Fujian in terms of junk type. Unlike the two types mentioned above, the typical junk employed by Hokkien and Teochiu merchants had a much deeper draught when loaded and a V-shape keel, a much more convenient design for long-distance ocean travel.[8] Taking into account that residents of Chaozhou or Teochiu had originally migrated from south Fujian and that people of this region shared a common dialect (Hokkien) with their fellows in south Fujian, it was understandable that merchants from south Fujian and Chaozhou utilized the same type of junks when sailing overseas.

When competition from Canton came to be added to the existing and very high customs' duties and extortion by Xiamen government officials, a gradual decline occurred in Xiamen's maritime shipping from the 1780s. More and more Hokkien junks were forced to shift their trade bases to Zhanglin, Leizhou Peninsula, Canton, and Hainan Island to avoid the Xiamen officials' squeeze. Some of them as a rule would first sail for Hainan or Zhanglin and reload their goods onto another junk before heading for ports in mainland Southeast Asia, an interesting fact that has long been overlooked by historians.[9] The shift of Hokkien merchants' commercial activity to the chief marts of Guangdong Province in the late eighteenth century explains the sudden rise of Hainanese and Cantonese trade with southern Vietnam.

As for Xiamen's trade with Nguyen-ruled Vietnam in the period under discussion, usually each year one junk of 7,000 piculs capacity would call at the port of Saigon, while four junks averaging 3,000 piculs each visited Hoi An. In addition, about the same number of junks would anchor at the roadstead of Hue. So many went to the Hue area because Xiamen junks shipped the most valuable commodities, principally wrought silks and teas, compared with the goods carried from other Chinese emporia.[10] Quite large numbers of Hokkien merchants, from 500 to 600 at a time, also often traveled to Cochinchina on Xiamen junks. An original receipt written by a Hokkien-speaking merchant named Li Kuan to certain captains of the English East India Company in 1809 provides an interesting example. According to the receipt, which is kept at the Public Records Office in London, Li Kuan (or Li Xilao) was the owner of Kun He Hong, one of the Xiamen guilds that specialized in maritime trade with southern Vietnam. Early in March 1809, Li Kuan organized a large group of Hokkien-speaking merchants to sail on a rented junk, *Jin shun yuan*, to Dong Nai in southern Vietnam. Eight days into the trip, the junk was wrecked by a storm in the dangerous *Wan-li-chang-sha* (South China Sea). Fortunately, two British East India Company vessels were passing through the same area and rescued all 561 Hokkien merchants. The British not only took them to Hoi An, but also lent them 210 Spanish dollars. It was for this reason that Li Kuan personally signed the receipt in question, together with the *Cai fu* (secretary in charge of finance) Zhou Pei, the *Hou zhang* (boatswain) Jiang Dan, and the junk owners Luo Kui and Ruan Yao. Together they expressed their profound gratitude to the Company captains and promised to repay the loan as soon as they returned to Canton.[11]

Guangzhou

Guangzhou, or Canton, is one of the oldest emporia in China. Its trade relations with mainland Southeast Asia can be traced back to 140 BC.[12] The eighth century saw the heyday of Canton's maritime trade when a large number of Persian and Arab merchants flocked to the city. During the thirteenth century, a family who emigrated from Champa, the *Pu*, even became the most wealthy and influential merchants here. In the late sixteenth century, thirty-six broker guilds were established to facilitate foreign trade. Like the rest of south China's emporia, Canton's economy was seriously hurt by the prohibition of maritime shipping from 1661 to 1683. But Canton reopened its doors to foreign trade in 1685 and actually became the only Chinese port allowed to deal with trading vessels from Europe after 1759.

With the development of trade with the European companies, a new type of broker guild came into being in Canton. These guilds, better known as the *Cong Hong*, acted as both foreign merchants' representatives when purchasing goods and their guarantors while they stayed in Canton. The number of these guilds fluctuated each year depending upon the economic situation, ranging from ten to more than forty.[13] It is interesting to note that among these broker guilds, seven specialized in trade with various ports on the China coast and with mainland Southeast Asia. At first, these seven guilds were called *Hainan Hong*, or guilds trading with Hainan Island, probably because this guild dealt with junks that were mainly involved in trade with Hainan. But the Canton authorities soon realized that a number of junks registered under the name of Hainan actually belonged to Hokkien- and Teochiu-speaking merchants who usually sailed to ports in Cochinchina. Accordingly, the Canton government changed these guilds' names into *Fu-chao Hong* or guilds dealing with Hokkien and Teochiu merchants.

According to John Crawfurd in the early 1820s, two junks from Canton visited Saigon annually, one with a capacity of 5,000 piculs and the other 8,000 piculs. As for Hoi An and Hue, six Canton junks averaging 3,000 piculs were recorded annually.[14] These numbers reflect Canton's rising dominance over the other south China ports in the late eighteenth century. By the nineteenth century it had become the main trade center insofar as the junk trade with Cochinchina was concerned, with eight junks per year normally visiting southern Vietnam.

Hainan Island

The Qing court's control over the junk trade in the geographically remote ports of Hainan Island was relatively lax. Realizing this, a large number of Chinese maritime merchants moved their activities to this island from south Fujian and Chaozhou. Generally speaking, junks sailing from Hainan were small in size, but with the advantage of being adjacent to Vietnam, this island usually supplied more junks to trade in the ports of mainland Southeast Asia. As a result, the cargoes they shipped back were actually no less in quantity than those carried by junks from other Chinese ports, but the cargoes were probably less valuable than those of Xiamen junks.

Thus, in the 1820s, Crawfurd reported fifteen to twenty junks from Hainan arrived each year in Saigon with a capacity ranging from 2,000 to 2,500 piculs each, while three similar sized junks visited Hoi An and Hue.[15]

Macao

Portuguese relations with southern Vietnam began in 1520s after they failed to establish direct trade links with China. Luso-Cochinchinese contacts increased gradually when the Portuguese established themselves in Macao in 1557. With the help of some Jesuits, the Portuguese entered into commercial activities in Nguyen-ruled Cochinchina. The years after 1620 saw the Portuguese in Macao consolidate their position in Cochinchina when they provided the Nguyen with cannons made locally in Bocarro's gun foundry.[16] Generally speaking, the Portuguese from Macao were the only Europeans to frequent the ports of Cochinchina regularly before the Tay Son rebellion. But that revolt and the ensuing civil war in the late eighteenth century ruptured trade relations between Macao and Nguyen Vietnam, with the Portuguese prevented from trading in southern Vietnam for nearly twenty years.

From earlier in the eighteenth century as well, the Cantonese government had tightened its control over Portuguese overseas trade from Macao. In 1725, the Canton governor, Kong Yuxun, submitted a memorial to the emperor asking that the number of Portuguese vessels allowed to trade overseas be limited to twenty-five and that the names of the Portuguese captains and of the ships be registered with the Canton customs. The Qing court approved his request and formally included it into the regulations governing the Portuguese of Macao. A full list of these twenty-five vessels can thus be found in all of Qing China's local gazetteers dealing with Macao.[17]

Under the strict control of the Chinese government, the junk trade from Portuguese Macao to Nguyen Vietnam was always a one-way operation. The Portuguese were allowed to voyage to Southeast Asia, but trading vessels from mainland Southeast Asia countries were generally forbidden from entering the port of Macao. Consequently, the Portuguese authorities in Macao were panic-stricken in August 1812 when a storm sent a Cochinchinese junk loaded with eaglewood drifting into the harbor. The Portuguese *Vereador* (governor) immediately sent a report to the Xiangshan county government asking for instructions. The Xiangshan authorities then ordered the *Vereador* to help the merchant from the Nguyen Vietnam to repair his junk and send him back with the Portuguese vessels. A series of correspondence between the *Vereador* and the Xiangshan authorities concerning this Vietnamese trade junk can be read in the National Archives of Lisbon.[18]

Closely related to the trade between Macao and Nguyen Vietnam is an interesting archival document, dated 30 April 1800, held in the Portuguese National Archives (*Torre do Tombo*). The document, written in Chinese by Nguyen harbor officials, asked the Portuguese captain *Ruo-se-an-zun-a-gu-liao* (Jost Antonio Aravjo?) to carry 10,000 Spanish dollars, 1,000 piculs of Chinese white zinc and 20 piculs of hemp rope to Cochinchina. If he did not agree, the port duties levied upon his vessel would be much higher. However, if the Portuguese would send two junks with double the quantity of the same cargoes in the following year, the Nguyen harbor officials would waive customs duties on the two vessels.[19]

Zhanglin

Junks from Chaochou or Teochiu were well known in eighteenth-century China. Though Chaochou junks were smaller than Xiamen junks, it did not hamper them from voyaging to foreign markets like Champa, Siam, Ryukyu, and Manila. Like Xiamen, the port of Zhanglin became important after 1684. As the emporium of Chaozhou district, Zhanglin's maritime trade developed rapidly in the eighteenth century when the Qing court encouraged rice imports.[20] While the major destination port of Zhanglin junks was Siam for more than a century, some Zhanglin junks also traded with Cochinchina.

Suzhou

Suzhou's maritime connections with mainland Southeast Asia can be dated to the 230s CE, when it became a commercial center of the Wu kingdom after Wu forces subjugated the region of present northern Vietnam.[21] In the 1750s, Suzhou was one of the most influential emporia of China and became the main center for the silk, cloth, and rice trades. By the 1790s, when the city's population had almost reached one million, it contained 183 merchant associations founded by traders from various parts of China, notably from south Fujian, Anhui, Shanxi, and Jiangxi.[22]

Suzhou merchants were often involved in coastal trading and known for their *Sha chuan* or sand junks, a special type of flat-bottomed vessel designed for shallow waters. However, they also traded with Japan and with southern Vietnam in the early nineteenth century. According to Crawfurd in the 1820s, six junks with a carrying capacity of 6,000 to 7,000 piculs each sailed regularly from Saocheu (Suzhou) to Saigon, while Hoi An attracted three junks of about 2,500 piculs burden each. In regard to Hue, it is likely that Suzhou junks shared the market with other Chinese junk fleets, as John Crawfurd only says in his journal that it "is also with the same ports, and amounts in all to about twelve junks, measuring from 2,500 to 4,000 piculs each, and to near 2,500 tons."[23] Given the description of Suzhou junks mentioned above and the fact that an influential Fujianese merchant community was active in the business life of south Vietnam, it is reasonable to assume that Hokkien- or Cantonese-speaking merchants owned the junks Crawfurd saw in the early nineteenth century.

Ningbo

Ningbo had been an important Chinese port from the late eighth century. Historically, it was the longest serving major emporium for trade with Japan and the Korean Peninsula, though merchants from Champa, Cambodia, Java, Borneo, and Palembang occasionally appeared there during the late twelfth and early thirteenth centuries. Some of these merchants even sojourned in Ningbo for a long period.[24] By 1800, almost all of Zhejiang's junks congregated at Ningbo port for maritime shipping.[25] According to the Zhejiang governor of the time, Ruan Yuan (1764–1849), there were between 600 and 700 junks based in Ningbo port.[26]

Junks commonly used on the Zhejiang coast belonged to a special type called *Dan chuan* or egg-shaped junks. This type of junk could be employed equally in Chinese coastal trading or for overseas shipping.[27] Like Suzhou, most of Ningbo's maritime trade focused on Japan, but a minority regularly turned up at the roadstead of southern Vietnam in the late eighteenth and early nineteenth centuries.

Emporia on the Cochinchinese Coast

A flourishing maritime trade between south China and ports on the southern Vietnamese coast can be seen as early as the early fifteenth century. In the seventeenth century and the first half of the eighteenth century, most international trade focused on the ports of Hoi An and Hue near the Nguyen capital of Phu Xuan, although a number of smaller destinations also attracted Chinese traders. In the far south, one of the main entrepôt ports of eighteenth-century Southeast Asia was Hatien, a tributary of Nguyen Cochinchina but ruled in an autonomous way by a Chinese emigrant family from Canton, the Mac. There were also several other smaller ports in Dong Nai and the Mekong Delta, one of which, Saigon (modern Ho Chi Minh City), began to emerge as a major destination toward the end of the eighteenth century and became the principal port in south Vietnam in the nineteenth century.

I want to look briefly at the central ports first as they formed an important component of the interregional trade network.

Hue

Hokkien-speaking merchants ranked Hue among the major Vietnamese commercial centers from the late sixteenth to the early nineteenth centuries. In March 1577, for instance, fourteen junks from Zhangzhou (south Fujian) loaded with copper, iron, and porcelain were reported off the roadstead of Hue,[28] while a south Fujian guide to maritime trade—Zhang Xie's *Dong-xi-yang kao* [A Study of the Eastern and Western Oceans]—put Hue on a par with Hoi An.[29] Hue retained this status for Chinese junk traders in the years after 1802 when Nguyen forces having defeated the Tay Son regime returned the capital there. Hue itself was situated five leagues upriver from the estuarine port of Thuan An and about eighteen leagues northwest of Tourane (Da Nang). It enjoyed good anchorage up to six fathoms deep. Local trade vessels of about one hundred tons burden carried out most short-distance coastal trading from here to other Vietnamese ports like Hatien, Saigon, and Hoi An. As a rule, business was conducted in the town and merchants from south China traded extensively there, with sometimes thirty junks in the river at one time.[30]

Hoi An

Hoi An, or Faifo to Europeans, was the most important eighteenth-century port for foreign trade. Nguyen Hoang had began to encourage trade early in his rule in Quang Nam, in the 1570s, shortly after the Chinese Ming court lifted its ban on maritime trade in 1567. Hoi An became a booming emporium in the late sixteenth century.[31] Its prosperity continued until the Tay Son rebellion in late eighteenth century when the town was taken by the Tay Son and mostly destroyed. It was the early nineteenth century before Hoi An began gradually to regain some of its former commercial importance.[32] Unfortunately, by then the river on which it was situated, which had formerly been navigable for large junks, had silted so badly that only junks of about one hundred tons burden could use it. Others had to remain in a river that communicated with Tourane Bay.

Newly arrived Chinese junks of two hundred tons burden as a rule would lie about three miles from the town in another river that communicated with Tourane Bay until they obtained permission from local authorities to trade. On the arrival of a junk, local officials would be sent on board until the captain had the king's approval and the duty to be levied on the junk had been agreed according to its size or cargo. Chinese merchants normally made a small present to the harbor official or *Cai-tau* in charge of shipping and foreign trade to expedite the official transaction. By the early nineteenth century, customs duty on all goods imported into Hoi An was 12 percent. Port charges for foreign vessels differed, however, with Portuguese vessels from Macao paying 3,000 *quan* annually while Chinese junks paid 1,500 *quan* to 2,000 *quan,* depending on their size.[33] Duty levied on foreign merchants had thus been reduced a little compared with the 1770s when, according to the Nguyen harbor archives, junks from south China were divided into five subcategories depending on their place of origin—Fujian, Guangdong (Canton), Shanghai, Hainan, and Macao—and duty levied accordingly. All foreign vessels had to pay duties on arrival and departure.[34]

The currency of Hoi An was a sort of cash made of tutenague, six hundred making a *quan,* which was equivalent to two rupees or one Spanish dollar. The *quan* was divided into ten mace of sixty cash each with a knot at each mace and the whole cash was strung together. Chinese maritime traders had the greatest share of the local market. Before the Tay Son rebellion and ensuing civil war, one hundred Chinese junks normally visited this port every year. The Chinese commercial influence in Hoi An is also shown by the fact that the weights widely used locally were the same as in China, and all goods were measured by the *datchin,* a Hokkien word for "steelyard."

Reportedly, the most desirable import into Hoi An was tutenague which was cast into coins used in daily transactions. The Nguyen ruler always took all that was imported for himself, usually at a price of fourteen *quan* per picul. Consequently, tutenague constituted the staple cargo for junks coming from south China and a large quantity of it entered Hoi An every year. During some years in the early nineteenth century, Chinese junks brought 10,000 piculs of tutenague to Hoi An, picking up locally produced sugar and sugar-candy, much esteemed in China, as a large part of their return cargoes. Usually the sugar was brought for sale in June, July, and August, although the greatest quantity was not available until the end of July when Chinese merchants were busy buying it up and sending it back to China.[35]

Saigon

The term *Cho Lon,* which means "great market" in Vietnamese, was given to the Chinese business town early in the nineteenth century.[36] The local Chinese usually called it *Cai-gun, Cai-jun,* or *Di-an* (Taignon). It had been established about 1778 by a group of Chinese businessmen who had been earlier based at Tran Bien, northeast of Saigon, and had moved to the Cholon area to escape the Tay Son. Despite this foresight, the Chinese who had fled to Cholon were ultimately overtaken by the rebellion and paid dearly for it because some Chinese took a hand in the conflict between the Nguyen and the Tay Son. In the spring of 1782, in revenge, the rebels massacred about 10,000 Chinese in Cholon and in Saigon, burning and looting the Chinese shops.[37] Saigon did not recover its vitality until after 1788 when Nguyen Anh, the future emperor Gia Long, returned from exile and took control of the Gia Dinh area. According to Trinh Hoai Duc, in the 1820s Chinese businesses thronged three streets in Saigon selling goods like satin, silk, porcelain, paper, pearls, books, medicines, tea, and food. Merchants from south China even established five *Huiguan* or regional associations in the town.[38]

Saigon was fortunate to be situated upon an excellent river. Chinese junks going upriver usually had to anchor first before Can Gio village, about a mile from the estuary. There they waited for a day or two for the local authorities' permission to proceed. Although they were allowed to trade at Can Gio village, the cargo had to be weighed before the junk was allowed to continue to Saigon. Junks and foreign vessels needed to be towed by local boats in several parts of the river because the channel was narrow and unlike the Mekong Delta not tidal.

Cholon stood about three miles from Vietnamese Saigon on the opposite bank of the river. Almost all commercial transactions were conducted in its market. As noted by the English merchant William Milburn, all manner of Chinese merchandise was in great abundance thanks to the number of Chinese junks that annually frequented Saigon. Mainly for this reason, the Nguyen emperor's warehouses were built nearby and the Portuguese from Macao also prefered to moor their vessels here.[39]

Some Chinese merchants in Saigon specialized in rice trading with Guangdong (Canton). Zhang Peilin from Xiangshan County, Guangdong, is an example. Zhang had his own firm named *Hong-tai-chang* in Saigon, and he lived there for more than thirty years. Each year he sent two junks loaded with locally produced rice to Guangzhou and shipped back Chinese products for the Saigon market. In time he became one of the wealthiest local merchants and a leader of the Chinese community.[40]

Hatien

Hatien was an overseas Chinese port-polity established around 1700 by Mac Cuu (or Mo Jiu), a Chinese from the Leizhou Peninsular of Guangdong Province, and his Cantonese followers. The town was located in the Cambodian area of Banteay Meas on the east side of Siamese Gulf. Contemporary Chinese documents called it *Gang-kou guo* (port country), *Ben-di guo* (country of Ponteamas), or *He-xian zhen* (town of Hatien or Hatien Tran), while European merchants knew it as Cancao (a Hokkien pronunciation for *Gang-kou* or port), Peam, or Ponteamas.[41]

According to Milburn, in the early nineteenth century Hatien was about four miles up from the estuary close to where Ponteamas had formerly stood. It enjoyed a regular trade with south China, especially with Canton. Local shipping and foreign trade was chiefly in the hands of Chinese merchants and every year about seven Cantonese junks traded there. Two commercial currencies circulated in Hatien at the time—Chinese coins and Spanish dollars. While all goods were bought and sold by Chinese piculs (60 kilos), all bargains were calculated in Spanish dollars. Among its main imports at the time was tutenague from south China. In some years, Milburn reported, about 1,600 piculs of tutenague were shipped into Hatien. Other goods imported by the Chinese junks were mainly articles of everyday consumption by the local Chinese community, such as porcelain, Chinese cutlery, furniture, ironmongery, lacquer-ware, silk goods of various sorts, sweetmeats, tea, various sorts of thread, vermilion, clothing, and so on. The junks loaded local products from Southeast Asia such as betel nut, tin, blackwood, nutmeg, clove, deerskin, dried shrimp, rattan, sappanwood, and pepper for their return.

Generally speaking, there were two observable trading patterns for Chinese junk activities on the Nguyen coast of Vietnam. While one involved junks that basically only plied directly between south China ports and Quang Nam (Hoi An), a normal and very frequent route among certain Chinese maritime merchants who could be described as specializing in the Quang Nam trade, another pattern involved junks that sailed from other Southeast Asian ports and called on Nguyen-ruled Quang Nam on their way back to south China in the hope of buying more tropical products as supplementary cargoes. The two patterns were not new insofar as the Chinese junk trade with the Nguyen Vietnam was concerned and their origins could be traced back at least to the late sixteenth century when the Ming court lifted its ban on maritime trade. In other words, these routes were actually a continuation of the earlier trade practice. Taken together they incorporated Nguyen Vietnam into a much larger regional maritime trade system by prolonging navigation routes and enriching transactions with goods collected from major Asian markets.

Conclusion

The brief survey above implies that two regional trade systems existed in terms of maritime trade between southern China and southern Vietnam during the late eighteenth and early nineteenth centuries. One was in China, where Xiamen and Canton functioned as its dual central markets, while the other was based in Mekong Delta. While Vietnamese coasting craft and itinerant merchants were busy trading with the small market ports dotting the Gulf of Siam or surrounding countries, the southern Chinese junk trade played an important role by bridging these two trade systems and acting as an external component of this integrated trade system. As the efforts of merchants from south China and Cochinchina interwove over time, an integrated trade system evolved almost unnoticed that connected southern China to southern Vietnam and beyond, a set of overlapping commercial networks that boosted commercial exchanges between two regions and the economic development on both sides.

Notes

1. See, for example, Sarasin Viraphol, *Tribute and Profit: Sino-Siamese Trade, 1652–1853* (Cambridge, Mass.: Harvard University, 1977); Jennifer W. Cushman, "Siamese State Trade and the Chinese Go-Between, 1767–1855," *Journal of Southeast Asia Studies* 12, no. 1 (March 1981): 46–61; Jennifer W. Cushman, *Fields from the Sea: Chinese Junk Trade with Siam during the Late Eighteenth and Early Nineteenth Centuries* (Ithaca: Cornell University, 1993).

2. Excellent studies and primary sources collections on the economic history of Nguyen Vietnam include Chen Chingho, "Shi-qi-ba shiji zhi Hui-an tangrenjie jiqi shang-ye" [The Chinese Town of Hoi An and Its Trade during the 17th and the 18th Centuries], *Xin-ya xue-bao* [Journal of New Asia College] 3, no. 1 (1960): 273–332; Nguyen Thanh Anh, *Tableau économique du Vietnam aux XVIIe et XVIIIe siècles* (Paris: Cujas, 1970); Yang Baoyun, *Contribution à l'histoire de la principauté des Nguyen au Vietnam méridional (1600–1775)*. (Geneve: Olizane/Etudes Orientales, 1992); *Southern Vietnam under the Nguyen: Documents on the Economic History of Cochinchina (Dang Trong), 1602–1777*, ed. Li Tana and Anthony Reid (Canberra and Singapore: ECHOSEA and ISEAS, 1993); Li Tana, *Nguyen Cochinchina: Southern Vietnam in the Seventeenth and Eighteenth Centuries* (Ithaca: Cornell University SE Asian Program, 1998).

3. Le Quy Don, *Phu bien tap luc* [Miscellaneous Notes on the Border Regions] (Saigon: Quoc Vu Khanh Dac Trach Van Hoa, 1973), *juan* 4, 35a–35b.

4. The most detailed study of Xiamen in English is Ng Chin-keong, *Trade and Society: The Amoy Network on the China Coast, 1683–1735* (Singapore: Singapore University Press, 1983).

5. Zhou Kai, *Xiamen zhi* [Gazetteer of Xiamen], 1832 edition, *juan* 5, "Chuan-zheng lue" [Brief Account on Junks], 21a–25b.

6. Zhou Kai, *Xiamen zhi*, *juan* 5, 27, 30–31; *juan* 6, "Tai-yun lue" [Brief Account on Navigation with Taiwan], 7a.

7. *Chenghai xianzhi* [Gazetteer of Chenghai County], ed. Li Shuji et al., 1815 edition, *juan* 6, "Fengsu" [Customs], 8a.

8. Lan Dingyuan (*c.*1820), "Caoliang jian zi haiyun shu" [Memorial on Rice Transportation and Maritime Shipping] in *Huangchao jingshi wenbian*, *juan* 48, 19a–21b.

9. Zhou Kai, *Xiamen zhi*, *juan* 5, 30a–31a.

10. John Crawfurd (1828), *Journal of an Embassy to the Courts of Siam and Cochin China*, reprint (Kuala Lumpur: Oxford University Press, 1967), 511–12.

11. Ch'en Kuo–Tung, "Qingdai zhongye Xiamen de haishang maoyi (1727–1833)" [Xiamen's Maritime Trade during the Mid-Qing Period, 1727–1833] in *Zhongguo haiyang fazhan shi lunwenji* [Collection of Papers on the Maritime History of China], ed. Wu Jianxiong (Taipei: Zhongyang yanjiuyuan, 1991) vol. 4, 90.

12. Ban Gu (*c.* 80), *Han shu* [History of the Han Dynasty] (Beijing: Zhonghua shuju, 1978 reprint), *juan* 28b, 1671.

13. Liang Jiabin, *Guangdong shi-san-hang kao* [Treatise on the Thirteen Hongs of Guangdong] (Shanghai: Guoli bianyiguan, 1937), 15–48.

14. Crawfurd, *Journal*, 511–12.

15. Crawfurd, *Journal*, 511–12.

16. For connections between the Portuguese and the Nguyen Vietnam, see P-Y. Manguin, *Les Portugais sur les Côtes du Viet-Nam et du Campa, Étude sur les routes maritimes et les relations commerciales, d'après les sources portugaises (XVIe, XVIIe, XVIIIe siècles)* (Paris: Ecole Française d'Extrême-Orient, 1972); George Bryan Souza, "Portuguese Society in Macao and Luso–Vietnamese Relations, 1511–1751," in *Boletim do Instituto "Luis de Camões"* 15, no. 1–2 (1981): 68–114.

17. Zhu Huai (1820). *Xiangshan xianzhi* [Gazetteer of Xiangshan County], *juan* 4, "Haifang" [Maritime Defense], 100a–105b.

18. Portuguese National Archives, numbers T1098, T1105, T1107, and T1110.

19. Archive number T1494.

20. Zhou Shuoxun ed., *Chaozhou fuzhi* [Gazetteer of Chaozhou Prefecture], 1762 edition, *juan* 12, "Fengsu" [Customs], 10; Li Shuji, *Chenghai xianzhi* [Gazetteer of Chenghai County], 1815 edition, *juan* 8, 8a–12b. In 1971, a typical redheaded Zhanglin junk was excavated at Nan-pan-zhou of Chenghai. It was thirty-nine meters long and thirteen meters wide, with a five-store cabinet built on board. See *Chenghai xian wenwu zhi* [Accounts of Historical Relics of Chenghai County], ed. Cai Yinghao et al., (Chenghai: Chenghai xian bowuguan, 1987, internal publication), 50–55.

21. Chen Shou, *San guo zhi: Wu zhi* [History of the Three Kingdoms: Wu Kingdom] (Beijing: Zhonghua shuju, 1979), *juan* 60, "Biography of Lu Dai," 1383–1387.

22. Shi Jun and Jin Guozheng, *Zongheng yunei de sushang* [Suzhou Merchants at Home and Abroad] (Hangzhou: Zhejiang renmin chubanshe, 1997), 8.

23. Crawfurd, *Journal*, 511–12.

24. For instance, Lou Yao, a famous Chinese literatus (1137–1213), recorded that a wealthy merchant from southern Cambodia lived in Song Mingzhou (Ningpo) for many years on business. When he died with no local offspring to inherit his fortune, the governor sent his property back to his family in Cambodia, together with the corpse. A year later, the Cambodian king sent a representative to Mingzhou to express the gratitude of the country and of the merchant's family. The family then donated all the dead man's property to build three commemorative Buddhist stupas in Mingzhou. Lou Yao, *Gong kui ji, c.*1210, *Si ku quan shu* edition, *juan* 86, 4b–5a.

25. For Ningbo's general maritime trading history, see Chen Gaohua and Wu Tai, *Song-yuan shiqi de haiwai maoyi* [Maritime Trade during the Song and Yuan Periods] (Tianjing: Tianjing renmin chubanshe, 1981); *Ningbo gang haiwai jiaotongshi lunwen xuanji* [Selected Papers on the History of Navigation and Maritime Trade of Ningbo Port], ed. Zhongguo haiwai jiaotongshi yanjiuhui (Ningbo: Internal publication, 1983).

26. Ruan Yuan (*c.*1820), *Haiyun kao ba* [A Treatise on Maritime Shipping] in Ruan Yuan, *Yan-jing-shi ji* [Ruan Yuan's Collected Writings], Part II, *juan* 8, 22a–22b.

27. Xie Zhanren (*c.*1820), "Haiyun tiyao" [Key Facts about Maritime Shipping] in *Huangchao jingshi wenbian* [Collection of Treatises on Politics and Economy of the Qing Dynasty], ed. He Changling, *juan* 48, 22a–32a.

28. Hou Jigao (*c.*1630?), *Quan-zhe bing-zhi kao* [Treatise on the Military System of Zhejiang], *juan* 2; appendix, "jin-bao wo-jing" (Tainan: Zhuang Yan wenhua shiye youxian gongsi, 1995 reprint), *Siku quanshu cunmu congshu: Zi bu*, Book 31, 176–77.

29. Zhang Xie (1617). *Dong-xi-yang kao* [A Study of the Eastern and Western Oceans] (Beijing: Zhonghua Shuju, 1981 reprint), *juan* 1, 9–20.

30. William Milburn, *Oriental Commerce*, 2 vols. (London: Black Parry Co., 1813), vol. 2, 457.

31. For more details on Hoi An and its foreign trade, see Chen, "Shi-qi-ba shiji zhi Hui-an," 273–332; and *Ancient Town of Hoi An*, ed. National Committee for the Interna-

tional Symposium on the Ancient Town of Hoi An (Hanoi: Foreign Languages Publishing House, 1991).

32. John Barrow, *A Voyage to Cochinchina in the Years 1792 and 1793* (London: Strahan and Preston, 1806), 310–11.

33. Milburn, *Oriental Commerce*, vol. 2, 456.

34. Le Quy Don, *Phu bien tap luc, juan* 4, 31b–32a; Seiichi Iwao, *Shuinsen boeki shi no kenkyu* [Studies in the History of Trade under the Vermillion-Seal Licenses of the Tokugawa Shogunate], revised edition (Tokyo: Yoshikawa Kobunkan, 1985), 345; Nguyen Dinh Dau, "The Birth and the Historical Evolution of Hoi An," in *Ancient Town of Hoi An,* 117–27.

35. Milburn, *Oriental Commerce*, vol. 2, 454.

36. J. Bouchot, "Notes historiques sur Cholon," *Extrême Asie* 23 (mai 1928): 582.

37. Trinh Hoai Duc, *Gia Dinh Thanh Thong Chi*, (c. 1820), reprinted in *Lingnan zhiguai deng shiliao san zhon*, ed. Dai Kelai and Yang Baoyun (Zhengzhou: Zhongzhou guji chubanshe, 1991), Entries of "Pho Sai-con" and "Tran Phan-an"; J. Bouchot, "Notes historiques sur Cholon," 581–85.

38. Trinh Hoai Duc, *Gia Dinh Thanh Thong Chi*, Entry of "Pho Sai-con."

39. Milburn, *Oriental Commerce*, vol. 2, 450–52.

40. Zhang Deyi, "Hanghai shuqi" [Navigation Accounts] in *Xiaofanghuzhai yudicongchao*, ed. Wang Xiqi (Beijing: 1891), Book 11, 58a–101b.

41. For primary sources on the history of Hatien and the Mac family, see Vu The Thuong, *Hatien Tran Hiep Tran Mac Thi Gia Pha*, 1818; Trinh Hoai Duc, *Gia Dinh Thanh Thong Chi*, 55–256. For the Chinese community in Hatien, see Émile Gaspardone, "Un chinois des mers du sud, le foundateur de Ha-tien," *Journal Asiatique* 240 (1952): 363–85; Chen Chingho, "He-xian-zhen ye-zhen mo-shi jia-pu zhu-shi" [Notes on the *Hatien Tran Hiep Tran Mac Thi Gia Pha*], in *Wen-shi-zhe xue-bao* 7 (1956): 77–139; Chen Chingho, "Zheng Haide zhuan Jiading tongzhi chengchizhi zhushi" [Annotation on the Township Section of Trinh Hoai Duc's *Gia Dinh Thanh Thong Chi*], *Nanyang xuebao* [Journal of South Seas Society] 12, no. 2 (1956): 1–31; Chen Chingho, "Mac Thieu Tu and Phraya Taksin: A Survey on Their Political Stand, Conflicts, and Background," in *Proceedings of the Seventh IAHA Conference*, 22–26 August 1977 (Bangkok: Chulalongkorn University Press, 1977), vol. 2, 1534–1575; and Nicholas Sellers, *The Princes of Ha-Tien (1682–1867)* (Brussels: Thanh-Long, Etudes Orientales no. 11, 1983).

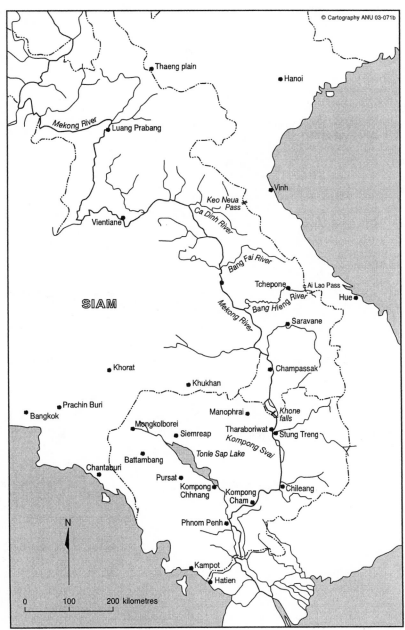

© Cartography ANU 03-071b

Thaeng plain

Hanoi

Mekong River

Luang Prabang

Keo Neua
Pass

Ca Dinh River

Vinh

Vientiane

Bang Fai River

Tchepone

Ai Lao Pass

SIAM

Bang Hieng River

Hue

Mekong River

Saravane

Khorat

Champassak

Khukhan

Prachin Buri

Manophrai

Khone
falls

Bangkok

Mongkolborei

Tharaboriwat

Stung Treng

Siemreap

Kompong Svai

Battambang

Tonle Sap Lake

Chantaburi

Pursat

Kompong
Chhnang

Kompong
Cham

Chileang

N

Phnom Penh

Kampot

Hatien

0   100   200 kilometres

Map 2: Delta and Upper Mekong to Laos

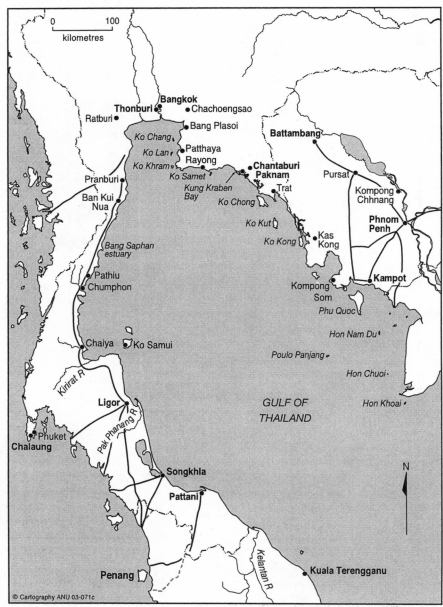

Map 3: Gulf of Siam and Road Networks in 1850

II

COMMERCIAL EDDIES AND FLOWS

5

The Late-Eighteenth- and Early-Nineteenth-Century Mekong Delta in the Regional Trade System

Li Tana

> Indo-China presents a remarkable picture of immigration, centuries old and un-changing. The groups within the country are steadily nourished and supplemented from identical groups from without.
>
> —V. Thompson[1]

The colonial notion of rigid, impermeable, and unchanging boundaries and un-changeable peoples in premodern Southeast Asia, enunciated here by Virginia Thompson but accepted by so many others at the time, has been challenged by scholars in the last few decades. Newly uncovered data further expose the wide gap between colonial perceptions and Southeast Asian historical experiences. Here I discuss the issues with respect to precolonial Southeast Asian trade. Together with the works of earlier revisionist scholars, new data challenge the nationalist historiographies that read back in time from the clear-cut boundaries of contemporary Southeast Asia. Unavoidably, questions are raised, such as what was "internal" and "external," "within" and "without," "local" and especially "national" in eighteenth-century Southeast Asia. With an eye to such questions, this chapter looks at the internal mechanism that made the region effectively one economic unit and explores the connections between the broader Mekong Delta region and its neighbors.

A Text that Unfolds a Picture, Reveals a Perspective, and Recovers an Experience

To illustrate some of the characteristics of this unit let us look at a Vietnamese text of the early nineteenth century that describes six major routes leading to different parts of the region around the Gulf of Siam. The text in question is the *Xiem la quoc lo trinh tap luc* [A Collection of Routes to the Kingdom of Siam].[2] Compiled by Tong Phuc Ngoan, a senior officer of the Nguyen government, it was presented to King Gia Long in 1810. The document details two land routes, three sea routes, and one mixed land and sea route between the various trading centers along coasts and rivers of the southern Water Frontier that connected Vietnam, Cambodia, Siam, and points further south. Information provided includes directions for the various routes, distinctive landmarks, and local products found on each route, the location of fresh water, and the distance between stopping places. The brief outline that follows gives a clearer understanding of the regional trade context.

The first route is called "the upper land route." Departing from Phnom Penh, it ran via Battambang to Bangkok up to Ayutthaya then down to the coast all the way to Chaiya. At some point it crossed the Malay Peninsula to Penang, from where it went up to Phuket and Chalaung. The second land route, called "the lower land route," is much shorter. It covers the area between Ko Chang, Chantaburi, Bang Pla Soi (Chonburi), and Petriu (Chachoengsao) to the east of Bangkok. It is worth noting that both land routes are described as departing from places other than the Mekong Delta, one from Phnom Penh and the other from Ko Chang. This was perhaps because the collection was submitted to Gia Long himself. As Prince Nguyen Anh, the king had been exiled in the region for many years and knew these places so well that it would have been stating the obvious to describe the routes from the Mekong Delta to Phnom Penh and Ko Chang.

The "coastal route" in the text departed from the Tranh De mouth of the lower Mekong branch, the modern Hau Giang and colonial Bassac River, and went via Rach Gia, Hatien, Ream, Ko Kong, and Chantaburi to Ko Kram Island in the Gulf of Siam. From there the route turned south to Pathiu, Chumphon, Chaiya, Nakhon Si Thammarat, Songkhla, Pattani, Sungei Kelantan, Terengganu, Singapore, and Penang before heading north to Chalaung. The "sea route" was a variation of the "coastal route." It left from Hon Khoai (Poulo Obi island) off Ca Mau point then sailed via Phu Quoc island to Ko Samet and Ko Si Chang islands in the Gulf of Siam before going down to Ban Pak Nam (or Packnam, about two miles from the mouth of the river Menam), Sam Roi Yat, Mae Nam Langsuan, Nakhon Si Thammarat, Pattani, and finally Chalaung, the present day Phuket.

The so-called cross ocean route[3] was a collection of short travel routes between the islands in the Gulf of Siam, such as those from Ban Plasoi to Mae Klong and from Phu Quoc to Poulo Panjang.

Finally the last, and perhaps most interesting, route was called "a port-to-port route." It contains detailed information about the major rivers of the Mekong Delta area as well as tracing their upper reaches. With its seventy-plus place-names along the Mekong and its description of their landscape, this text has to be the earliest extant document we have about the Mekong Delta, predating Trinh Hoai Duc's better-known *Gia Dinh Thong Chi* by more than a decade. Further, and unlike the Gia Dinh gazetteer, Tong Phuc Ngoan's collection of trade routes contained information extending far beyond Vietnamese borders, including in its final description a route reaching as far north as Chiang Mai.

This document highlights the hybrid culture that characterized the Water Frontier. Both the compass used for directions and the way the compiler calculated distance (*geng*) were Chinese, but the text used distinctively Vietnamese measures for length, the *thuoc* (about 0.44 meters) and the *tam* (2.2 meters) rather than the Chinese maritime measure of *tua* (about 2.5 meters).[4] Almost all the islands in the Gulf of Siam were given Vietnamese names, expressed in demotic Vietnamese (*nom*) characters and arranged according to Vietnamese grammar.[5] Penang, for example, was called "Cu Lao Cau" in the text, totally different from the Chinese name Binlang Yu (Palm Island). While the word *Cau* is Vietnamese, the word *Cu Lao* for "island" came from Malay *Pulau*.[6] The fascinating material compiled in this text surely indicates the extensive regional experience of southern Vietnamese before 1810. All this knowledge—the Vietnamese names for even quite small places, detailed directions, carefully noted water depths, features of the landscape, and products available for trade in each place—had to be accumulated from lengthy contacts between the peoples of the Water Frontier, which enabled these terms and knowledge to be so naturally absorbed into each other.

This observation led me to consider the principal contributors acknowledged in the compilation. They were named as Vietnamese with quite different occupations: a Buddhist monk, *Sai* Thuy; an army officer, Thinh; an interpreter, Bien; two Vietnamese merchants from Phu Quoc island, An and Tam; and some Vietnamese migrants in the area.[7] Among them the most interesting for my purpose here are the two Vietnamese merchants. The text used a particular term for "merchant," the *nom* character *lai*. According to Thanh The Vy, the authority on Vietnam's commercial history, *lai* was only used to describe rich merchants handling trade in large quantities.[8] It was also, linguistically speaking, a relatively late term in common parlance, with *lai* or *cac lai* not becoming widely used until the Tay Son period, that is, from approximately the 1770s onward.[9]

A Liberated Rice Market in the Regional Trade

Rice trade was the heart of the Mekong Delta regional economy. Although rice had always been produced virtually wherever Vietnamese settled, before the

Nguyen won increasing control of the far south it had never been produced as a large-scale export commodity. The development of the Mekong Delta region as an area of commercial rice production for the export market was undoubtedly one of the most momentous events in eighteenth-century Cochinchina. It was also a significant episode in Vietnamese history, since it represented a real departure from Vietnamese agricultural practices and the prevailing economic order.

For much of the eighteenth century, the Nguyen government in the Hue area of modern central Vietnam levied a substantial amount of this rice for sale cheaply to the capital area. After civil war broke out between the successful Tay Son rebels and Nguyen forces (1773–1802), the changed circumstances seem to have provided southern rice growers and boat owners with a singular chance for greater economic autonomy. Before the Tay Son period, the government in Hue reportedly levied 341 boats annually to transport rice from the south,[10] removing an amount of between 5,000 and 6,000 tons from the export market.[11] However, all the old political and economic bonds between Hue and the far south were cut by the Tay Son rebellion by the mid-1770s. Although this produced the most devastating famine for a century in central Vietnam, in the south it freed the local rice market to an unprecedented extent and enabled it to offer its product on a far broader Chinese and Southeast Asian market. To this extent, the Tay Son rebellion created the environment that facilitated the rise of big Vietnamese merchants—the *lai*.

As *lai* was designated for rich merchants handling trade in large quantities and the word *lai* originally meant "sail," it is reasonable to assume that the merchants known by this term originally sailed large trading vessels and became rich on this basis. This group must have grown numerous enough to be socially visible, to be recognized as separate from petty traders. More important, the term distinguished sea from land traders. It is thus telling that the term *lai* became well known in the Tay Son period after the economic controls of the former Dang Trong (Cochinchina) Nguyen government had been destroyed by the rebellion.

Lai is also most likely a southern usage that originated from commercial rice transporting. This required a large quantity of junks that in turn required an abundance of accessible hardwood. The Mekong Delta region answered this demand beautifully.[12] It had been reputed as the best place for logging since early Vietnamese settlement in the later seventeenth century. Le Quy Don reported, on the basis of official documents from the later eighteenth century, that merchants in Nam Bo Chinh (in modern Quang Binh Province) would make trips to the Mekong Delta specifically for shipbuilding there. "They would build over a hundred big ships, and each would sell for thousands of *quan* [when they went back to Nam Bo Chinh]."[13] This would mean at a minimum well over 100,000 *quan* in sales from one district alone. To set this amount in context, it can be compared to the figure given for Nguyen state revenue in the same source. According to the same author, in the mid-eighteenth century Nguyen government revenue ranged between 338,100 and 423,300 *quan*, although this does not include the Nguyen rulers' other more lucrative sources of revenue. Even so, it is striking to note that the money produced by shipbuilding and re-sale in one district totaled about one-fourth of the state revenue. It is also worth considering how many craftsmen must have been involved in this huge ship-building business. All these were crucial ingredients for the rise of big mer-chants, the *lai*. The development of these big merchants resulted directly from the freed rice market of the Mekong Delta.

An Extensive Arena—the Gulf of Siam

The zone of most active trade involving people from the Mekong Delta region, be they Vietnamese *lai* or local Chinese, stretched from Saigon to the Gulf of Siam and its south. Certainly the Gulf of Siam area was familiar to Nguyen Anh, who constantly "moved among the islands [in the Gulf]." In an urgent situation in 1783, for instance, as later Nguyen court records reported, an army officer of Nguyen Anh was "sent to Chan Bon (Chantaburi) to seek Ba Da Lac (Bishop Pigneaux)" to take charge of the prince's young son, Canh. But as chance had it, Nguyen Anh found the bishop himself later in 1784 as both parties were leaving the Gulf of Siam, the exiled prince en route to Batavia or Malacca to seek for-eign assistance against the Tay Son and the missionary taking his pupils to Pondicherry to escape the chaos of civil war in southern Vietnam and Cambo-dia.[14] This suggests that there was already a fairly good knowledge of the islands and coastal areas along the Gulf of Siam among certain southern Vietnamese of the late eighteenth century. In this regard it is particularly interesting to observe that the area of most detailed knowledge contained in the *Collection of Routes* lay from the Hau Giang (Bassac) river southwards, that is, the area facing the Gulf of Siam. A good number of Vietnamese probably lived on this line of con-tact. Apart from the well-known Vietnamese community in Chantaburi, archival materials held in the Missions Étrangères de Paris also routinely mention Cochinchinese settlements on a number of islands in this region in the late eighteenth century,[15] not to mention the many thousands who lived in Hatien before its destruction in 1771. More specifically, a European traveler also noted in 1826 that Vietnamese merchants trading to Bangkok stopped over on the Siamese island of Koh Si Chang where they had built a temple.[16] Koh (Ko) Si Chang appeared in our text as part of the sea route between Ca Mau and Phuket in modern southern Thailand.[17]

This active trading conducted by people from the Mekong Delta region con-tributed considerably to the flourishing commerce in the Gulf of Siam area, which in turn attracted the Chinese junk trade. Although Chinese junks were noted in this region by European travelers in earlier centuries, the fact that the junk trade was reportedly at a peak in the Gulf of Siam in the late eighteenth and early nineteenth centuries was surely related to the prosperity generated at that time by the dense trading network that linked coast and hinterland from Saigon to the Malay States.[18] A saying among the Chinese trading to Southeast Asia, most likely coined before the 1830s, compares the degrees of prosperity of the three major ports in Southeast Asia: "The first is Siam, and second Ba (Batavia). The third is Selat (Singapore)."[19] The factors leading to the prosperity of the Siam trade were varied. Setting aside demand for rice for southern China, there was an expanding market for rice in the territory between the Gulf of Siam and the archipelagoes. This was the area in which, as Carl Trocki has shown, an off-shore production system was created by expatriate Chinese labor organizations (*kongsi*) in the late eighteenth century. This system of "offshore" production was linked directly into the broader Chinese trading system. By the 1780s, Trocki noted, "a significant number of these 'coolie' settlements had been formed in . . . Phuket, Kedah, Terengganu, Kelantan, Sambas, Pontianak, Bangka, Brunei, or . . . Chantaburi and Trat."[20] Interestingly, this list of ports coincides closely with the ports mentioned in the *Collection of Routes.*

That the Vietnamese visited the ports cited above is also confirmed by an English observer in 1833 in regard to Terengganu: "In the afternoon a Cochin-chinese vessel came into the river from Annam, laden with salt and rice. She was about 50 tons burthen, built after a European model."[21] Terengganu was one of the rice deficit ports in the area that the Cochinchinese had good reason to visit.[22] It had long been a meeting place for English, Portuguese, Chinese, and Bugis traders and a dissemination point for opium and firearms. From 1784 it became an important outlet for the tin and pepper previously taken to Riau.[23]

This 1833 observation brings our attention to the southern Vietnamese maritime tradition. The French merchant and adventurer Pierre Poivre observed disdainfully in the mid-eighteenth century that Cochinchinese vessels were "al-ways hugging the coast."[24] This was certainly confirmed by the sea routes mentioned in the early-nineteenth-century Vietnamese text *A Collection of Routes to the Kingdom of Siam,* all of which indeed hug the coast and its long string of minor ports. This typical Vietnamese maritime tradition, however, did not seem to hinder Viet trade from the Mekong Delta to the Gulf of Siam. As the regional trade system was fairly well developed in this period, it was in fact to the Viet advantage to hug the coast. Carried by strong coastal currents and prevailing winds, they could visit the smaller ports without paying port taxes and trade their rice for local products such as iron, tin, and pepper with little capital re-quired.

This characteristic made Saigon's trade similar to that of Bangkok, although on a smaller scale. Crawfurd observed in the 1820s that "Bangkok carries on a coasting trade with the ports of Champon, Chaiya, Bandon, Ligor, Sungora, and Talung, on the western coast of the Gulf, and with Banpasoi, Banpakung, Bang-prah, Banpomung, Rayong, Passeh, Chantabun, Tungyai, and Kokong on the eastern coast. The great object of this trade is to collect produce for the Chinese markets."[25]

From this point of view, Hatien was only one of the major ports flourishing in the regional trading system in the Gulf of Siam area in the eighteenth century. It was better known because for most of the eighteenth century there was no other major commercial center on the gulf. The founding of Saigon and Bangkok in the late eighteenth century, the liberation of the Mekong Delta rice trade, and the emergence of a significant number of Chinese laborer settlements in coastal Southeast Asia created a thriving trade system most noticeably in the Gulf of Siam area. Although ultimately linked to the Chinese trade system, it also had a life of its own.

Medium and Small Boats—the Backbone of the Regional Trade

The backbone of this system was medium- and small-sized junks rather than larger ones. This suggests a strong local or regional, rather than long-distance, trade. Medium to small boats formed perhaps the most numerous and active group in the Gulf of Siam area at the time. Crawfurd reports that in the 1820s there were about 280 junks based in Bangkok, 80 of them trading to China and 40 or 50 to Vietnam, "all small." [26] Those trading to China would also sometimes stop in Saigon to trade before heading to China.

It was these groups who supplied Vietnamese demand for iron and tin. Crawfurd said that Saigon's "exports from Siam consist of unwrought iron, iron pans, tobacco, opium, and some European Chinese goods. They take back mats for bags and sails, wrought and unwrought silks, &c."[27] Iron was always in great demand in Cochinchina of the predynastic Nguyen era, and this exchange must have been an ongoing practice present in the region for a long time as suggested by the name of Sa Dec as the "iron market." The need for iron became acute during the Tay Son period. To encourage merchants to bring the strategic items (pig iron, wrought iron, tin, and sulfur) he most needed, in 1789 Nguyen Anh allowed Chinese junks bringing these commodities to Saigon to take away large amounts of Mekong Delta rice tax free.[28] Although nineteenth-century Nguyen court records clearly used the term "Qing (i.e., Chinese) junks," the list of favored imports strongly suggests that the 1789 regulation was mainly targeting those Chinese based and trading in the Gulf of Siam area and its south where such commodities were easily available, rather than those who came directly from China.

The need for iron was expressed more explicitly in the tax regulation of 1809, which was concerned exclusively with vessels trading to Saigon from Hatien and Siam. According to this, anyone who brought more than 4,000 *can* (two tons) of wrought iron or 2,000 *can* (one ton) of pig iron from Siam to sell in Saigon could buy unrestricted amounts of items like silk, silk fabric, cotton, silkworm cocoons, and sugar without paying port tax. Those who failed to bring any iron to Saigon, however, would not have access to the listed items.[29] By the 1830s this large Cochinchinese demand for iron seemed to have stimulated the iron industry in northern Siam in Tha Chanuang. There Siamese made a living by collecting large lumps of iron carbonate, which were scattered on the surface over a large area, and taking it by boat loads to sell to the Chinese foundries whose five to six hundred men worked day and night. With numerous Chinese in the area, a distillery was founded and the little China town established there became one of the two towns noted as having an exceptionally strong Chinese presence in northern Siam.[30]

A Regional Trade System Including Chinese Small Traders

As the foregoing shows, the Chinese operating medium- or small-sized junks and based in the ports along the Gulf of Siam and its south, in the later eighteenth and early nineteenth centuries, were an important element in the short to medium distance regional trade system. One illustrative example comes from a local history of the Qiong Shan District of Hainan Island. There it was reported that two junks were built in the early nineteenth century that headed for the port of Ban Pak Phanang, from where they started their business of *bo zai* (junk transportation) between Siam and Singapore. From Siamese ports they transported rice and teak to Singapore, bringing back European products to sell in Siam. As the distance between the two was short, they could make four to five journeys a year. When they had earned sufficient money, they brought rice, teak, and European products back to Hainan.[31]

Another example of the importance of Chinese small traders in the regional context of Southeast Asia comes from the report of an English observer in 1833 about some Chinese traders in a small vessel he met in Hoi An: "They told me that they had come from Foochowfoo [Fujian] four months ago, that they had been trading on the coast of Cochinchina ever since; that they were going up to Turon [Danang] in a week or so, to load with sugar for Singapore."[32]

This observation from Vietnam was equally reflected in the experiences of some of the people from the same district of Hainan Island as discussed above. One happy story was about a certain Rao Xinxiao, who built eighteen junks in the Mekong Delta and twelve berths at the ports along the coast. His junks traveled between these ports carrying both people and cargoes and made a fortune.[33] None of these traders seemed to have paid port taxes to anyone, a major attraction of this region to the Chinese and other traders.

Rao's story might have been a common experience of many Chinese small traders operating in the regional trade system in the early nineteenth century. A similar story can even be found in the Nguyen chronicles of 1837. According to this source, Emperor Minh Mang was furious to hear that a Chinese called Huang Ye had engaged in an extensive regional trade for more than ten years and had paid no tax to the Nguyen government by pretending that the government had levied his junk. What upset Minh Mang most was this pretense. A government levied boat (*nhieu thuyen*), which carried an official identification plate, looked completely different from a Chinese junk and thus he should have been easily recognized and taxed. Yet this corrupt Chinese had successfully made his fortune with the support of local officials who had known what he was doing and profited from it for an outrageously long ten years or more.[34]

What Minh Mang saw in this case was the corruption of government officers. What he did not know was that he was looking at one unit in a massive trade system in which thousands of people in the Mekong Delta and the Gulf of Siam, be they Chinese, Vietnamese, Khmer, or Siamese, made their living. Looking at the political map of the region between the fifteenth and the late eighteenth centuries, one striking factor stands out: for almost three hundred years, not a single major political center existed along the thousands of miles of coast from Phan Rang in modern central Vietnam to Ligor (Nakhon Sithammarat) on the Malay Peninsula.[35] With waterways going everywhere and rice ready as cash, for those living in the Mekong Delta and beyond trade was a long-established custom and way of life, while notions of government control and tax obligations were recent and alien. This Mekong Delta experience and perspective formed an important basis for the Le Van Khoi rebellion of the 1830s. It is interesting to note, in this context, the stereotype of the inhabitants of southern Siam as being "pugnacious, impatient of authority, given to lawlessness."[36] Similar, almost word-for-word descriptions can be found on the people from the Mekong Delta.

Trade between the Mekong Delta and Phnom Penh

River-borne trade was just as integral a part of this regional trading system as maritime trade, especially trade between the Mekong Delta and Cambodia. As the Mekong Delta region was covered with rivers and canals, water routes were the easier option for trading in this area. As Crawfurd described Saigon, "the residence of the Chinese merchants . . . is intersected with many canals communicating with the main river, and boats come up and unloaded at the merchants' doors. From here there is a communication by water with the great river of Kamboja."[37]

The backbone of this hinterland trade between the delta and Cambodia, however, was Vietnamese traders. Different types of boats and ships were made in the Mekong Delta for different purposes ranging from rice boats, fishing boats, firewood boats, to pleasure boats. One type of bigger boat, called *Ghe be*, had a large capacity and was made for trading to Cambodia.[38] This was most likely what the Nguyen chronicles termed *thuyen hanh thuong Tran Tay* (boats trading to the "western protectorate," that is, to Cambodia). These craft were different from and more heavily taxed than *thuyen hanh thuong Luc Tinh* (boats trading within the six southern provinces), which were described as shorter, narrower, and shallower than those trading to Cambodia.[39] According to Son Nam, a Vietnamese expert on the Mekong Delta, the origin of the place-name Cai Be—"the place where *be* are gathered"[40]—derives from the custom of *ghe be* anchoring at that part of the Tien Giang Mekong arm before and after trading to Cambodia. Cai Be in modern Tien Giang Province, the town that grew up on the trade between Saigon and Cambodia, is still called by the same name.

Besides its convenient location between Saigon and Cambodia, Cai Be possessed another advantage in its closeness to My Tho. My Tho was important to the Cambodian trade because it produced betel nuts, one of the major items that Vietnamese carried to Cambodia. Indeed, proximity to the Cambodia market might have directly stimulated commercial betel nut production here. Certainly Son Nam identified an area called *"muoi tam thon vuon trau"* (eighteen villages specializing in growing betel nuts) in the My Tho area.[41]

Another item that Vietnamese traded to Cambodia was salt. A special kind of red salt, said to be particularly tasty for processing salted fish, was produced in modern Kien Giang Province on the Viet–Khmer border. In the early nineteenth century local Chinese traded this salt to Cambodia. They would "pack the salt into bags, each bag containing 56 *can* [2.53 kilos] of salt, 40 bags would make one Khmer *xe* [a measure of about 100–120 kilos]. This trade [was] very profitable when the salt [was] sold in Cambodia."[42] For their return trip, Vietnamese purchased canoes cheaply in Cambodia[43] where big tree trunks were readily available. The Nguyen chronicles of the early nineteenth century often mentioned logging in Cambodia and the Mekong Delta to make big ships for the court.[44] In the Gia Long era all the boats seem to have brought back quantities of deerskin since the chronicles say every Viet trading boat returning from Cambodia had to pay a special tax in deerskin of fifteen to forty-five pieces, depending on the size of the boat. Minh Mang abolished this tax in 1820.[45] In addition, traders with the specialized vessels required to transport them would bring back buffaloes, particularly from the Takeo area.

If we consider the trade items above, it strongly suggests that this trading system existed from very early in the Vietnamese history of the Mekong Delta. Certainly in regard to the buffalo traded from the Takeo area, it was critical for the opening of the Mekong Delta region as an area of commercial rice production. We know that early-nineteenth-century Saigon was the present-day Cholon, and Ben Nghe was modern Saigon/Ho Chi Minh City.[46] In its written form Ben Nghe was also called Ben Trau or Nguu Chu.[47] All these are Vietnamese versions of one Khmer name, Kompong Krabei,[48] which means "ferry for young buffaloes." Surely this name hints at an economic interchange between Vietnamese and Khmers in the eighteenth century.[49] The location of this "ferry of young buffaloes" strikes me as significant because buffaloes were crucial for large-scale rice cultivation in the Gia Dinh and Bien Hoa area. As Trinh Hoai Duc noted in the early nineteenth century, "land in the Phien An and Bien Hoa areas needs buffaloes to cultivate it. Such land could yield one hundred *hoc* of rice for one *hoc* of seeds planted." Land in the Bassac area colonized much later by Vietnamese did not "require the use of buffalo."[50] In the old place-name for Saigon, it seems, lurks the memory of a trading practice critical to the opening of the Mekong Delta. The regular supply of draft animals sometimes came from even further away, from Siam. In 1778, for example, thirty Vietnamese traders were said to have come to purchase cattle at Khukhan in northeastern Siam and from there they returned to Phnom Penh.[51] Only in the context of a regional trade in cattle can we understand how some rich Vietnamese families in the Mekong Delta area could possess 300 to 400 oxen and buffaloes each, as reported in the late eighteenth century.[52] This astonishing number of draft animals owned by one family would have been almost literally unimaginable to anyone residing in the old territories of Vietnamese-speaking people, but not in the Mekong Delta.

Setting aside Saigon as an old port of the buffalo trade, we can find other such links elsewhere in the Mekong Delta region. The buffalo–oxen trading link between Vietnamese and Khmers definitely existed, and Cambodia remained the major source for oxen and buffaloes for southern Vietnamese provinces for centuries. So regular and profitable was this trade that it prompted some Vietnamese to specialize in it at the Takeo market in the bigger, heavier vessels that were previously mentioned.[53] As late as the 1950s, each year 40,000 of the 70,000 oxen (or nearly 60 percent) exported from Takeo and Pong Tom went to the Saigon–Cholon area and all of their 10,000 buffaloes.[54] This large and regular supply of farm animals, something only possible by trading with Khmer and uplanders in the region, was indispensable for the mass production and commercialization of rice. In other words, the opening of far southern Vietnam depended on a regional economic and commercial system in which Vietnamese interacted with various other peoples in the region and from which the vitality of the region arose.

Conclusion

Lying at the crossroads of several different trade currents, the Mekong Delta region formed a crucial link in an active trading system in the eighteenth and early nineteenth centuries as the early nineteenth century Vietnamese text *A Collection of Routes to the Kingdom of Siam* clearly demonstrates. What this shows us is a well-known and well-used series of trade routes by land and by sea, which connected mainland and insular Southeast Asia in various ways and had been in operation long before it came to Crawfurd's attention in the 1820s. Both the future primate cities of Saigon and Bangkok were originally built on the basis of this tightly woven regional trade network and its wider connections. In this respect it is interesting to note that this region produced at the same time not one but three of the most important political figures of mainland Southeast Asia in the late eighteenth and early nineteenth centuries: Nguyen Anh from the Mekong Delta, Taksin from Chantaburi, and Rama I from Ratburi. In light of the discussion above, I do not believe that their appearance at the same time and in the same region can be properly understood without relating these men and their accomplishments to the regional trade network that made possible so much of their success.

Notes

1. Virginia Thompson, *French IndoChina* (New York: Octagon Books, 1968), 168.

2. Tong Phuc Ngoan and Duong Van Chau, *Xian luo guo lu cheng ji lu* [A Collection of Routes to the Kingdom of Siam], introduced by Chen Chingho (Hong Kong: New Asia Institute, Chinese University of Hong Kong, 1966) [hereafter *Xian luo guo*].

3. The translation of the names of this route and some others in this article are from Geoff Wade, "A Maritime Route in the Vietnamese Text: *Xiem-La-Quoc Lo-Trinh Tap-Luc*," in *Commerce et Navigation en Asie du Sud Est (XIVe-XIXe siècles)*, ed. Nguyen The Anh and Yoshiaki Ishizawa (Paris: L'Harmattan, 1999), 143–44. A new, abridged excerpt from the coastal route appears as an appendix to this volume.

4. See Chen's comment in *Xian luo guo*, 19.

5. *Xian luo guo*, 21.

6. Alexander Woodside, *Vietnam and the Chinese Model* (Cambridge, Mass.: Harvard University, 1988), 245.

7. *Xian luo guo*, 1.

8. Thanh The Vy, *Ngoai thuong Viet Nam hoi the ky XVII, XVIII va dau XIX* [The Overseas Trade of Vietnam in the Seventeenth, Eighteenth, and Early Nineteenth Centuries] (Hanoi: Su Hoc, 1961), 173.

9. Thanh The Vy, *Ngoai thuong Vietnam,* 173.

10. Le Qui Don, *Phu Bien Tap Luc* [Miscellaneous Border Records (seized in 1775—1776)] (Saigon: Phu quoc vu khanh dac trach van hoa, 1973), vol. 4, 41.

11. The average tonnage of Southeast Asian junks in the early nineteenth century was 20 to 28 tons. Anthony Reid, "A New Phase of Commercial Expansion," in *The Last Stand of Asian Autonomies: Responses to Modernity in the Diverse States of Southeast and Korea, 1750–1900*, ed. Anthony Reid (London and New York: MacMillan and St Martin's Press, 1997), 68. A reasonable guess for the average Viet junks of this period would be 15 tons.

12. John White observed in 1820 that local "shiptimber, and planks, excelled anything I had ever seen." *A Voyage to Cochinchina*, reprint (Kuala Lumpur: Oxford University Press, 1972), 235.

13. Le Quy Don, *Phu bien tap luc*, in *Le Quy Don toan tap* [Complete Works of Le Quy Don] (Hanoi: Social Sciences Press, 1977), 104.

14. *Dai Nam chinh bien liet truyen, so tap* [First Collection of the Primary Compilation of Biographies of Imperial Vietnam] (Tokyo: Keio Institute of Linguistic Studies, 1962), vol. 28, 1322. Copy of letter from Pigneaux, 8 July 1785. Archives of the Missions-Étrangères de Paris, "Cochinchine", vol. 801, 71–73. Private communication from Nola Cooke, January 2002.

15. Private communication from Nola Cooke, January 2002.

16. Christopher Goscha, *Thailand and the Southeast Asia Networks of the Vietnamese Revolution, 1885–1954* (Richmond: Curzon, 1999), 15.

17. *Xian luo guo*, 17.

18. Tien Rukang, *Shiqi zhi shijiu shiji zhong ye zhongguo fanchuan zai dongnan yazhou* [Chinese Junks from the Mid-Seventeenth to Nineteenth Centuries in Southeast Asia] (Shanghai: Shanghai People's Press, 1957), 33–34.

19. Yuan Zuzhi, "Ying hai cai wen ji shi" [A Traveler's Account of Overseas] quoted from *Wanqing haiwai bi ji xuan* [Selected Chinese Travelers' Accounts of the Late Qing Era] (Beijing: Maritime Press, 1983), 18.

20. Carl Trocki, "Chinese Pioneering in Eighteenth Century Southeast Asia," in *The Last Stand of Asian Autonomies,* 195.

21. Trocki, "Chinese Pioneering," 191.

22. Anthony Reid, *Southeast Asia before the Nation-State: An Economic History*, unpublished manuscript, chapter VII, 14.

23. Barbara Andaya, *To Live as Brothers: Southeast Sumatra in the Seventeenth and Eighteenth Centuries* (Honolulu: University of Hawaii Press, 1993), 222.

24. "Description of Cochinchina, 1749–50," in *Southern Vietnam under the Nguyen: Documents on the Economic History of Cochinchina (Dang Trong)*, ed. Li Tana and Anthony Reid (Singapore: ECHOSEA, ANU/ISEAS, 1993), 73.

25. John Crawfurd, *Journal of an Embassy to the Courts of Siam and Cochin China* (Oxford University Press, 1987), 413.

26. Crawfurd, *Journal*, 414.

27. Crawfurd, *Journal*, 414.

28. *Dai Nam Thuc Luc, De Nhat Ky* [Veritable Records of the Imperial South, First Reign] (Tokyo: Keio Institute of Linguistic Studies, 1962), vol. 4, 350 [hereafter *DNTL*].

29. *Kham Dinh Dai Nam Hoi Dien Su Le* [Official Compendium of Institutions and Usages of the Imperial South] (Hanoi: Social Science Press, 1993?), *tap* 4, vol. 48, 430.

30. B. J. Terwiel, *Through Travellers' Eyes* (Bangkok: D. K. Book House, 1989), 128, quoting the French missionary Bishop Pallegoix.

31. Pan Gan, "Qiong shan zui zao chu yang fang chuan dui sing shuai shi" [The Ups and Downs of the Earliest Junk Crews Going Overseas from the Qiong Shan District], *Qiong Qiao Chun Qiu* [Journal of the History of Overseas Chinese from Hainan Island] 1 (1990): 12.

32. Edward Brown, *Cochin-China and My Experience of It: A Seaman's Narrative of His Adventures and Sufferings during a Captivity among Chinese Pirates, on the Coast of Cochin-China, and Afterwards during a Journey on Foot across That Country, in the Years 1857-58* (London: Charles Westerton, 1861), 161.

33. Brown, *Cochin-China*, 13.

34. *DNTL, De Nhi Ky*, vol. 179, 4054–55. Also see Choi's chapter in this book.

35. *Southeast Asia in the Early Modern Era: Trade, Power, and Belief*, ed. Anthony Reid (Ithaca and London: Cornell University Press, 1993), 4.

84 *Li Tana*

36. Lorraine M. Gesick, *In the Land of Lady White Blood: Southern Thailand and the Meaning of History* (Ithaca: SEAP, 1995), 9.

37. Crawfurd, *Journal*, 587–88.

38. Son Nam, *Ben Nghe Xua* [Saigon's Yesteryears] (Ho Chi Minh City: Van Nghe, 1992), 40–41.

39. *DNTL*, vol. 179, 4050–4051.

40. Son Nam, *Ben Nghe Xua*, 40.

41. Son Nam, *Dong bang song Cuu Long* [The Mekong Delta] (Ho Chi Minh City: NXB Ho Chi Minh City, 1993), 36. This place also seems to have been closely associated with Chinese residence and perhaps occupation. See Li Tana, "*Cang hai sang tian:* Chinese Communities in the 18th Century Mekong Delta" (paper presented at the International Conference on "China and Southeast Asia: Changing Links through History," Centre of Asian Studies, University of Hong Kong, 19–21 July 2001), 6.

42. Trinh Hoai Duc, *Gia Dinh Thanh Thong Chi* [Gia Dinh Gazette] (Saigon: Phu Quoc vu khanh dac trach van hoa, 1972), vol. 3, 7b.

43. Son Nam, *Ben Nghe xua*, 40.

44. Son Nam, *Dong bang song Cuu Long*, 38.

45. *DNTL, De Nhi Ky,* vol. 179, 4054–4055.

46. Crawfurd, *Journal*, 223.

47. "Gia Dinh that thu vinh" [Song about the Loss of Gia Dinh] in Truong Vinh Ky, *Gia Dinh phong canh vinh* [Odes to Gia Dinh], introduced by Nguyen Dinh Dau (Ho Chi Minh City: Tuoi Tre, 1997), 47, fn 1.

48. Truong Vinh Ky, *Petit cours de géographie de la Basse Cochinchine* (Saigon: Imprimerie du Gouvernement, 1875), quoted in Nguyen Dinh Dau, "Dia ly lich su thanh pho Ho Chi Minh" [Historical Geography of Ho Chi Minh City] in *Dia chi van hoa Thanh pho Hochiminh* [A Cultural Gazette of Ho Chi Minh City], ed. Tran Van Giau et al. (Ho Chi Minh City: NXB Ho Chi Minh City, 1987), 223.

49. "Ben Nghe" [*Nguu Chu*] first appeared in the Nguyen chronicles in 1775. This is later than many place names in the Mekong Delta like Saigon or Dong Nai. *Dai Nam Thuc Luc, Tien Bien* [Veritable Records of the Imperial South, Early Period] (Tokyo: Keio Institute of Linguistic Studies, 1961), vol. 12, 165.

50. Trinh Hoai Duc, *Gia Dinh Thong Chi*, vol. 5, 3b.

51. Quoted from Puangthong Rungswadisab, "War and Trade: Siamese Interventions in Cambodia, 1767–1851", Ph.D. thesis, University of Wollongong, 1995, 77.

52. Le Quy Don, *Phu Bien Tap Luc,* 243a.

53. Son Nam, *Dong bang song Cuu Long*, 38.

54. *Nanyue Gaomian huaqiao shiye* [Overseas Chinese Enterprises in South Vietnam and Cambodia], ed. Chen Jixing (Saigon: n.p., 1955), 8. Buffalo and cattle for the Red River Delta came from the northern highland provinces of Lang Son, Thai Nguyen, and Yen Bai, from Nghe An and Thanh Hoa in the central region, and from Laos. Ta Thi Thuy, "Rice Cultivating and Cattle Raising in Tonkin in the First Half of 20th Century," in *Quantitative Economic History of Vietnam*, ed. Jean-Pascal Bassino, Jean-Dominique Giacometti, and Konosuke Odaka (Tokyo: Institute of Economic Research, Hitotsubashi University, 2000), 101.

6

The Nguyen Dynasty's Policy toward Chinese on the Water Frontier in the First Half of the Nineteenth Century

Choi Byung Wook

In the seventeenth and eighteenth centuries, Chinese merchants from Fujian, Quangdong, and other southern Chinese ports had been welcome to trade with or sojourn in Nguyen Cochinchina (Dang Trong). After the fall of the Ming dynasty, this contact expanded as a wave of émigrés from southern China appeared seeking asylum from the Qing. Because these newcomers maintained an outward allegiance to the fallen dynasty in appearance and customs, Vietnamese called them Ming loyalists (*Minh Huong*.) The overwhelming majority of them were men who freely intermarried with local women, whether Viet or Khmer. Once established in the Nguyen realm, Minh Huong usually put down roots in local society and an unknown number probably merged into it over time, although others continued to maintain a sense of separate identity through their registration in special Minh Huong association. By the early nineteenth century, when Gia Long took the throne after three decades of civil war, many Minh Huong were already third-generation locals who had long supported the Nguyen cause.

As population pressure increased in China during the eighteenth century, a different exodus occurred from southern Chinese ports, especially after the Qing court relaxed its opposition to emigrant Chinese returning from abroad. Men seeking to make their fortunes in Southeast Asia, without necessarily intending to leave China permanently, began appearing in large numbers in the region. Unlike the earlier Minh Huong, these newcomers conformed to Qing norms of appearance, so Viets categorized them as "Qing men" (*Thanh Nhan*) to distinguish them from the Minh loyalist community even if they ultimately settled in Dang Trong. For greater ease of administrative control, the Nguyen required both groups be organized either into associations (*bang*) of common dialect speakers or collectives of Minh Huong, with the earliest recorded Minh Huong association in far southern Dang Trong being created at the same time as Gia Dinh *phu* in 1698.

From the early 1780s and especially after Prince Nguyen Anh returned from exile in Siam, these local Chinese became an important component in his ultimate success. In 1788, the Nguyen finally founded a solid power base in the Saigon region after years of unsuccessful struggle there. This power base, called here the Gia Dinh regime (1788–1802), was the means through which Nguyen Anh ruled and mobilized support for more than another decade of continuing warfare. Nguyen Anh drew on all the resources of Gia Dinh to strengthen his rule, including its Chinese population. Due to their long acquaintance with local society, Minh Huong Chinese like Le Quang Dinh, Trinh Hoai Duc, and Ngo Nhan Tinh, to name but a few, were welcome to participate alongside Viets in the Nguyen ruling group and rose to high positions in the Gia Dinh regime.[1] From 1789, Thanh Nhan immigrants were also mobilized as soldiers in proportion to their numbers in each dialect association in Gia Dinh. Even Chinese immigrants in more peripheral areas like Tra Vinh, Soc Trang, and Hatien were organized into military plantation units.[2] Even so, the most prominent Chinese role in the Gia Dinh regime was economic as the providers of supplies and equipment. From 1789, they brought strategic materials like iron, black lead, and sulfur to Gia Dinh to exchange for rice, cotton fabric, and raw silk.[3] When the Nguyen-controlled area expanded and local people began to experience instability in rice prices, it was to these same Minh Huong merchants that Gia Dinh leaders turned to import rice from Siam in 1791.[4]

During the Gia Long reign (1802–1820), both Chinese communities in the Gia Dinh region enjoyed the favor of the Hue court in gratitude for their vital support during the long struggle against the Tay Son. As both Minh Huong and Thanh Nhan had contributed to the king's final victory, Hue made no distinction between the two communities. Because of this royal favor, preexisting Chinese dominance of commerce in far southern Vietnam continued during the first reign, for Chinese merchants were directly protected by the regional government Hue set up to administer the area from 1808 to 1832, the *Gia Dinh Thanh Tong Tran* (or Gia Dinh general government). Gia Long's greatest generals headed this administration, with Nguyen Van Nhan, Nguyen Huynh Duc, and Le Van Duyet all in turn holding the position of *tong tran quan* or governor general. All local men themselves, under their administration the Gia Dinh general government naturally continued the Gia Dinh regime's practice of appointing many Chinese to official positions.

However, circumstances began to change under the second Nguyen king, Minh Mang (1820–1841), who perceived a negative impact from Chinese settlement in the far south. According to his public statements, the new king's settlement in the far south. According to his public statements, the new king's biggest concern regarding Chinese settlers was rice smuggling. Some recent scholarship has supported this. Fujiwara, for instance, provided evidence for the smuggling of rice and opium under the Nguyen and noted the probable involvement of Chinese.[5] In my view, however, the implications of smuggling here were much wider, and the issue can only be fully explained in the context of the Nguyen dynasty's changed policy toward Chinese settlers. Such an approach reveals that Hue's strong opposition to rice and opium smuggling was related to Minh Mang's goal of depriving these settlers of their important role in the southern Vietnamese economy.

This chapter explores this wider approach by first examining the question of rice and opium smuggling in order to apportion responsibility for it and then discusses Chinese influence in Gia Dinh before ending with a consideration of Minh Mang's policy of discriminating against Chinese settlers, whether Ming Huong or Thanh Nhan. This approach allows us to glimpse Ming Mang's real intentions in continually raising the issue of rice and opium smuggling and also provides an opportunity to probe the increasing role of southern Vietnamese in commercial life along the Water Frontier in the half-century before French colonization.

The Gia Dinh Overseas Rice Trade

The supply and consumption of rice in the northern and central regions of Nguyen Vietnam depended on southern rice. The situation began with nineteenth-century unification after which southern rice surpluses played a key role in the state economy. The court in Hue was deeply concerned with the rice price in Gia Dinh. Until 1827, Gia Dinh officials had to report the local rice price twice a month, while other areas reported only monthly.[6] Although the dynastic chronicles recorded that 500,000 *can* of rice, or more than 300 tons,[7] was exported to the Philippines in 1804,[8] this was a rare case. Rice export was normally strictly controlled and foreigners were prohibited from exporting it. Each vessel departing the country was only allowed to carry a strictly limited amount for provisions, in proportion to the number of the crew and the anticipated length of the journey. The penalty for violating these regulations was decapitation.[9]

Nevertheless, the rice price continued to increase in the later 1820s. According to Nguyen The Anh, between 1825 and 1829–1830 its price rose by 50 to 100 percent in the north,[10] with a similar situation in the south. An 1829 report from Gia Dinh confirms that the rice price had climbed sharply toward the end of the 1820s: "Previously, the rice price was very low. One *phuong* [38.5 liters] of rice was no more than 5–6 *mach* [0.5–0.6 *quan*]. These days, however, the rice price hardly drops below 1 *quan*."[11] In this situation, the court suspected Gia Dinh rice was illegally flowing out of the country: "Gia Dinh has very fertile soil and produces more grain than any other region [in Vietnam]. Until now, the northern area from Binh Dinh up has depended on southern rice. Once the Gia Dinh rice price jumped, the rest of the regions followed. Smuggling rice outside [the country] is a serious affair that relates to the management of the state economy."[12]

Where did the Gia Dinh rice go? The court believed it was destined for southern China, Cambodia, and Siam, with island Southeast Asia the most popular destination. Possibly basing his comparison on information from subjects who had been sent to China and island Southeast Asia, Minh Mang claimed the Vietnamese rice price was half that of the most expensive rice elsewhere.[13] Given its competitiveness, Gia Dinh rice was clearly welcome in foreign markets, regardless of its being an illegal export.

It was not only the higher price that encouraged smugglers to take rice abroad. Foreign goods like knives, swords, muskets, metal teapots, serge, flannel, broadcloth, calico, and linen from the Western colonies were very attractive in Vietnam. In normal trading, a round-trip between Vietnam and Singapore would yield a profit of 200 to 400 percent;[14] but for illegal goods such as rice and opium the profit was much higher. Opium, especially, was the most profitable commodity traded in the British colonies in island Southeast Asia. Generally, in the first half of the nineteenth century, the main market for British opium was China. Occasionally, however, British opium could be provided to traders from Vietnam quite cheaply if export to the Chinese market was frustrated.[15] Gia Dinh was the main place of entry for opium into Vietnam as Minh Mang complained in 1832 just before the death of Le Van Duyet, the last *tong tran quan* of Gia Dinh Thanh Tong Tran: "As Gia Dinh Thanh neglects to patrol the seas, cunning people secretly carry away rice and sell it. . . . Basically, rice is very important for my people, so it should not be sold outside Vietnam . . . [these cunning people] return with opium to make more profit. This situation is most serious in Gia Dinh."[16]

The Chief Suspects: Chinese or Vietnamese?

Hue blamed the Chinese for trading rice for opium, but was the court correct? Drawing on his local experience, the Gia Dinh governor general Le Van Duyet diagnosed the problem rather differently. He gave three reasons for the increased rice price: Chinese junk passengers (*thanh thuyen thap khach*) were consuming more; cunning merchants (*gian thuong*) were secretly buying up rice; and government-hired rice junks transporting rice to the center and the north (*dai dich thuyen*) were illegally trading in rice.[17]

We should consider his arguments more closely. By "Chinese passengers" Le Van Duyet meant Thanh Nhan emigrants on Chinese-owned and Chinese-crewed junks from south China. At this time, Gia Dinh was one of the most attractive destinations for southern Chinese emigrants to Southeast Asia and the Gia Dinh government was concerned about this new rice-consuming population. It is hard to believe, however, that such junks carried only passengers. To make the journey more profitable, whether as crew or passengers, they naturally loaded other valuable items. Though what follows is a list from 1857, it gives an interesting insight into the sort of items imported by earlier southern Chinese immigrants: tea, beans, wheat, lead, Chinese coins, and opium.[18] It can be inferred, therefore, that opium was entering Gia Dinh not only from island Southeast Asia but also from China. That is why Le Van Duyet denounced junk passengers for luring Gia Dinh people to smoke opium.[19]

Next, what of the "cunning merchants" who were accused of buying up rice in Gia Dinh? They could have been Thanh Nhan or Minh Huong, but equally they might have been local Vietnamese. This latter possibility is supported by the third element in Le Van Duyet's list, the transport of rice by government junks.

Rice was supposed to be shipped to different regions in Vietnam to balance demand and supply, though it mainly went from Gia Dinh to the central and northern regions. Basically, government junks were responsible for the task, although private junk owners might sometimes ship rice also. In such cases, it can hardly be expected that government fees always satisfied the junk masters.[20] Once a boat was under way, we can imagine that a master seeking greater profits could sell some of the rice to Chinese traders waiting at prearranged meeting places at sea. Certainly, in the Minh Mang reign, junks ventured far out to sea. One court official reported in the mid-1830s that transport junks had been sailing as far as island Southeast Asia, Guangdong, and Hainan.[21] According to John Crawfurd, who encountered thirteen small junks on his way to Hue, the capacity of each junk was "from five to seven hundred piculs burden."[22] The owners of these rice transport junks were local Vietnamese. As Le Van Duyet argued in an 1829 report, they were among the main suspects in the illegal rice trade. As long as rice trading was profitable and local Vietnamese monopolized its transport,[23] it was inconceivable that they would not attempt to buy up rice too. That is why the "cunning merchants" could be Vietnamese as easily as Chinese settlers.

Le Van Duyet's analysis thus allows an important insight into a change in the Gia Dinh economy from the previous century: Vietnamese were rising in the field of commerce from the early nineteenth century. Formerly, Chinese had dominated commerce in Gia Dinh, and evidence of this dominance persisted into the nineteenth century. Western visitors like John White, John Crawfurd, and his subordinate George Finlayson all reported Chinese active in Saigon's commercial life in the years 1819 to 1822. Indeed, they often favorably compared the Chinese role in trade with Vietnamese inferiority in this field. White, for instance, described streets filled with lively Chinese and with products from China:

These industrious and enterprising people are the butchers, the tailors, the confectioners, and the peddlers of Cochin China: they are met with in every bazaar, and in every street . . . they are also the bankers, and money-changers . . .

Many of the cooking utensils, and a principal part of the clothing of the Onamese [Vietnamese], are brought from China, from whence they also have their porcelain, tea, many of their drugs and medicines, cabinet-work, and, in short, almost every article of convenience which they possess. [24]

But these descriptions of Saigon require some explanations. First, what Westerners called Saigon was in fact Chinese Cholon, the place where "the *'hoi quan'* [buildings of the Chinese associations] of Phuc Chau (in Fujian), Quang Dong (Guangdong), Trao Chau (Teochiu), On Lang (Wen Ling), and Chuong Chau (in Fujian) are located."[25] In the 1820s Saigon proper was still known by its original name of Ben Nghe, the place a few miles from Cholon where Nguyen Phuc Anh had established his fortified administration in the late eighteenth century.[26] Second, such reports were based on limited experience in Vietnam: whether in Saigon or Cholon, the Westerners had spent all their time in urban areas.

To assess the situation in rural areas we need to rely on evidence from the next decade. After central court officials took over the administration of Gia Dinh in 1832, they found rather large numbers of local people had been pursuing what they called *mat nghiep*, or the lowliest occupation, by which they meant trade or commerce. This was both because of the ease with which waterborne commerce could be carried out here and because no taxes had been levied on it. In 1835 a Hue appointed official, Truong Phuc Cuong, reported of the region west of Hau Giang (the Bassac or lower Mekong) that:

> The six provinces of southern Vietnam have fertile land, but people are idle and many of them carry out professions [i.e., commerce] by means of ships and boats. Thus fertile land is abandoned. Until now, no tax has been charged on the trading boats [with the exception of the trade ship to Cambodia]. If we tax these boats, the people can be recalled from the lowliest occupation to farming.[27]

As this indicates, a noticeably high proportion of Gia Dinh's Vietnamese population engaged in commerce alongside the Chinese settlers. During the first half of the nineteenth century, residential areas to the west of Saigon were crisscrossed by streams. Much to his surprise, in 1833 the northern mandarin Doan Uan discovered that "in the land of southern Vietnam, only the region around Saigon is solid. In other regions, you find water if you only dig about 30cm below the ground. Streams cross like the warp and weft of cloth. There is no land access between villages. Once you go out the gate, you cannot reach other villages without using boats."[28] Settlements were scattered and isolated from each other. Once the rainy season came villages were inundated, forcing them to rely on the supply of goods from the outside. Local conditions, therefore, made trade by boats essential in southern Vietnam.

Even around Saigon where Chinese had dominated commerce certain Vietnamese merchants apparently controlled trade in large amounts of sugar in

1819–1820. When John White sought to purchase cargo for his ship in 1819, Vietnamese women traders had approached him offering sugar, silk, cotton, gamboges, and other items but at 50 to 100 percent higher than the usual price. This caused the American to try to buy sugar via a different route, possibly from Chinese merchants who were connected to a high-ranking Chinese official in the Gia Dinh administration. Whatever the case, the attempt caused an angry reaction, which White himself witnessed, by the Vietnamese merchants against the Chinese official, who, they insisted, had flouted their privileges.[29]

There is also evidence that local Vietnamese merchants had enough maritime experience to sail to island Southeast Asia. White's observations in the Saigon area convinced him that local maritime skills were of a high standard. Vietnam, he recorded, was "perhaps, of all the powers in Asia, the best adapted to maritime adventure . . . the Vietnamese rivaling even the Chinese as sailors."[30] Then in 1823, when Minh Mang decided to resume the state-run overseas trade from Hue that had stopped in 1801,[31] he was startled to find his selected captain insisted on using Gia Dinh ships to ensure a safe journey to Ha Chau (island Southeast Asian ports).[32] These two examples suggest the superiority of Gia Dinh's maritime experience over any other region of Vietnam. Gia Dinh Vietnamese traveled as a matter of course between southern Vietnam and parts of island Southeast Asia such as the Straits of Malacca, Batavia, Singapore, and the Philippines. Vietnamese and Cochinchinese junks were frequently found in these regions as local sources recorded during the 1820s and 1830s.[33] But such records did not capture the reality of Vietnamese commercial activity because they did not differentiate between junks from Cochinchina sailed by Vietnamese and those sailed by Chinese settlers. In this respect, Vietnamese records are more reliable. Official reports of state-run trade missions occasionally recorded sighting illegal Vietnamese ships in island Southeast Asia, but "once [the private traders] saw the state vessels, they scattered to the four winds . . . [because] in exchange for rice, they bring back opium."[34]

We can even find the commercial ability of Gia Dinh Vietnamese demonstrated in state-run trade if we read the court chronicles of the reigns from Minh Mang to Tu Duc carefully. One name appears frequently during this period in connection with foreign trade with the Western world. He was a Gia Dinh regional graduate (*cu nhan*) of 1825 from the district of Long Thanh in Bien Hoa Province, who had changed his more conventional name of Dao Tri Kinh to the more eccentric Dao Tri Phu, meaning "accumulation of wealth."[35] He went on to meet a gruesome end in 1854, being torn to pieces for participating in the failed coup of Tu Duc's elder brother Hong Bao, on whose behalf he had tried to exploit his overseas contacts to procure military support.[36] The court chronicle, therefore, was not very friendly toward him, yet it still acknowledged his contribution to state-run trade. Dao Tri Phu was the principal central official in charge of purchasing foreign goods from island Southeast Asia and the eastern coast of India. When not overseas, he worked in the Hue Board of Finance. Phu was said to be so accurate in his work that he could faultlessly complete an account book overnight, even when drugged on opium as he often was when overseas. Because of his talents for business and foreign languages, he accumulated great wealth from his frequent trading trips. As the Nguyen dynasty's "state businessman," he was also the one who introduced steamships to Vietnam.[37] In all, Dao Tri Phu was an exemplary Gia Dinh man with a talent for commerce.

Given this supporting evidence, Le Van Duyet's analysis gains strong ground. It was not Chinese alone who ran the illegal rice and opium trade; local Vietnamese also participated. Even court mandarins accepted his position as correct.[38] Yet Minh Mang and his chosen officials continued to fix their eyes on the Chinese settlers. In 1827, when Thanh Nhan immigrants in Gia Dinh asked to participate in the rice shipping business, something that Le Van Duyet seems to have approved locally, the Hue court rejected the request because it claimed "the cunning Thanh Nhan" were already secretly trading rice with Chinese merchants in distant islands.[39]

The Chinese in Gia Dinh Thanh

Just as during the late-eighteenth-century Gia Dinh regime, many Chinese continued to help rule Gia Dinh, notably senior officials like the Minh Huong Trinh Hoai Duc and Ngo Nhan Tinh or the Thanh Nhan settler Nguyen Huu Nghia.[40] Huu Nghia had been a retainer of Le Van Duyet since the early Gia Long reign when the general had been in Hue. After Le Van Duyet was appointed *tong tran quan* of Gia Dinh Thanh, Huu Nghia had followed him south where Duyet soon appointed him head of the local office of justice, *hinh tao*.[41]

Another example was Luu Tin. No immigrant from China, Tin was a rich, Hoi An–born merchant who, like many of his expatriate countrymen, had kept his identity as Chinese. He was twenty years old before he actually visited the land of his ancestors. After making business trips to the north, south, and China, he eventually decided to settle in Gia Dinh. Luu Tin represented another type of southern Thanh Nhan. In Gia Dinh his business prospered thanks to his relations with Governor-General Le Van Duyet. In this case, a personal relationship—Le Van Duyet had adopted Tin[42]—developed into an official relationship when Duyet appointed him to the agency in charge of Gia Dinh's foreign trade (the *hanh nhan ty*).[43]

While it is possible, as Shimao has claimed, that Le Van Duyet's group received financial support from Chinese merchants like Luu Tin,[44] what cannot be denied is that Chinese immigrants in Gia Dinh benefited from the favor of the local government thanks to their connections with Chinese-descended officials, including Trinh Hoai Duc and Luu Tin. Moreover, these Chinese officials might themselves be directly involved in commercial activities. As White observed during his stay (1819–1820), the acting governor of Gia Dinh, who doubled as a petty dealer in sugar and other merchandise, had his own Chinese business agent and close contacts with other petty dealers.[45] It might have been impossible for the American to recognize him, but the mandarin in question was the long-serving Minh Huong official Trinh Hoai Duc, who was acting governor at the time when the serving governor general, Nguyen Van Nhan was visiting Hue.[46]

Given that Chinese influence was strong in Gia Dinh Thanh, in what ways were Chinese able to use their position locally to frustrate central government decisions that impacted negatively on Chinese settlers? One example is how the tax system worked. When new immigrants landed in Gia Dinh in the early nineteenth century, the heads of local Chinese dialect associations (*bang*) were supposed to enlist them in the appropriate group according to their origins in China; but this did not always happen. Some were accepted into a Minh Huong association (*xa*) instead, so that new immigrants might receive visits from leaders of both Thanh Nhan and Minh Huong associations.[47] From this stage, newcomers could hide in *bang* or Minh Huong associations and quickly settle down in the new land under the protection of whichever group they belonged to.

The problem with all this, as Le Van Duyet discovered, was that new immigrants often managed to be indefinitely exempted from tax payments. Usually newcomers were registered as extremely poor laborers (*cung co*) or as men without property (*vo vat luc gia*) and were thus waived tax; but if they later accumulated property, their status was seldom upgraded to taxpayers.[48] In 1827, Le Van Duyet proposed to the court that ordinary Thanh Nhan pay a tax of 6.5 *quan*, with a continued exemption for empty-handed newcomers.[49] The problem was how to define the empty-handed. Le Van Duyet's proposal left too much room for Thanh Nhan to avoid taxes. Minh Mang's response was more logical and realistic in terms of identifying the taxpayers: "I know the newcomers are really poor, but my paradise will not let them stay poor, then they will be able to pay tax."[50] Minh Mang preferred that new Chinese immigrants be levied the full amount in principle, though only half should be collected from those judged as extremely poor for the first three years. After that, they would also have to pay the full amount. This was the decision sent to Gia Dinh.

Even so, it was not long before Minh Mang and his Hue coterie found this clear rule was not being applied to all Thanh Nhan in Gia Dinh. The so-called extremely poor Thanh Nhan were still being exempted from paying tax there. This clear violation of a royal directive may have strengthened the king's desire to impose his will on the southern administration. Certainly, from 1830 when Minh Mang and his chosen officials began to assume greater power over the administration of Gia Dinh, the 1827 tax rule was finally implemented in Gia Dinh. In Hatien Province, local Chinese fared even worse with the amount of tax levied on a Thanh Nhan rising steeply, even to almost triple what it had been.[51]

After Hue banned resident Chinese from engaging in the rice transporting business in 1827, Gia Dinh Chinese still found ways to elude central government control. As long as the multiple connections between Chinese associations and the ruling group of Gia Dinh Thanh continued, Chinese settlers could find ways around the ban. They could, for example, register their junks under the names of

Vietnamese colleagues or the names of their own Vietnamese wives or concu-
bines. Considering that court documents report most ships in the Gia Dinh region
were registered under women's names, this possibility seems very likely.[52] Another method was to transport rice with forged official permission, something
that required links with at least some Gia Dinh Thanh officials to be successful.
In one such case, by the time one of Minh Mang's handpicked officials uncovered this collusion in 1837, a local Thanh Nhan had been doing business like this
for ten years.[53]

The Court Seeks Ways to Limit Chinese Activities

The court's basic policy was to weaken Chinese influence on the trade of Gia
Dinh in particular and of Vietnam in general. Thus Chinese were deliberately
excluded from the profitable annual trading expeditions of state vessels to parts
of island Southeast Asia, the eastern coast of India, or to Guangdong.[54] As mentioned above, Chinese were also prohibited from transporting rice by sea. Ten
years after their first request to be allowed to take part in this trade was rejected
by Hue in 1827, Gia Dinh Chinese presented the same request again, but this
time with disastrous results for southern Chinese settlers and immigrants. Hence-
forth, all Chinese, whether Thanh Nhan or Minh Huong, were to be prohibited
from either building or purchasing ships for overseas travel. In other words, the
Chinese immigrant population was supposedly banned from maritime trade for-
ever.[55]

After Le Van Duyet died in 1831, Gia Dinh Thanh was reorganized into six
provinces under the direct control of the court. In the eyes of newly appointed
Hue government officials, local Chinese settlers still remained at the center of
illegal trading activities; but at last they were within the direct reach of central
bureaucrats. For possibly the first time, government officials tried to carry out a
rigorous examination of local Chinese commercial networks and their involvement in illegal trade. One of the first things the new officials discovered was that
some of Le Van Duyet's soldiers had been illegally cutting and selling timber in
most cases to local Chinese.[56] As far as Hue was concerned, Chinese settlers
would have to pay the price for their illegalities. Not only were no Thanh Nhan
allowed to deal in overseas trade from 1837 on, but, in a decision of 1838, Minh
Mang decreed that no resident member of a Thanh Nhan association could work
on any maritime trade vessel in any capacity: "As for all Thanh Nhan who immi-
grate [to my country] and live here, only allow them to trade by river, and do not
permit them to trade by sea. No trade vessel (*thuong thuyen*) which crosses the
sea to do business (*viet hai doanh thuong*) may hire Thanh Nhan, either as
helmsman or crew."[57]

In addition, the court set out to assimilate Thanh Nhan. In 1839, Minh Mang
experimented in Cambodia with a significant new technique of Chinese assimilation that sought to abolish the Thanh Nhan's little world or his shelter, his dialect

association (*bang*). In this land newly absorbed by Vietnam in 1835, Thanh Nhan were not allowed to form their own associations. New Chinese immigrants to Cambodia were required to live with Vietnamese in Vietnamese villages and to become Vietnamese: "If you [Vietnamese officials in Cambodia] have Vietnamese and Thanh Nhan who recently immigrated to your place and live around the administrative center, have them [Vietnamese and Chinese immigrants] build villages according to their numbers. Have them influence each other to make all of them Vietnamese (*han dan*). You do not need to organize the Thanh Nhan separately by *bang*."[58] Had the experiment given a positive result in Cambodia, the same method might have been implemented in Vietnam afterward. In practice, however, it was impossible for the Nguyen government to totally destroy the *bang* system of organizing Chinese immigrants. Nonetheless, it should still be regarded as an ambitious attempt by Hue to Vietnamize Chinese settlers.

Minh Mang's basic assimilationist policy was pursued by his successor Thieu Tri (1841–1847) although using different methods. From the court's perspective, it must have seemed too hard to force Thanh Nhan to abandon their identity quickly, so the Nguyen government devised another method to encourage assimilation. This time Hue tried to use the existing Minh Huong associations to act as a collective mediator between Thanh Nhan and Vietnamese. In 1842, a new regulation decreed that locally born Thanh Nhan had to become Minh Huong, meaning in effect to become Nguyen subjects. Any newly arrived Thanh Nhan could still live as a member of one of the dialect associations, but any son or grandson born after his arrival was forbidden to wear the Qing hairstyle. Once the child reached eighteen years, the head of the Thanh Nhan association had to register him as a member of a Minh Huong association. If no Minh Huong association existed in any particular area, one had to be established when at least five eligible sons of Thanh Nhan were available.[59]

No regulation ever called for this sort of general discrimination against Minh Huong. Yet it may be that some covert discrimination existed against them in the state examinations as the century progressed. Unlike Thanh Nhan, Ming Huong enjoyed the right to contest the examinations and, under Le Van Duyet's administration, two Minh Huong became regional graduates in 1825 and 1831 from four examinations that produced fifty-seven graduates (1821 to 1831). After Gia Dinh Thanh Tong Tran was abolished and the assimilation policy launched, however, no Minh Huong graduated from Saigon during the remaining three regional examinations under Minh Mang (1835 to 1840).[60] During eleven years from 1835 to 1846, Gia Dinh produced ninety graduates, but again not one of them was Minh Huong. In the 1840s, regional and metropolitan examinations were routinely biased in favor of candidates from former Nguyen Dang Trong, and Hue and Saigon enjoyed disproportionate success rates,[61] yet no Minh Huong graduated at Saigon until 1847 and then only because Thieu Tri allowed four extra graduates due to the high increase in candidate numbers. That year one Minh Huong scraped into the twenty regional laureates, but thereafter none followed him. This means that from 1835 to 1858, only one Minh Huong ap-

peared among 182 graduates of the Gia Dinh site, and none were successful at
the metropolitan and palace examinations where imperial preferences played a
significant role.[62] Of course, it is not impossible that this result reflected a general Minh Huong preference for commerce over administration, so that relatively
few of them actually contested the examinations from the 1830s on. But even so,
their near total collective failure in the Saigon examinations over several decades
seems suggestive of bias, to say the least.

The Resistance of Chinese Settlers

The Nguyen court's anti-Chinese policy, as might be expected, met with the resistance of Chinese settlers in the south, especially the Thanh Nhan. In particular, after the Gia Dinh general government was dismantled in 1832 and the south
integrated into the new provincial system run from Hue, a major revolt broke out
in 1833 led by Le Van Duyet's adopted son, Le Van Khoi. One source reported
that in less than ten days thousands of people joined the rebel army in the Saigon
region alone. The slogan that attracted people was to reject the legitimacy of the
Nguyen dynasty and avenge their benefactor Le Van Duyet, whom Minh Mang
has posthumously dishonored.[63] Almost as soon as revolt erupted in the Saigon
citadel in the fifth lunar month of 1833, it spread quickly to the other provinces.
Within three months, rebels had captured the fortresses in all six provincial centers.

One of the leading forces in the revolt were the Chinese settlers who were
already suffering financially from Minh Mang's hostility and stood to suffer
much more if Hue tightened its control. After the revolt was quelled, six principal leaders were sent to Hue to be executed. Among them was Luu Tin, the
Thanh Nhan Chinese adopted son of Le Van Duyet, who had actively organized
Chinese settlers into rebel forces right from the outbreak of the revolt.[64] In 1833,
just before the rebels entered Gia Dinh citadel for their final stand, the royal
army swept through the Cholon Chinese settlement in response to the Chinese
rebels' attempt to turn the area into a military base. Royal forces killed or captured over one thousand Chinese settlers in Cholon alone and confiscated their
property. Any Chinese believed to have participated in the rebellion had his
property confiscated and four fingers of his right hand cut off before being exiled
even if he had surrendered.[65]

The court's savage repression of the 1833 uprising did not deter Thanh
Nhan Chinese from joining other antidynastic and anti-Vietnamese revolts during the troubled years of minority uprisings and Cambodian insurrections under
Thieu Tri (1841–1847). Indeed, resentment at the repression may have encouraged defiant resistance among those who had not fled to Siamese or other jurisdictions. Certainly, in these latter disturbances, Thanh Nhan living in Cambodia
were often found among Khmer insurgents, cooperating in battles against Vietnamese.[66] Other Thanh Nhan perhaps unwilling to fight openly might have fled

from Gia Dinh Province to Cambodia where they acted as spies against the Vietnamese, as one court official complained in 1845.[67]

It was official Nguyen oppression that called forth these armed reactions from southern Thanh Nhan Chinese. Under the first Nguyen king, they had been quietly increasing their role and influence in southern Vietnam through links with a local ruling group whose members had long included local Chinese settlers. As court policy changed to one of limiting Chinese activities, settlers reacted by using their local influence to resist the center. In turn, the Nguyen became more determined to destroy the identity of the Chinese and to assimilate them into the Vietnamese population. This tense cycle of mutual hostility would persist until the Chinese settlers of southern Vietnam finally encountered their future protectors the colonial French, from 1859.

Notes

1. For a longer discussion of this period see Choi Byung Wook, "Southern Vietnam under the Reign of Minh Mang (1820–1841): Central Policies and Local Response," Ph.D. dissertation, ANU, 1999, chapter 1.

2. *Dai Nam Thuc Luc Chinh Bien, De Nhat Ky* [Primary Compilation of the Veritable Records of the First Reign of Imperial Vietnam, 1848] [hereafter *DNTL* I] (Tokyo: Keio University Institute of Cultural and Linguistic Studies, 1968), vol. 5, 15a.

3. *DNTL* I, vol. 4, 12b; vol. 8, 5.

4. *DNTL* I, vol. 5, 23a.

5. Fujiwara Riichiro, *Tonanajiashi no kenkyu* [Study of Southeast Asian History] (Kyoto: Hozokan, 1986), 283–302.

6. *Dai Nam Thuc Luc Chinh Bien De Nhi Ky* [Primary Compilation of the Veritable Records of the Second Reign of Imperial Vietnam, 1861] [hereafter *DNTL* II] (Tokyo: Keio Institute of Linguistic Studies, 1963), vol. 45, 12b.

7. One *can* equaled 0.604 kilos. Do Bang, *Kinh Te Thuong Nghiep Viet Nam duoi Trieu Nguyen* [The Commercial Economy of Vietnam during the Nguyen Dynasty] (Hue: Thuan Hoa, 1996), 21.

8. *DNTL* I, vol. 23, 18a.

9. John White, *A Voyage to Cochinchina* [1824] (Kuala Lumpur: Oxford University Press, 1972), 234.

10. Nguyen The Anh, "Quelques aspects économiques et sociaux du problème du riz au Viêtnam dans la première moitié du 19 siècle," *Bulletin de la Société de Etudes Indochinoises* (ns) XLII, no. 12 (1967): 9.

11. *DNTL* II, vol. 61, 6.

12. *DNTL* II, vol. 26, 10.

13. *DNTL* II, vol. 79, 26b.

14. Edward Brown, *Cochin-China, and My Experience of It. A Seaman's Narrative of His Adventures and Sufferings during a Captivity among Chinese Pirates, on the Coast of Cochin-China, and Afterwards during a Journey on Foot across That Country, in the Years 1857–1858* [1861] (Taipei: Ch'eng Wen Publishing Company, 1971), 198–99.

15. *DNTL* II, vol. 201, 24b.

16. *DNTL* II, vol. 79, 27.

17. *DNTL* II, vol. 61, 6b–7a.

18. Brown, *Cochin-China,* 82.

19. *DNTL* II, vol. 61, 7a.

20. For example, in 1836 the government only paid three *quan* to the junk master who had brought one *thong* (about 2,200 liters) of rice from Gia Dinh to Hue. Nguyen archives, *Chau Ban,* Menzies Library, ANU, microfilm reels 60–64, lunar 25th day (January), 1836.

21. *DNTL* II, vol. 167, 15b–16a.

22. John Crawfurd, *Journal of an Embassy from the Governor General of India to the Courts of Siam and Cochin China* [1828] (Singapore: Oxford University Press, 1987), 230.

23. *DNTL* II, vol. 46, 28b–29a.

24. White, *A Voyage,* 261–62.

25. Trinh Hoai Duc, *Gia Dinh Thanh Thong Chi* [Gia Dinh Gazetteer], Ecole Francaise d'Extreme Orient microfilm A. 156, 6, 18.

26. George Finlayson, *The Mission to Siam and Hue, the Capital of Cochin China, in the Years 1821–22* [1826] (Singapore: Oxford University Press, 1988), 305.

27. *DNTL* II, vol. 159, 13.

28. Doan Uan, *Doan Tuong Cong Hoan Tich* (or *Thu Tinh Tu Tap Ngon*) [Minister Doan's Chronicle of Office, or Thu Tinh Tu's Miscellaneous Notes], 1842. Hanoi: Vien Han Nom, A 2177, vol. 13, 15.

29. White, *A Voyage,* 208, 245, 246–47, 271, 332.

30. White, *A Voyage,* 265.

31. Chen Chingho, "Gencho shoki no 'Kashukomu' ni tsuite" [Comments on 'The Official Affairs of the Ha Chau' in the Early Nguyen Dynasty], *Sodaiajiakenkyu* (Tokyo, 1990): 75–76.

32. *DNTL* II, vol. 16, 18b–19a.

32. Wong Lin Ken, "The Trade of Singapore, 1819–1869," *Journal of the Malayan Branch of the Royal Asiatic Society* 33 (1960): 155; Crawfurd, *Journal,* 226.

33. *DNTL* II, vol. 166, 33b.

34. Cao Tu Thanh, *Nho Giao o Gia Dinh* [Confucianism in Gia Dinh] (Ho Chi Minh City: NXB Thanh Pho HCM, 1998), 124–125; and Cao Xuan Duc, *Quoc Trieu Huong Khoa Luc* [Record of Regional Examination Graduates under the Current Dynasty] trans. Nguyen Thuy Nga, Nguyen Thi Lam (Ho Chi Minh City: NXB Thanh Pho HCM, 1990), 151.

35. Tran Tan Gia, *Ba Tam Huynh Kinh Luc* [An Account of Compassionate Hearts and Hanging Mirrors], 1897. Hanoi: Vien Han Nom A 2027, 102–03.

36. *Dai Nam Thuc Luc Chinh Bien, De Tam Ky* [Primary Compilation of the Veritable Records of the Third Reign of Imperial Vietnam] [hereafter *DNTL* III] [1894] (Tokyo: Keio Institute of Cultural and Linguistic Studies, 1977), vol. 41, 8a.

37. *DNTL* II, vol. 167, 15b–16b.

38. *DNTL* II, vol. 46, 28b–29a.

39. *Le Cong Van Duyet Su Trang* [Accounts of Matters for Le Van Duyet], n.d. Hanoi: Vien Han Nom A 540, 16.

40. *DNTL* II, vol. 7, 14a.

41. Dinh Xuan Lam, Nguyen Phan Quang, "Bon Bang Thu, mot tai lieu co gia tri ve cuoc khoi nghia Le Van Khoi (1833–1835)" [Bon Bang's Letter, a Valuable Document about Le Van Khoi's Revolt], *Nghien Cuu Lich Su* 178 (1978): 77.

42. *Dai Nam Chinh Bien Liet Truyen, So Tap* [First Collection of the Primary Compilation of Biographies of Imperial Vietnam] [1889] (Tokyo: Keio Institute of Linguistic Studies, 1962), vol. 45, 2a.

43. Shimao Minoru, "Meimeiki (1820–1840) Vetonamu no nankichiho tochi ni kansuru ichi kosatsu" [A Study on Vietnamese Rule of the South during the Reign of Minh Mang] *Keio gishoki daigoku gengo bunka kenkyusho kiyo* 23 (1991): 180.

44. White, *A Voyage*, 287, 332.

45. *Dai Nam Chinh Bien Liet Truyen, So Tap*, vol. 11, 6a.

46. *Kham Dinh Dai Nam Hoi Dien Su Le* (Official Compendium of Institutions and Usages of Imperial Vietnam), n.d. Hanoi, Vien Han Nom, VHv 1570, *Thanh Nhan,* 5. This is important evidence that, in the nineteenth century, Minh Huong association members were not always descendants of Ming refugees as they are usually described. From 1843, the court required locally born children of Thanh Nhan to be registered as Minh Huong (*Hoi Dien Su Le, Thanh Nhan,* 8), although the majority also joined Thanh Nhan associations and had their names registered on the *bang* lists.

47. *DNTL* II, vol. 40, 17b–18a.

48. *DNTL* II, vol. 40, 18a.

49. *DNTL* II, vol. 40, 18a

50. *DNTL* II, vol. 173, 13a.

51. *DNTL* II, vol. 183, 42b.

52. *DNTL* II, vol. 179, 29b.

53. Instead, there is evidence that Westerners were hired as important crew members. For instance, a Portuguese called An Ton commanded a vessel on a mission to Batavia in 1830 (Phan Thanh Gian, *Luong Khe Thi Thao* [Poetry of Luong Khe] manuscript, compiled 1876. VHv 151, Vien Han Nom, Hanoi, vol. 10, 170). In 1837, Minh Mang authorized a monthly salary of fifty Spanish dollars to a Western helmsman. Nguyen archives, *Chau Ban*, 5th lunar day (October), 1837.

54. *DNTL* II, vol. 177, 27b–28a.

55. *Dai Nam Chinh Bien Liet Truyen, Nhi Tap* [Second Collection of the Primary Compilation of Biographies of Imperial Vietnam] [1909] (Tokyo: Keio University Institute of Cultural and Linguistic Studies, 1981), vol. 45, 1b.

56. *DNTL* II, vol. 196, 26a.

57. *DNTL* II, vol. 196, 26a.

58. *DNTL* II, vol. 205, 8b.

59. *Hoi Dien Su Le, Thanh Nhan,* 8.

60. *DNTL II*, vol. 212, 7a–11a.

61. Nola Cooke, "Nineteenth-Century Vietnamese Confucianization in Historical Perspective: Evidence from the Palace Examinations (1463–1883)," *Journal of Southeast Asian Studies* 25, no. 2 (1994): 307–11.

62. Cao Xuan Duc, *Quoc Trieu Huong Khoa Luc*, passim.

63. *Liet Truyen Nhi Tap*, vol. 45, 4a.

64. *Liet Truyen Nhi Tap*, vol. 45, 3b, 26b.

65. *DNTL* II, vol. 103, 21–22; vol. 104, 7a.

66. *DNTL* III, vol. 3, 27; vol. 11, 24a; vol. 23, 9b; vol. 25, 16.

67. *DNTL* III, vol. 46, 17b.

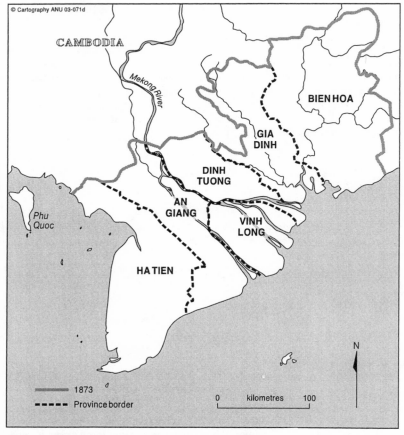

© Cartography ANU 03-071d

CAMBODIA

Mekong River

BIEN HOA

GIA
DINH

DINH
TUONG

AN
GIANG

VINH
LONG

Phu
Quoc

HA TIEN

——— 1873
----- Province border

0   kilometres   100

N

Map 4: The Six Southern Provinces in 1836

7

Siam and the Contest for Control of the Trans-Mekong Trading Networks from the Late Eighteenth to the Mid-Nineteenth Centuries

Puangthong Rungswasdisab

After the destruction of Ayutthaya in 1767, Siam's politico-economic order was devastated. Yet by the early to mid-nineteenth century, Siam was arguably the major political and economic power in the region. This remarkable turnaround has been mainly explained as the result of expanding overseas trade in the late eighteenth and early nineteenth centuries. But how a country whose economy had been so wasted by warfare and disease was able so quickly to find or produce goods suitable for export has not been fully explained. The main interpretation has pointed to the influx of Chinese immigrants who helped to expand the Thai economy as junk crews, merchants, craftsmen, cash crop producers, or wage laborers.[1] While they undoubtedly played an important role, it is still true that the principal exports of Siam under Kings Taksin (r. 1767–1782) and Rama I (r. 1782–1809) were forest products, whose best-known source of supply in the immediate post-Ayutthaya decades was the Khorat Plateau and the trans-Mekong basin. Given its export significance, Bangkok rulers could not afford to ignore this vital economic hinterland, whose produce fed the export economy of their maritime commerce. It was very much in the monarchy's financial interest to tie these areas closely to Bangkok. Commercial interest drove an expansionary policy so that, by the mid-nineteenth century, annual tribute and local tax flowed to Bangkok from northeast Siam, the Lao kingdoms, and northwest

Cambodia. So well entrenched was Siamese authority that local officials were even able to conduct semi-regular censuses in these areas.[2]

The remarkable nineteenth-century advance of Siamese political and economic power owed much to the Thonburi and Bangkok dynasties' policy of controlling forest produce exports. Yet the consequences of this policy have rarely been adequately related to Thai policy toward neighboring states on the Water Frontier and its hinterland. Along with the attempt to rehabilitate the country's economy went the suppression of smaller neighboring states in the lower Mekong hinterland, along the trans-Mekong basin and in Cambodia and up to Laos. However, the Thai attempt to monopolize the trade and resources of this zone did not go uncontested by the Nguyen kingdom in eastern Indochina. Intense competition between the two over export items largely for the Chinese trade led to protracted warfare from the late eighteenth to the mid-nineteenth centuries over the control of the coast and then later over the trans-Mekong basin hinterland. This chapter introduces that long politico-economic struggle before focusing on Thai activities in Cambodia.

Trading Networks

Several trade routes had long existed along the trans-Mekong basin that ultimately connected the forested hinterland with Water Frontier commercial riverine and coastal ports. Although documentation is fragmentary, it is possible to identify five passages in the middle Mekong basin north of Cambodia that served in times of peace as trade routes. They were the basins of the Ca Dinh, Bang Fai, and Bang Hieng Rivers, the Phuan state, and the Thaeng (Dien Bien Phu) plain. From the east, people could travel between Vietnam and the Mekong left-bank basin through three passes: Keo Neua, Mu Gia, and Ai Lao. From the left-bank Lao towns, people could then go on to reach northeast Siam.[3] George Vinal Smith refers to Lao traders coming to trade with Ayutthaya. They supplied export goods, such as benzoin, gumlac, and gold to Ayutthaya, and in return they carried back Indian cloth, red yarn, and opium.[4]

Outside Siam, Cambodia was an alternative route by which merchandise from the middle Mekong basin went down to the sea. The account by Wuysthoff tells of local trade along the Mekong River between Laos and Cambodia. In the seventeenth century in this border region between Laos and Cambodia was situated the commercial town of Sombok, which was also the main place from which Cambodia obtained goods from the uplanders.[5] Traders usually transported goods downriver by boat or bamboo raft until they arrived at the impassable Khone falls in southern Laos, where they would abandon the river and continue by cart to Cambodia.[6] This old trading traffic continued at least until the late nineteenth century, with Laotian and uplander products joining other Cambodian goods at Phnom Penh before going down the Mekong to reach foreign vessels at Saigon–Cholon or branching off near Chau Doc to take the canal to Hatien.

Vietnamese were also active traders in the region. In particular, they traded with uplanders in the central area around the present-day borders of Vietnam, Laos, and Cambodia. These tribal people were important to the Nguyen rulers as the major suppliers of forest products for Vietnam's foreign trade. The export commodities they supplied included eaglewood, cinnamon, ebony, and other precious woods, many of which were royal monopolies in the eighteenth century. So significant was the area that the Nguyen rulers began to assert their political influence there from the mid-eighteenth century onward.[7]

Northwest Cambodia provided an alternative route for Laotian and uplander goods, some of which were sent to northeast and central Siam. Despite the Khone falls, the route that ran from Bangkok to Prachin Buri then to northwest Cambodia and southern Laos was favored by travelers, who wanted to avoid the malaria-infested Dong Phrayayen range while taking advantage of the abundant food along this northwest Cambodian route. Products from western Cambodia could also reach the Siamese Water Frontier ports of Chantaburi and Trat, which were important collection centers for forest commodities from Cambodia and Vietnam bought by junks for sale in China.

The overland routes seem to have activated trade in coastal ports. John Crawfurd described a distinct trading network along the Siamese Gulf in the early nineteenth century, including Bang Plasoi, Bang Pakong, Bang Lamung, Rayong, Chantaburi, and Thung Yai (Trat) in Siam, Kampong Som and Kampot in Cambodia, and Hatien, Rach Gia, Ca Mau (Long Xuyen), and Saigon in Vietnam.[8] The commercial network linked Siamese, Cambodian, southern Vietnamese, Chinese, and Western merchants trading in coastal ports with the multitude of traders that brought export commodities to the coast. For instance, documents in the National Library of Thailand confirm that trading vessels from southern Vietnamese ports came to Hatien to purchase wax, ivory, other forest goods, and rice, while pepper attracted them to Kampot where they offered salt in exchange.[9]

Siamese junks on the way to China also often visited those coastal ports in order to collect luxury products for the Chinese market. In return, imported Chinese, Western and Indian trade goods were reexported to Cambodia and Vietnam by Siamese junks visiting those ports. Also part of this trade were Siamese-manufactured goods such as metal, sappanwood, iron pans, tobacco, opium, and rice. The number of Siamese junks involved in this traffic was estimated at between forty and fifty in the early nineteenth century, but they were mostly small junks with carrying capacity ranging from 60 to about 180 tons.[10]

Thus products from the trans-Mekong hinterland had access to several different coastal ports along both Thai and Vietnamese sectors of the Water Frontier. A major factor in deciding which routes to take and networks to participate in was whether the areas involved were peaceful or not. However, by the late eighteenth century changing politico-economic conditions saw Siam and Vietnam both seek to tighten their control over the area.

Encroachment

After King Taksin of the Thonburi dynasty (r. 1767–1782) had consolidated his internal power, he quickly moved to recover Siam's earlier preeminence in regard to surrounding states. In the lower Mekong region, King Ang Ton of Cambodia refused to send tribute to the new Siamese ruler; but the more serious affront came from the lord of Hatien, Mac Thien Tu, whose antagonism to Taksin had caused him to obstruct the new Thai king's early attempts to rebuild Siam's shattered economy. First, Thien Tu provided asylum to Taksin's enemies, the governor of Chantaburi and two Ayutthayan princes, Chao Srisang and Chao Tuy. Then in 1768, Thien Tu sent his son-in-law, Tu Dung, to capture Taksin by a trick, but the plot was uncovered and Tu Dung executed. Next, in 1769, a Hatien naval force attacked Chantaburi and Trat, but again without success. Mac Thien Tu even sent a letter to the Chinese court to discourage it from recognizing Taksin as the new Siamese king. Without such recognition, the Thonburi regime would not have been able to reestablish the Sino-Siamese tribute trade, meaning its disrupted economy could hardly revive. In the early stages, the Chinese court was inclined to believe Thien Tu, but after Taksin had demonstrated his supremacy it reversed the earlier decision and granted him recognition.[11]

After Mac Thien Tu's son-in-law was executed, he retaliated by banning all trade between Hatien and Siam, which at the time relied on rice imported from Hatien and Cambodia.[12] This ban must have adversely affected the commerce of Chantaburi and Trat, both of which were closely connected with the adjacent interior and coastal ports. This Water Frontier coast became remarkably important for Siam in the Thonburi period, as it was King Taksin's political and economic base and the Chinese there had played a significant role in assisting him to consolidate power. Moreover, these two provinces were great assets for Taksin, enabling him to secure essential goods from overseas because they continued their normal junk trade with China.[13]

The significance of Chantaburi increased even more in the early Bangkok period when Siamese foreign trade was expanding. Bishop Pallegoix recorded that in 1838 twelve Chinese junks visited the port of Chantaburi,[14] which was the most important center of pepper production in Siam[15] as well as a key center of Siamese shipbuilding.[16] This eastern Water Frontier coast of Siam thus played a great part in the commercial profits of the Siamese ruling class, as a number of trading junks based here belonged to the Siamese kings and nobles.[17]

For all these reasons, it became economically indispensable for Siam to urgently consolidate its domination over the eastern coast and its trans-Mekong hinterland. Taksin first responded to Mac Thien Tu's aggressive policy by encouraging Teochiu adventurers settled along the Water Frontier, from eastern Siam down to southern Vietnam, to revolt and seize Hatien. The conspiracies failed, however.[18] Finally, in 1771 he decided to launch a campaign himself against Hatien and Cambodia, which ultimately compelled Thien Tu to take refuge in southern Vietnam.[19] The Siamese seizure of Hatien was nevertheless short-lived, and in March 1773 peace talks took place between Taksin and Thien

Tu. But not long after that the rapid expansion of the central Vietnamese Tay Son rebellion (1772–1802) into the Mekong Delta forced Thien Tu to seek asylum in Thonburi in 1777, leaving Hatien to the rebels. In 1782, Mac family members accompanied Nguyen Anh on his return from Bangkok asylum to fight the Tay Son, and Hatien was again under the government of the Mac family.[20]

Although the Thai seizure of Hatien in 1771 did not last long, it is interesting to note that Taksin did not require the evacuation and resettlement of people from Hatien as the Thai always did elsewhere in order to increase manpower for Siam. Instead, Taksin ordered Siamese troops stationed there that they "must neither capture nor kill Chinese and Vietnamese traveling to trade in Hatien, but should seek to persuade people to settle and continue working. Those who violate the order will be punished by death."[21] This passage is clear evidence that the attempt to control Hatien was influenced by Siamese trade interests. In this respect it is also noteworthy that Taksin appointed a fellow Teochiu, *Phraya* Phiphit, as governor of Hatien. *Phraya* Phiphit was well versed in the commerce of this area since he had formerly served as a high-ranking official of the Krom Tha.[22]

While Taksin was leading Thai troops from Hatien to attack Phnom Penh, another Siamese army marched overland to Cambodia to occupy Battambang, Siemreap, and Pursat. Taksin placed his Cambodian protégé Ang Non on the throne and put the Khmer *okya* Ta-la-ha Baen in control of Battambang and Pursat. Then the middle Mekong basin kingdoms of Vientiane and Champassak were brought under Siamese suzerainty in 1779, with Luang Prabang to follow soon after. The three Lao kingdoms were then reduced to the status of dependent principalities. Thus, between the reigns of Taksin and Rama I, Thai kings had successfully consolidated their political power throughout the trans-Mekong region bringing the major commercial centers of Vientiane, Champassak, Battambang, and Phnom Penh under Siamese domination.

During this time, the Thai probably also benefited commercially from the political turmoil in late-eighteenth-century Vietnam. Despite the scarcity of documentation, some factors indicate trouble on the overland route in Vietnam during the Tay Son revolt. Hickey mentions the disruption of trade between Vietnamese and the highlanders who supplied forest products for export.[23] French missionary records state that Vietnamese traders in Tonkin, who wanted to avoid the route running through this turbulent area of Vietnam, had to shift their activities to Laos.[24] It is very likely that similar disruptions affected trade between Vietnam and the Mekong basin. Local traders from Laos and Cambodia would naturally be discouraged from going to war-torn Vietnam and instead be attracted to carrying their products to the Chaophraya basin. Siam consequently had the opportunity to establish and maintain a near-monopoly on forest products from the trans-Mekong area at the time.

However, conditions ceased to favor the Thai after Emperor Gia Long took the Vietnamese throne in 1802. Thai domination over Cambodia and Laos began to be challenged. After three decades of political unrest in Vietnam, the need for economic recovery must have been very urgent and required the restoration of local and foreign trade. The Vietnamese began to make great efforts to re-establish their former power and influence.

As far as Hatien was concerned, after the Mac descendant Tu Thiem died in 1809, Gia Long moved quickly to appoint his own mandarin as governor. The Vietnamese king informed Rama II (r. 1809–1824) after the event, claiming the Mac claimant was an incapable ruler. Apparently Bangkok felt unable to refuse the arrangement and could only maintain Siamese symbols of suzerainty over Hatien by granting the newly appointed Vietnamese governor a set of insignia.[25] Hatien resumed its maritime trade. Although by the early nineteenth century foreign vessels were more attracted to Saigon–Cholon, Hatien remained a place for Siamese junks to obtain Cambodian products into the 1820s.

Vietnam's success in depriving Siam of Hatien ultimately disadvantaged Siamese ventures along this stretch of the Water Frontier coast. In the 1830s the Vietnamese tightened their control by reimposing a customs post in Hatien. The new regulation was directed especially against vessels from Southeast Asian ports,[26] plus those from Canton, Shanghai, and Macao, which were all obliged to pay the highest duties, while Teochiu junks paid a middling rate and those from Hainan least of all.[27] Further, foreign vessels were no longer allowed to sail up to Cambodia but had to trade through Vietnamese agents.[28] One French archival document reveals that in 1862 all goods exported from Phnom Penh attracted a 20 percent levy, with half paid to the Cambodian government and the other half to the Vietnamese customs post at Chau Doc.[29] As a result, Siamese traders were confronted with higher costs for Cambodian and Laotian merchandise coming through Hatien.

Along with installing their administration in Hatien, the Vietnamese also sought to extend their control to Cambodia and the Lao middle Mekong basin. Under King Chan (r. 1806–1835) and his sister Queen Mei (r. 1835–1840), Cambodia came under increasing Vietnamese domination ending in the late 1830s with direct Vietnamese control imposed by force.[30] In regard to the middle Mekong basin, tributary relations had been restored with Vientiane as early as 1801, when Chao Inthavongse, Chao Anu's brother, sent a tributary mission to Hue. After Inthavongse died in 1804, Anu consistently pursued this policy.

The Nguyen equally renewed their efforts to reassert administrative control over uplanders with the dual aim of effective control of trade and of Vietnamese resettlement in the upland area. Tributary relations with the uplanders' rulers, the so-called King of Fire and King of Water, were made to work again. In 1802 and 1803, Hue restored the former tax on uplander trade and reorganized the administration in their area. According to Hickey, up until the Minh Mang era (r. 1819–1841), Vietnamese penetration into upland areas increased greatly. In the Lao region, Vietnamese military organization was imposed over the east Mekong bank between the 16th and 17th parallels in the basin of the Bang Hien River. Once secure, they then reorganized the tribute from the local towns and the administrative posts in the Lao area of Tchepone, Lao Bao (Ai Lao pass), and Lang Co. Small military posts were created throughout to supervise the timber trade.[31]

Thus by the Minh Mang reign the trading zone from the middle Mekong basin to its coastal delta was under Vietnamese domination. This situation must have reduced Thai benefits considerably. Although evidence is limited, it seems likely that a political settlement in Vietnam, followed by the reestablishment of Nguyen tributary relations with Laos, Cambodia, and the uplanders, would have encouraged the growth of trade between Vietnam and the Mekong left-bank area. The 1830 travel account of Charles Gutzlaff hints at exactly this consequence for Thai commerce. According to his account, the cause of the war between Siam and Vientiane in 1827–1828 was a very brisk trade in southern Laos, which the Siamese governor in the northeast wanted to control.[32] This account appears to conform to that in the Lao history of Vientiane, *Phun Wiang*, which analyzed the causes of the Chao Anu revolt in 1827–1828.[33] *Phun Wiang* attributed the Chao Anu revolt to the Siamese attempt to appropriate manpower in the Champassak principality, including Sithandon, Saenpang, Saravane, Attapeu, Khamthong Yai, Chieng Taeng, and Khong. With respect to trade, the text states that Bangkok authorized the Siamese authority, the Yokrabat of Khorat, to undertake conscription in the northeast and southern Laos. During this time, the Siamese conscription unit based itself at Ban Don Khong (now in Sithandon), impeding the river route along which local merchants usually traveled. The Thai authorities even went so far as to conscript traveling traders. The harshness of this measure caused tremendous suffering for local people, as traders no longer dared to come.

Thus *Phun Wiang* suggests that the Siamese authorities in the northeast wanted to control Champassak because they did not gain substantial benefits from the lucrative trade of the southern Lao towns. The Thai disadvantage was possibly due to local traders changing their route, since stability and Vietnamese influence was likely to have attracted them eastward to Vietnam or southward to Cambodia and the Mekong Delta, instead of heading west to Siam. Whatever the case, such a decline in trade would have resulted in a loss of importance for both the local and central Siamese authorities. Added to this was the very serious threat posed by the Chao Anu revolt, which had included the Vientiane and Champassak principalities. Although the Chao Anu war ended in early 1828, a series of Thai expeditions and depopulation campaigns were subsequently launched along the whole Mekong left-bank area from the Phuan state in northern Laos to Cambodia. When the news of the 1833 Le Van Khoi revolt in far southern Vietnam reached Bangkok, Rama III finally decided on war between Siam and Vietnam. A Siamese army briefly invaded the Mekong Delta region, but the real battlefield was to be in Cambodia.

Devastation versus Construction in Cambodia

The strategic objective of the Thai expedition to Cambodia was to destroy the Vietnamese garrison and to besiege as many Cambodian towns as possible, particularly in the vicinity of Phnom Penh. The Thai expedition formed two land columns and a naval force. From Siam, one column moved overland toward Battambang; the other went through the Champassak territory in southern Laos and then to northern Cambodia. The naval force moved to attack the Vietnamese stations along the Gulf of Siam and continued to Phnom Penh from Hatien.[34] However, as the east bank and the coastal areas were major Vietnamese strong-holds and difficult to besiege, Thai troops instead turned to widespread burning of villages and the full-scale deportation of local people and captured Vietnam-ese soldiers. Thai records of the fourteen-year war are filled with descriptions of the devastation in Cambodia. Phnom Penh, Hatien, and probably Sombok were the worst devastated areas.[35] The most furious fighting was concentrated in the areas under strong Vietnamese influence, the east bank and coastal areas. The Vinh Te canal joining Chau Doc and Hatien was also a major military target of the Thai campaigns. The Thai made an unsuccessful endeavor to fill up the canal in order to obstruct the access of the Vietnamese naval forces, but they were confronted with massive numbers of Vietnamese troops who protected the canal.

But this was not all. Thai troops also sought to prevent Vietnamese from the Mekong Delta from being able to move into the devastated area. Bangkok had ordered local officials to prevent Vietnamese resettlement and trade, and to de-port to Bangkok any Vietnamese who came to settle or trade in Cambodia. In other words, the Thai objective was to destroy an area if they could not control it, so that the Vietnamese could not benefit from it either. Evidence for this atti-tude is clearly expressed in the order from *Chaophraya* Bodin, the Thai army commander, to the Thai military unit chiefs in Hatien, Kampot, and Kampong Som, "to evacuate the people, to burn down the houses in every town, and to demolish the town, so that only the forest and the rivers are left."[36] Similar or-ders were sent to the troops of the client Cambodian princes Im and Duang in Phnom Penh. At the time Khmer unrest was helping the Vietnamese against the Thai, so Bodin ordered Im and Duang:

> Now the Khmers are revolting in many towns; therefore, it is difficult to retain Cambodia. The army commanders in Phnom Penh must demolish all ramparts, and turn Phnom Penh into a charnel ground. Do not allow the Khmer rebels to use it as a base. Then you must transport the Khmer, Indian (Cham), Chinese, and others in Phnom Penh to Battambang.[37]

Breazeale and Sanit have suggested that the purpose of Thai depopulation campaigns in Laos was to prevent the area from being used by Vietnamese troops because a human desert could not provide logistical services.[38] This was no doubt the case in Cambodia, too. But I believe there was also another reason behind the Thai campaigns here, that is, the attempt to control trade and to ac-quire the existing resources (products and manpower) of the area. A devastated area certainly could not sustain its former commercial activities. Traders would naturally try to avoid routes that crossed it and shift their trade to more secure paths. In this context, trade between Laos and Phnom Penh must have been dis-rupted, leaving three alternative routes for traders from Laos. First was eastward to Vietnam; second was westward to the Khorat Plateau and the Chao Phraya basin; third was southwest to the Battambang region and from there to central Siam. As mentioned above, after the Chao Anu revolt both Vientiane and Champassak were tied more firmly to the Thai administrative system in the northeast, so that their economies would have been increasingly drawn toward the Thai side. Besides, since the Second Reign, the area under Thai occupation in northwest Cambodia had expanded to cover Mlou Prei and Tonle Ropeou (in Thai, Manophrai, and Tharaboriwat, respectively). French officials later reported that there were roads and *sala* (shelters) built by the Thai all the way from the two provinces to Champassak.[39] In addition, the governors of Pursat and Kampong Svai had already submitted to an alliance with Bangkok.

Therefore, the Thai were able to secure the major Laos–Siam and Laos–Cambodia–Siam routes. The Thai seem to have been so secure in the area between southern Laos and northwestern Cambodia that during the Third Reign, *suai* (or head tax) payments from the southern Lao towns—Champassak, Sithandon, Attapeu, Chieng Taeng (present-day Stung Treng), Saenpang, Saravane, Khamthong Yai—were sent to Bangkok via Battambang and Prachin Buri.[40] This was a more favorable route for travelers than the way across the dangerous Dong Phrayayen range on the Khorat Plateau, so the security of the road certainly facilitated trade toward Siam. On the other hand, it is understandable why the Thai wanted to advance their control to northwest Cambodia.

Although it might not have been possible for the Thai to induce all merchants from Laos and Cambodia to travel west, they took every opportunity for local officials to use their power to influence the itinerary of local traders. Moreover, as local officials often participated in trade, Bangkok's preference surely shaped their choice of route, if only because the caravan of *suai* payment was usually associated with royal trade expeditions. Bangkok often ordered officials in charge of collection to purchase local goods, usually with the *suai* money from the area, and to consign them with the *suai* caravan to Bangkok. These local commodities then became valuable Siamese export items.[41]

It is evident that the Thai attempted to prevent trade between Laos and the Vietnamese-controlled areas in Cambodia so that they themselves could secure maximum profits from the trans-Mekong basin. This was quite clear when *Chaophraya* Bodin left Cambodia in 1847. Before his departure, he imposed a trade embargo between the lower Lao towns—Champassak, Sithandon, and Saenpang—and Cambodia, in order to protect Bangkok's commercial position. As a Thai document bluntly stated, "Cambodian and Vietnamese goods would be sold to foreign countries, not to Bangkok. There are also many Lao goods. So if we lift the barrier, the Chinese Laotians would become bold enough to bring valuable goods to sell in Cambodia and Vietnam. Bangkok would thus gain fewer goods."[42] Although the official embargo was imposed after the war ended, it had probably been informally implemented during the fourteen-year conflict as well. Wartime arrests of local traders traveling between Cambodia and southern Laos by the Siamese army show that the Thai had indeed kept the area under surveillance.[43]

While the Thai were maneuvering to obstruct or destroy trade in the Vietnamese bases in Cambodia, they made efforts to strengthen commercial links between Siam and their own base in Cambodia. Given this, what happened in the Battambang region was entirely different from the experience of the Vietnamese zones. Bangkok's policy was in fact to strengthen the Battambang region as its politico-economic base, with a resulting increase in Thai economic interest in the area.

First, after the Khmer king Chan died in 1835, Rama III had received a report that the Cambodian *okya* wanted Bangkok to send Princes Im and Duang to rule Cambodia since Chan only had daughters. In 1837 Bodin returned to Battambang with the first duty of building up the city itself, including a new city post and a walled palace for Im and Duang. The reason for this activity was "that (Battambang) would be stronger and more prosperous; this would glorify the status of Prince Im, who rules Battambang, and it would also be convenient for the Khmers to flee to a more peaceful place."[44] The city of Siemreap was similarly strengthened in the following year. Later, the Thai established a new town in the north of Battambang. The former village of Mongkolborei was raised to the status of a town (*muang*) because "Rama III wanted the news to spread to the Vietnamese that this side [Battambang] was well populated."[45]

Second, I have discovered no forced migrations from Battambang and Siemreap during the protracted war in Cambodia, but only from the areas under Vietnamese influence. The relative stability in the Battambang region is indicated by the ongoing rice cultivation in the area.[46] Third, it was obvious that the Thai tried to keep Battambang's people content. For instance, in 1827 after one hundred able-bodied men (*lek*) of Battambang and Siemreap escaped to Kampong Svai and Staung because of their oppression by local officials, Bangkok ordered the local officials to search them out and prevail upon them to return, promising that local authorities would allow people to settle where they wished.[47] This goal was also explicitly indicated in Rama III's advice to *Chaophraya* Bodin:

> [he] should try to teach Prince Im to govern and nourish with mercy the people, nobles, monks, nuns, and Brahmans in Battambang and its subordinate towns. Tell Prince Im to rule with justice in accordance with the traditions and customs of Battambang. Do not damage the customs of Battambang and trouble the people.[48]

Further evidence indicating the Thai objective was to build up the Battambang region relates to the prospect of economic benefits from the area in the form of *suai* (head-tax payment) and trade. The *suai* account of Battambang first appears in the 1830s and Battambang's subsequent payments show little evidence of local economic disruption as a consequence of the protracted war. Existing records reveal that Battambang and Siemreap began payments to Bangkok in the Third Reign (see table 7.1). Pursat, whose governor had been allied with the Thai since the Second Reign, also levied *suai* for Bangkok (see table 7.2). The

Table 7.1: Battambang *Suai* Payment in Piculs of Cardamom, 1835–1847

Year	Number of payers	Quantity
1835	1634	65.36
1836	1500	60.00
1837	1604	64.16
1838	1657	66.28
1839	1349	52.68
1840	1442	60.04
1841	1594	63.76
1842	1542	62.80
1843	1582	63.28
1844	n.a.	n.a.
1845	1000	40.00*
1846	1328	66.16
1847	n.a.	61.71

Note: *Drop caused by an epidemic.
One picul (*hap*) equaled 60 kilos, or 100 catties. Each taxpayer had to provide 4 catties, or 2.4 kilos.
Sources: My calculations from archival records (*Chotmaihet*) held in the Thai National Library. For the Third Reign, CMH. R. III C.S. 1202/83, C.S. 1203/51, C.S. 1204/63, C.S. 1208/60, C.S. 1211/2. For the Fourth Reign, CMH. R. IV C.S. 1213/125, C.S. 1215, 1217, 1218/195, C.S. 1218/49, C.S. 1219/154, C.S. 1226/316.

Table 7.2: Pursat *Suai* Payment in Piculs of Cardamom, 1835–1856

Year	Quantity	Year	Quantity
1835	22.00	1850	50.54
1836	15.00	1852	49.70
1840	34.26	1853	47.68
1844	70.00	1854	49.21
1845	70.00	1855	50.54
1846	70.00	1865	50.54
1847	60.50		

Note: Each taxpayer here had to provide 14 catties, or 8.4 kilos.
Sources: As in table 7.1

accounts show that the region paid *suai* fairly regularly throughout the 1830s and 1840s, with the size of Battambang's *suai* units remaining relatively constant. *Suai* payments from Battambang and Pursat were mostly composed of cardamom (*krawan*), a highly valuable forest commodity on the Chinese market. Siemreap, less fertile than Battambang, usually sent less valuable goods like bastard cardamom, and beeswax.[49]

Cardamom was one of the most important forest goods because of its high price on the Chinese market. It was a court monopoly until Rama III abandoned

Table 7.3: Value of Cardamom *Suai* from Battambang and Pursat, 1835–1854

Year	Combined quantity (piculs)	Money value at 120 *baht* per picul#	Gross export revenue (220 *baht* per picul)*
1835	87.36	10,483.2	19,219.2
1836	75.0	9000.0	16,500.0
1840	94.36	11,316.0	20,746.0
1845	110.0	13,200.0	24,200.0
1846	136.16	16,339.2	29,955.2
1847	122.21	14,665.2	26,886.2
1852	99.54	11,944.8	21,898.8
1854	100.77	12,092.4	22,169.4

Conversion rate based official purchase rate.
* Conversion rate based on export price to Canton in 1844, in *Chotmaihet* R. III C.S. 1206/49.
Source: Amount of *suai* payment taken from tables 7.1 and 7.2.

the royal monopoly system in 1826. The constant number of *lek suai* (or of able-bodied men liable for tax payment) and the regularity of payment in the Battambang region suggest that local *suai* payers were neither conscripted into military service nor forcibly resettled in Siam, as happened to those captured in Vietnamese-controlled areas. The records of regular *suai* payment enable us to infer that the policy of maintaining peaceful conditions in the Battambang region convinced *suai* payers not to flee Thai authority. Moreover, the regularity of *suai* payment explicitly demonstrates Thai capacity to control an efficient manpower system in the region, with the high value of cardamom sufficient to convince Thai authorities to keep the *lek suai* at work.

Table 7.3 gives an idea of the money value of the cardamom *suai* from Battambang and Pursat and of the expected royal revenue from exporting it. The value of this cardamom is better understood when compared to table 7.4, which tabulates the annual *baht* value of the *suai* paid to Bangkok in the same period from the eastern Lao provinces (*huamuang lao fai tawan-ok*) and the Forest Khmer provinces (*huamuang khamen padong*), including Champassak, Khamthongnoi, Khamthongyai, Khongchiam, Sithandon, Saravane, Chieng Taeng, Saenpang, Nongkhai, Mukdahan, Kalasin, Roi Et, Yasothon, Suwannaphum, Det Udom, Ubon, Khemarat, Khong, Samia, Khon Kaen, Chonlabot, Surin, Sangha, and Khukhan. The comparison between tables 7.3 and 7.4 reveals that except for the year 1845 the value of cardamom from Battambang and Pursat formed about half of the total revenue Bangkok secured from various towns on the Khorat Plateau.

The Battambang region was Siam's major source of cardamom since it appears to have been available only in Chantaburi; but this Chantaburi cardamom was considered inferior to that of Cambodia. The Battambang region was also a center for marketing cardamom. *Suai* payment in money from the lower Lao

Table 7.4: The Money Value of *Suai* from Northeast Siam and Laos, 1830–1855

Year	Total (*baht*)	Year	Total (*baht*)
1830	13,291.38	1847	24,838.63
1832	28,007.25	1848	31,971.13
1833	8682.25	1849	11,845.13
1834	9638.78	1850	54,773.88
1835	14,677.50	1851	16,952.88
1836	18,670.00	1852	38,225.75
1837	20,429.76	1853	12,101.50
1840	21,300.63	1854	26,629.76
1845	52,485.63	1855	27,706.75
1846	26,949.01		

Source: Junko Koizumi, "The Commutation of *Suai* from Northeast Siam in the Middle of the Nineteenth Century," *Journal of Southeast Asian Studies* 23 (1992): 91–93.

towns and northeast Siam was usually sent to Battambang and Pursat to buy cardamom to send to Bangkok with the annual *suai* caravan. Thus, a dispatch from *Chaophraya* Chakkri to *Chaophraya* Bodin, who was stationed in Battambang in 1842, said that Rama III wanted Bodin to purchase cardamom with the *suai* money collected from Champassak and then sent it to Bangkok. Also, Rama III ordered Bodin to press for *suai* arrears from the eastern Lao towns in order to get money to buy cardamom for Bangkok. If the money was insufficient, Bodin was asked to report it to Bangkok and the government would then send him more.[50] Cardamom from the Battambang region, both in the form of tax and of purchases by the royal treasury, contributed a high proportion to the estimated total quantity Siam produced each year. Henry Burney indicates that Siam secured about 800 piculs of cardamom annually, most of which was sold to China, with only 100 piculs being retained for domestic consumption.[51] In 1846, Battambang and Pursat contributed 168.84 piculs of cardamom, or onefifth of the whole Siamese supply excluding what was purchased by local traders traveling between the central Chaophraya basin and the Battambang region. The average annual amount of cardamom sold to China by Siam was valued at about 140,000 *baht*.[52]

Evidence shows that Thai nobles were also commercially active in the Battambang region. *Phraya* Chodoc Ratchasetthi, for example, appointed Chinese business agents to trade in Battambang on his account, bringing cloth and ironwares to sell in exchange mainly for cardamom. Battambang's Chinese traders also went to deal with the Bangkok cardamom tax farmer named *Khun* Thepthipphol. They brought cardamom and other Cambodian forest goods such as gamboge, stic-lac, varnish, rawhides, horns, and ivory to sell in Bangkok for money that they then used to purchase trade goods there. *Khun* Thepthippol also acted as agent for a high-ranking official, *Chaophraya* Ratchasuphawadi, who participated in the Thai expedition in Cambodia.[53] As *Chaophraya* Bodin was fully responsible for the Thai court's commercial activities in the area, he also shared in the profits of their trans-Mekong ventures. As one record shows, *suai* that was sent to Bangkok from Saravane in lower Laos through Battambang included goods belonging to Bodin.[54]

Concerning the currency for purchasing cardamom, if money was sent from Bangkok it was usually *ngoen tra thai* (silver Thai *baht* coins). If the *suai ngoen* (tax in money/silver) came straight from the northeast and Lao towns, it also contained Thai *baht* but mixed with various kinds of local monies, including Lao coins and others called *ngoen naentu* and *ngoen* that originated in Vietnam.[55] Thai officials usually had to commute them into Thai *baht* before they could buy trade goods because Bangkok wanted to circulate Thai money in preference to local silver coins. In one instance, when the *suai* money from the northeast and Laos arrived at Bangkok in the form of local coinage, the Bangkok authorities recast them before using them to purchase cardamom in Battambang. The value of local silver coins was usually reduced by the smelting fee. Local officials in Battambang and Siemreap, however, made no difficulty in accepting other currencies that seem to have been in common use among the local people. This suggests that the cross-border trade between Siam, Cambodia, Laos, and Vietnam was long established.

The Battambang region also had trade relations with Phnom Penh and southern Vietnam. But since it was under Thai control, these particular trade relations inevitably faced intervention from Bangkok. Sources from the 1860s indicate that while there was no customs duty on trade between Battambang and the Siamese side, exports from Battambang to Phnom Penh and French Cochin China attracted a duty of 10 percent of the purchase value, first at Bac Prea customshouse (in Thai, Peam Sema) at Battambang, then at the Cambodian customshouse in Phnom Penh, and finally once more at the Vietnamese customs post at Chau Doc.[56] As the customs duty revenue belonged to the governor of Battambang, it was undoubtedly enforced.[57] Though transport between Battambang and Bangkok was longer and more laborious, these high duties made the general expense of the two routes almost the same. These customshouses thus obstructed the flow of trade between Battambang and Vietnam, while encouraging its flow to Siam by the absence of any customshouse between Battambang and Bangkok. In this way as in others, Thai influence over the Battambang region was used as an effective means of stimulating local traders in the Water Frontier hinterland to favor with Siam over her eastern Indochinese rival.

Conclusion

Since the trading networks between Water Frontier coastal ports and the trans-Mekong hinterland connected together several different parts of the region, changes in any one area were likely to bring tensions or changes to others. As this chapter has argued, the economic intervention and expansionism of the Thai state brought about major changes. It encouraged growing economic relations between Battambang and Siam, and tied the nineteenth-century Battambang area's economic life to the Siamese economic center. But the advance of Thai control over the Battambang region can itself be perceived as a response to earlier Thai-Vietnamese military competition over controlling access to Cambodia via the important eighteenth-century port of Hatien, a contest Vietnam ultimately won. Expansion of Thai power to Battambang substituted for its loss of access to Cambodia by way of Hatien and also provided an important source of high-quality export commodities (like cardamom) that helped feed the vital Sino-Thai trade. As the example of Battambang shows, the ability to protect vital trading interests in the Thai competition with Vietnam for control of lucrative forest exports to China was one of the main reasons for the expansion of the Siamese state under Taksin and the early Bangkok dynasty.

Notes

1. Sarasin Viraphol, *Tribute and Profit: Sino–Siamese Trade, 1652–1853* (Cambridge: Harvard East Asian Monographs 76, 1977), chapter 8; Nidhi Aeusrivongse, "Watthatham kadumphi kap wannakam ton rattanakosin" [Bourgeois Culture and Literature in the Early Bangkok Period] in *Pakkai lae bai-rua* [A Quill and a Sail] (Bangkok: Amarin kanphim, 1984), 107–28; Jennifer W. Cushman, *Fields from the Sea: Chinese Junk Trade with Siam during the Late Eighteenth and Early Nineteenth Centuries* (Ithaca: Southeast Asian Program, Cornell University, 1993), chapter 5.

2. Boonrod Kaewkanha, *Kan kep suai nai samai rattanakosin ton ton* [*Suai* Collection during the Early Bangkok Period], M.A. thesis, Chulalongkorn University, 1964; Theerachai Boonmatham, "Kan kap suai nai hua muang lao fai tawan–ok nai chuang ton samai rattanakosin" [*Suai* Collection in the Eastern Lao Provinces during the Early Bangkok Period], *Warasan Thammasat* 12, 4 (1983): 154–67.

3. Kennon Breazeale and Sanit Smuckarn, *A Culture in Search of Survival: The Phuan of Thailand and Laos* (New Haven: Yale University Southeast Asian Studies, Monograph Series 31, 1988), 1–5; Charles Gutzlaff, *Journal of Two Voyages along the Coast of China in 1831 & 1832* (New York: John P. Haven, 1833), 35.

4. George Vinal Smith, *The Dutch in Seventeenth-Century Thailand* (Dekalb: Northern Illinois University, Center for Southeast Asian Studies, 1977), 61–62.

5. Jean Claude Lejosne, *Le Journal de voyage de G. van Wuysthoff et de ses assistants au Laos (1641–1642)* (Metz: Editions du Centre de Documentation du Cercle de Culture de Recherches Laotiennes, 1987), 101–3, 117.

6. Anthony Reid, *Southeast Asia in the Age of Commerce, 1450–1680*, 2 vols. (New Haven: Yale University Press, 1988, 1993); vol. II, 55; Gaspar da Cruz, "The Treatise of Fr. Gaspar da Cruz," in *South China in the Sixteenth Century*, ed. C. Boxer (London: The Hakluyt Society, 1953), 76–78.

7. Gerard Hickey, *Son of the Mountains: Ethnohistory of the Vietnamese Central Highlands to 1954* (New Haven: Yale University Press, 1982), 159–60; Li Tana, "'The Inner Region': A Social and Economic History of Nguyen Vietnam in the Seventeenth and Eighteenth Centuries," Ph.D. dissertation, Australian National University, 1992, 132; *Southern Vietnam under the Nguyen: Documents on the Economic History of Cochinchina (Dang Trong), 1602–1777*, ed. Li Tana and Anthony Reid (Singapore: Institute of Southeast Asian Studies, 1993), 110–13.

8. John Crawfurd, *Journal of an Embassy from the Governor General of India to the Courts of Siam and Cochin China,* reprint (Kuala Lumpur: Oxford University Press, 1967), 407–14.

9. National Library, Thailand [hereafter TNL], *CMH. R. III C.S.* 1204/1/kho/6.

10. Crawfurd, *Journal,* 413–14; Henry Burney, *The Burney Papers,* vol. II (Bangkok: The Vajirayana National Library, 1911), 82.

11. Chen Chingho, "Mac Thien-tu and Phraya Taksin," in *Proceedings of the Seventh IAHA Conference* (Bangkok: Chulalonghorn University Press, 1977), 1546–1548; Nidhi Aeusrivongse, *Kan muang thai samai phrachao krung thonburi* [Thai Politics in the Reign of King Taksin] (Bangkok: *Sinlapa watthanatham* special issue, 1986), 90–93.

12. Dhiravat Na Pombejra, "Ekkasan hollanda ruang chumchon thonburi nai pi kho so 1767–1768" [Dutch Documents about the Thonburi Community in 1767–1768], *Ruam bot khwam prawattisat* 10 (February 1988): 103–13.

13. Chen, "Mac Thien-tu and Phraya Taksin," 1551; Nidhi, *Kan muang thaithonburi,* 68–71.

14. Pallegoix, *Description du Royaume Thai ou Siam,* reprint (Hants: Gregg International Publishers, 1969), vol. 1, 73.

15. Adisorn Muakphimai, *Krom Tha kap rabop setthakit thai* [Department of the Port Authority and the Thai Economy], M.A. thesis, Thammasat University, 1988, 246, 301, 309.

16. B. J. Terweil, *Through Travellers' Eyes* (Bangkok: Duang Kamol, 1989), 187; Pallegoix, *Description du Royaume,* 73–74.

17. Crawfurd, *Journal,* 413.

18. Chen, "Mac Thien-tu and Phraya Taksin," 1550, 1552.

19. "Chotmaihet raiwan thap samai krung Thonburi" [Records Concerning Expeditions in the Thonburi period] *Prachum Phongsawadan* [hereafter *PP*+Part] *Part 66* [Collected Chronicles] (Bangkok, Kurusaph, 1985) 134–64.

20. Nicholas Sellers, *The Princes of Hatien (1682–1867)* (Brussels: Editions Thanh Long, 1983), 127–28.

21. "Chotmaihet raiwan thap," *PP 66,* 143.

22. "Chotmaihet raiwan thap," *PP 66,* 143. Krom Luang Narintharathewi, *Chotmaihet khwam songcham khong krom luang Narintharathewi* [Memoir of Krom Luang Narintharathewi] (Bangkok: Cremation Volume for Princess Wapi Busabakon, 1983), 5, 91. Chen Chingho suggests *Phraya* Phiphit was probably a leader of the Teochiu in the area and had led an unsuccessful plot against Hatien in 1767. Chen, "Mac Thien-tu and Phraya Taksin," 1552–1553.

23. Hickey, *Son of the Mountains,* 164–67.

24. "Chotmaihet khong phuak bathluang farangset nai phaendin phrachao ekathat, khrang krung thonburi lae khrang krung rattanakosin ton ton" [Records of the French Missionaries during the Periods of King Ekathat, Thonburi, and the Early Bangkok Era], *PP 39* (Bangkok: Kurusapha, 1968), 193.

25. *Chotmaihet ratchakan thi song cho.so. 1173* [Records of the Second Reign, Lesser Era 1173 (AD 1811)] (Bangkok: Department of Fine Arts, 1971), 60.

26. Only Siamese junks with cargoes of at least 80 percent rice were exempt from Hatien customs tax, according to the Vietnamese annals cited in Alexander Woodside, *Vietnam and the Chinese Model* (Cambridge, Mass.: Harvard University Press, 1971), 258.

27. Sarasin, *Tribute and Profit,* 203 and footnote 82, 332.

28. Archives Nationale, depôt d'outre-mer, Aix-en-Provence [hereafter AOM (Indochine)], *Amiraux 10144*, "Rapport du M. Aubaret à M. le Vice Amiral de la Grandière, Gouverneur et Commandant au chef en Cochinchine, 9 juillet 1867."

29. AOM (Indochine), *Amiraux 12705*, "Rapport sur le Cambodge, Voyage de Saigon à Battambang par Spooner, 30 décembre 1862."

30. David Chandler, *Cambodia before the French: Politics of a Tributary Kingdom*, Ph.D. dissertation, University of Michigan, 1973, chapter 3.

31. Hickey, *Son of the Mountains,* 164–67.

32. Gutzlaff, *Journal of Two Voyages*, 35. He traveled to Laos in 1830, just two years after the Chao Anu revolt.

33. See Thawat Punnothok, *Phun Wiang: Kansuksa prawattisat lae wannakam isan* [A History of Vientiane: A Study of the History and Literature of the Northeast] (Bangkok: Thai Khadi Studies Institute, Thammasat University, 1983). A full text of *Phun Wiang* is published in Pratheep Chumphol, *Phun Wiang* [A History of Vientiane] (Bangkok: Samnakphim Adit, 1982).

34. *Chotmaihet ruang thap yuan khrang ratchakan thi sam* [Records Concerning Expeditions against Vietnam during the Third Reign] (Bangkok: Cremation Volume for General Phraya Singhaseni, 1933), 9.

35. K. S. L. Kulap, *Annam sayamyuth* [The Annam–Siam War] (Bangkok: 1971), 286–287.

36. Kulap, *Annam sayamyuth*, 612.

37. Kulap, *Annam sayamyuth*, 657–58.

38. Breazeale and Sanit, *The Phuan of Thailand and Laos*, 20.

39. AOM (Indochine), *Gouvernement Général 14474*, "Le Chargé de la Résidence à M. le Résident Supérieur de France au Cambodge, 20 juin 1892."

40. TNL, *CMH. R .III C.S. 1201/87; CMH. R .III C.S. 1202/42; CMH. R. III C.S. 1203/110.*

41. Junko Koizumi, "The Commutation of Suai from Northeast Siam in the Middle of the Nineteenth Century," *Journal of Southeast Asian Studies* 23 (1992): 302; TNL, *CMH. R. III C.S. 1200/68.*

42. TNL, *R .5 M.2. 12ko/3.*

43. TNL, *CMH. R.III C.S. 1193/17*; "Chotmaihet kieokap khmen lae yuan nai ratchakan thi sam" [Records Concerning Cambodia and Vietnam during the Third Reign], *PP 67*, vol. 42 (Bangkok: Kurusapha, 1969), 43–45, 119.

44. "Chotmaihet kieokap khmen lae yuan, *PP 67,* vol. 42, 119.

45. TNL, *CMH. R .IV C.S. 1223/58.*

46. "Chotmaihet kieokap khmen lae yuan," *PP 67*, vol. 42, 21.

47. TNL, *CMH. R .III C.S. 1189/12*, in *Chotmaihet ratchakan thi sam* [Records of the Third Reign] (Bangkok: Published on the Occasion of the 200th Anniversary of Rama III, 1987), vol. 4, 28–33.

48. "Chotmaihet kieokap khmen lae yuan," *PP 67*, vol. 42, 12.

49. For further information on the *suai* system in the Battambang region see my doctoral dissertation, "War and Trade: Siamese Interventions in Cambodia, 1767–1851," University of Wollongong, 1995, 111–13.

50. TNL, *CMH. R. III C.S. 1204/6.*

51. Burney, *Burney Papers*, vol. 1, 103–07.

52. Cushman, *Fields from the Sea*, 144, 148 note c.

53. TNL, *CMH. R. III C.S. 1212/128.*

54. TNL, *CMH. R .III C.S. 1199/52.* Bodin had been involved in the Chinese trade with his own junk when he had been *Phraya Kasetraksa.*

55. Luang Phadung Khwaenprachan, "Ruang ngoen khong ratsadon phak isan" [Money Used by People in the Northeast] in *Latthi thamniam tang tang* [Beliefs and Traditions] (Bangkok: Khurusapha, 1961), 50–56.

56. AOM (Indochine), *Gouvernement Général 26143*, "Rapport du Lieutenant Maitret sur sa mise à Battambang, 1897."

57. Francis Garnier, *De l'Exploration en Indo-Chine effectué pendant le années 1866, 1867 et 1868* (Paris: Librairie Hachette, 1987), 222; F. Méré, "Une promenade de Saigon à Battambang et aux ruines d'Angkor," *Bulletin de la Société des Études Indochinoises de Saigon* 15, no. 2 (1888): 395.

8

Ships and Shipbuilding in the Mekong Delta, c. 1750–1840

Li Tana

1841. Vietnam as a Maritime Power: A View from the North

In 1841, Lin Zexu, former governor general of Guangdong and Guangxi and central figure of the Opium War in 1840, was sitting in the house of one of his old colleagues in Zhenhai, Zhejiang Province. Over the previous two years Lin had written many memorandums to the Qing court calling on the government to build ships and cannons, but in vain. Charged with responsibility for losing the war, Lin was stopping over in Zhenhai on his way to exile in remote Ili. When conversation turned to defense against the British, and especially the urgent need for warships, Lin laid out the plans of eight different types of ships that would serve the purpose. Half of them came from Vietnam.

First was the "warship of Annam," which used wheels instead of rowers. Second was the "*Dashi chuan* of Annam," which had two masts built in three joints following the British style, and whose cables were managed with capstans. Next was the "*buxuo chuan* of Annam," which was a small vessel similar to Western ones, but with two rudders at each of its ends. Last was the *Shi chuan* and the "big head sampan of Annam," whose sides were covered with several layers of ox hide and whose bow was higher than its stern, both measures that increased its defensiveness.

To contemporary Chinese eyes, each was strong, quick, flexible, and superior in both attack and defense. In these modern Vietnamese ships might lie the future of the Chinese navy if one-third of its force, all large ships, were styled on the Vietnamese *dashi* and warships and the rest on the smaller Vietnamese *boxuo* and sampans. If such effective Vietnamese-style vessels were stationed in strategic locations like Canton, Xiamen, Zhenhai (Zhejiang), Shanghai, and Tianjin, thought the Chinese officers, surely the British could not invade China.[1]

This story certainly shows the desperation of mid-nineteenth-century Chinese officers, but it also reveals an important aspect of Vietnamese history that has received little attention from scholars. When a high-ranking Chinese official with experience in Canton looked to the contemporary maritime power in his region to improve the Chinese navy, his eyes went first to Nguyen Vietnam. This was not a view shared by Westerners a century later. J. B. Pietri's classic late-colonial account of Vietnamese ships and junks, for instance, concluded their dominant characteristic was that they were distinctly area oriented and rarely found far from the region in which they had been built.[2] Lin Zexu's praise for the precolonial Vietnamese shipbuilding industry found no echo in the colonial era or for many years after, despite readily available evidence in contemporaneous accounts.

What I want to discuss here is a lost Vietnamese experience of the southern Water Frontier, a time and place when for a few short decades centuries of Vietnamese social and economic order fractured and Nguyen Vietnam became an important maritime state in Southeast Asia. All the information that I have seen on this subject points to one conclusion, that there was a remarkable shipbuilding industry in late-eighteenth and early-nineteenth-century southern Vietnam, beginning in Dang Trong (or Cochinchina) and persisting until at least the 1830s. This industry, going hand in hand with rice trade, formed the new economic foundations for southern Vietnam and integrated it into the Water Frontier of Southeast Asia at a level never before seen in Vietnamese history.

Cochinchinese Ships, c. 1830

It was not only Lin Zexu who admired Cochinchinese maritime expertise in the early to mid-nineteenth century. John White, an American merchant who visited Vietnam in 1820 and criticized almost every aspect of Vietnamese society, had a remarkably high opinion of the ships he saw. "About 50 are schooner-rigged, and constructed partly in the European style: their sterns are completely European, while their bows are a mixture of that and the Onamese [Annamese] model." As for southern Vietnam itself, he concluded: "Cochin China is perhaps, of all the powers in Asia, the best adapted to maritime adventure."[3]

Ten years later the *Singapore Chronicle* reported the arrival of two Cochinchinese ships and a brig in the following approving terms:

> The Cochin Chinese ships have touched here on their way to Bengal. . . . This information we ascertained from the interpreter attached to one of the ships who is a native of Macao, and speaks the Portuguese and Malay languages well

... in each ship there are 80 sailors and 10 officers of different grades, including two captains—one in charge of the ship, and one of the cargo. They are acquainted with the use of the compass and have English charts ... the Cochin Chinese brig ... was but lately built and launched in Cochin China, under the direction of an European resident here. The Cochin Chinese, he states, have 10 square-rigged vessels altogether, some of which are employed as men-of-war, or cruisers.[4]

In 1837, one of these Cochinchinese men-of-war called in at Macao. Its arrival was recorded as follows:

That recently at Macao, a man-of-war, was about 400 tons measurement, being about 90 feet long with 20 feet beam. . . . The hull of the vessel was constructed of teak, and apparently very strongly put together. The masts were well made, though the spars and rigging were not in very good proportion. A flag, bearing the characters *kin chae* [*qin chai* in Chinese characters, meaning "imperial envoy"] hung from the stern.[5]

Vietnamese ships in nineteenth-century Chinese eyes were distinctively Western in construction. In 1831 Emperor Minh Mang sent officers to escort back to Xiamen a retired Chinese district officer from Zhaohua, Li Zhenqing, his family, and followers, who had been shipwrecked earlier. The name of the ship sending them was *Rui Long* (*Thuy Long* in Vietnamese—"auspicious dragon").[6] The *Xiamen Gazette* recorded this trip and emphasized that the mast was in three joints and the sails were made of cotton fabric.[7] The masts were thus radically different from Chinese ones, which were made of one piece rather than in joints. Smaller vessels owned by ordinary people from Cochinchina were also built after the European model, as was observed in 1833 in Terengganu: "a Cochinchinese vessel came into the river from Annam, laden with salt and rice. She was about 50 tons burthen, built after an European model, and with the exception of the Batavian fishing-boats, appeared to be better adapted from fast sailing than any native vessel I had hitherto seen."[8]

This information raises some interesting points regarding the vessels being built in Cochinchina. The first relates to their wide variety. They ranged from the blue-water men-of-war, brigs, and schooners in the above sources. The second relates to their quality and style. The oceangoing vessels could be very large and solidly built, and a European style was widely adopted for smaller boats and bigger ships, especially with respect to their masts and sterns.

Nguyen Anh's support for local shipbuilding and shipyards made the industry strikingly successful in terms of numbers produced and the pace of ship production. According to the Hue court chronicle, between 1778 and 1819 Nguyen Anh/Gia Long built 1,482 ships of various sorts. They included 235 *gai bau* (Cham-Malay-style prahu), 460 *sai thuyen* (bigger galleys), 490 *chien thuyen* (war boats), 77 *dai chien thuyen* (large war junks), 60 big and small Western-style vessels or schooners, 100 *o thuyen* (black junks), and 60 *le thuyen* (carved and decorated galleys). Nguyen Anh's ships were not the only official vessels being built in Dang Trong at the time. Nguyen Anh's enemy, the Tay Son, also had a formidable naval force comprised in large part of Chinese pirates sailing junks built in Vietnam. According to the testimonies of captured Chinese pirates, they had been recruited, given vessels and titles by the Tay Son, and sent to fight the Nguyen, and then later to rob merchant junks in the South China Sea. Their Tay Son patrons would sell the booty in Vietnam and give the pirates a share ranging from 20 to 40 percent. The vessels provided by the Tay Son were no ordinary watercraft. As Dian Murray has pointed out, "Vietnamese ships, with masts more than 80 feet tall and sides protected by layers of ox-hides and nets, were larger and sturdier than any pirates could obtain on their own."[9] From Murray's description, this seems to be the type called *Shi chuan*, as mentioned above, which was also used by the Nguyen navy. It had in fact been invented by a Nguyen general of Chinese descent, Do Thanh Nhan, in 1780. He ordered ironwood be shaped into long rudders and the decks covered with bamboo to protect the oarsmen from being attacked while soldiers on the upper deck fought the enemy. "From then on maritime travel became more effective and the skills of the navy became more capable and vigorous."[10]

This scale of shipbuilding required a large amount of timber, and the main logging sources were the Quang Hoa and Tan Chau areas of present-day Tay Ninh and Song Be Provinces. These two areas are repeatedly mentioned in the Nguyen chronicle as useful for logging. From there timber would presumably be rafted down from the East Vam Co River or the Saigon River, to where Nguyen Anh had constructed a major dockyard in 1790. It was a spectacular dockyard, according to Vietnamese and Western observers,[11] running for about 1500 meters along the Saigon River to the Thi Nghe River. "All types of ships were built and displayed there," the Nguyen chronicle reported.[12] But this was not the first or the only dockyard in the Mekong Delta area. Various sources reveal the existence of others. One mid-eighteenth-century dockyard we know of was located on the south bank of the Dong Nai River in Bien Hoa. Ruined during the Tay Son period, it was consequently abandoned.[13] Other dockyards were set up by local officials serving Nguyen Anh as occurred, for example, in 1791 when the prince gave permission to build a shipyard in Sa Khe (near My Tho).[14] Some areas even specialized in purpose-built vessels. Villages along the Cai Be River in Dinh Tuong, for example, built a particular type of large capacity for trading to Cambodia.[15] Nevertheless, the state shipyards northeast of Saigon along the riverbank remained the main center of the local shipbuilding industry right through the Nguyen period and even under the French.[16]

Private Shipbuilding and the Rice Trade

There is little doubt that this official shipbuilding was formed on the technical basis of the private shipbuilders. The large war junk of the Nguyen, according to the Nguyen chronicle, was built after the style of the merchant junk (*thuong thuyen*) but with no awning and was smaller in size.[17] Although shipbuilding had always been going on in Dang Trong, there seemed to be a rather sudden shipbuilding boom in mid-eighteenth-century Dang Trong, and this had an intimate relation with rice trade to China.

Although the Qing government had started an incentive scheme to encourage the rice trade between Southeast Asia and China in 1722, the condition that allowed it to be taxfree—that merchants should trade in rice alone—meant most traders quickly lost interest. Rice was hardly profitable from the merchants' point of view—freight costs were high, and the cargo was bulky and of low value.[18] Merchants soon made it clear that they would be more enthusiastic about the rice trade if they were allowed to build ships overseas and bring rice back in the ships they built. As shipbuilding costs in Southeast Asia were only half those in China, the profits from shipbuilding were sufficient to cover the cost of the rice trade and make the trip worthwhile. Official permission to build ships overseas was slow and was not finally given by the Qing government until 1747. But when it did come, it caused an instant upsurge of Chinese shipbuilding in Southeast Asia. From this point of view, rice trade and shipbuilding were twin offspring of the eighteenth-century Chinese overseas trade with mainland Southeast Asia. In the words of Professor Chen Xiyu, the authority on Chinese junk building, there was "an indissoluble bond" between the Chinese rice trade and the shipbuilding industry in Southeast Asia.[19] In light of this insight, it is not surprising to note that the largest Chinese junks were reportedly built in the Mekong Delta and the Gulf of Siam, two major centers of export rice production. The special trade conditions of Qing China seemingly dictated the two major elements of an eighteenth-century Southeast Asian trade center dealing with China—rice and ships. Both Saigon and Bangkok were first built up on this basis.

Dang Trong had been reputed as a fine source of shipbuilding wood as early as the seventeenth century: in the 1690s, an English envoy, Thomas Bowyear, reported that Spanish merchants from the Philippines frequented Cochinchina for the purpose of logging and shipbuilding there.[20] The Mekong Delta region was an even greater resource for the same purpose. As late as 1820, the American John White praised its quality.[21]

> The ship-timber, and planks, excelled anything I had ever seen. I measured one plank, whose dimensions were one hundred and nine feet long, more than four inches thick, and perfectly square to the top, where it was two feet wide. It was sawed out of the trunk of a teak tree, and I believe there is no part of the world where these gigantic sires of the forest arrive at such magnitude as in Cochinchina. I have seen in the country a tree that would make a natural mainmast for a line of battle ship, clear of knots; and this, I learnt, is not unusual.

In the 1770s, the northern scholar-official Le Quy Don, who worked as a senior administrator in Hue after the successful northern incursion early in the Tay Son war, reported that in one small district alone there were a hundred big ships and over 100,000 *quan* of cash in sales.[22] This amount equaled about one-fourth of the state revenue of mid-eighteenth-century Dang Trong. The economic impact of this trade must have been enormous in the south, involving thousands of workers from the initial logging to the expert craftsmen who finished the product.

This lucrative business attracted the early interest of Nguyen officials, as the story of Li Wenguang, a Cantonese who rebelled against the Nguyen in 1748, indicates. According to Li, he went to Hue in 1744 with some friends to trade in Chinese medicine, but they were soon sent to the Dong Nai area (near modern Bien Hoa) to log timber and build ships for some Nguyen officers. To that end he recruited a further forty or so Chinese craftsmen to do the actual work. When he started his rebellion four years later Li had more than three hundred followers, presumably all more or less involved in his shipbuilding industry.[23] The ships Li provided were most likely controlled by the officers for their private benefit, rather than used for government business. In this connection it is interesting to note that in 1768 in the Mekong Delta, the area where most ships and boats were being built, there were only seven boats being officially levied by the Nguyen government to transport rice out of a known total of some 341 in the country.[24]

If hundreds of ships were being built in the Mekong Delta for Bo Chinh alone in this decade, many of them must have been commissioned privately and most likely sold to China. The ships taken to Bo Chinh might also have been sold to Chinese merchants. When Li Wenguang was captured and sent back to China, he found himself on just such a Chinese ship that had been newly built in Dang Trong. This private shipbuilding industry made lower Cochinchina and Siam appear similar at the time. From the mid-eighteenth century, specially built big ships from Siam carried rice back annually to Xiamen in China.[25] The situation persisted in the early nineteenth century, according to the dynastic chronicles of the Bangkok Era, which noted: "These ships were either built in Bangkok or in provincial areas outside the capital. They were loaded with merchandise to be sold in China every year. Some ships sold only their cargoes of merchandise; some sold both their cargoes of merchandise and the ships themselves as well. The profits from this junk trade were tremendous."[26] Roberts confirmed this in 1833. "To the Siamese trade may be added that of ship building, which is carried on very extensively. A great number of Chinese junks are built here annually; the timbers are of very hard wood called *marbao*, and the plank is of the finest teak in the world. Many of these vessels are of a thousand tons' burden."[27]

As documents on eighteenth-century Macao reveal, Western merchants based in Macao and Manila also used small ships built in Dong Nai. One example comes from a 1798 statement by a Portuguese ship that had purchased several thousand piculs of betel nuts from Cochinchina. "Since all the space of the ship was taken, we had to buy a small ship [*tau*] to carry back the several hundred piculs left over."[28] This practice might have been perhaps the norm, with Portuguese merchants coming on their own ships and purchasing local products while looking for a suitable ship to carry their cargoes back. If so, Portuguese merchants from Macao were no different from Chinese merchants based in Canton or Amoy. After all, trading ships might be the most profitable part of their journey. In May 1805, for example, a Macao merchant who was carrying betel nuts, sappanwood, dry fish, and rice back to Macao in his "small barbarian ship," was kidnapped by the pirate Zheng Yi near Canton. According to the Chinese report of this incident, this "small barbarian ship" [*xiao yi chuan*] had been purchased in Cochinchina.[29] The same thing happened in the same year to a Spanish ship based in Luzon [Manila], the only difference being that the Spanish merchants seemed specifically to have gone to Vietnam to buy the ship.[30]

It is interesting that the Chinese report made it clear that the ship the Macao merchant brought back was a "small barbarian ship," suggesting that the ship was built in a Western style. It is not inconceivable that Western merchants based in Southeast Asia may have transferred some of their shipbuilding technology to the Chinese and Vietnamese craftsmen in Dong Nai when they placed their orders there. Whether true or not, there is little doubt that private shipbuilding in mid-eighteenth-century Dong Nai provided the crucial foundation for the shipbuilding industry of Nguyen Anh, under whom the adoption and adaptation of Western techniques became manifest during the later years of his war with the Tay Son. At this time, shipbuilding would become the crucial element that determined the Nguyen victory over the Tay Son.

An important qualification should be made here. When I say "Cochinchinese" it does not necessarily refer to Vietnamese-speaking people but to all the peoples living within the territory of Cochinchina in this period. Cochinchina's flourishing shipbuilding industry, for instance, was by no means an exclusively Viet specialty. Do Thanh Nhan, the Cochinchinese general who reputedly invented the *Shi chuan* model, was a Minh Huong Chinese from Huong Tra County, Thua Thien, who had migrated to Phien An in the Mekong Delta.[31] The story of Li Wenguang also indicates that if shipbuilding in Dang Trong had largely been supported by the Nguyen government or its officials, it was mainly carried out by the Chinese. Chams also participated, if the large number of *gai tau* vessels (the Cham-Malay *prahu* type of galleys) being built in the early period of Nguyen Anh is any guide. Interestingly, Chams may also have participated in the Siamese shipbuilding industry at the same time. It was said that Taksin had brought a number of Chams back with him from Cambodia, who were then settled on the Bangkok waterfront and employed by the navy.[32] Last but not least in Dang Trong were Westerners, especially the French. It is no exaggeration to say that among all mainland Southeast Asian countries, late-eighteenth-century Cochinchina saw the most extensive involvement of Westerners, from politics through to supplying war materials to directly participating in battles. Their most lasting influence, however, was in building citadels and ships.

Shipbuilding on the Water Frontier: Vietnamese Vessels and Siamese Aid

Does the foregoing discussion make eighteenth-century Cochinchina seem comparable to contemporaneous Siam? After all, shipbuilding in Siam was a well-known activity among scholars of Southeast Asia and China; and Vietnam's prosperous neighbor was ultimately able to keep its independence. At first glance, it may seem that Vietnamese naval power had been too pitiful to prevent its fate of being colonized by France. A more careful examination, however, suggests that Siam's supposed advantage in naval forces over Vietnam is much less clear-cut. If Siamese naval power did become stronger than Vietnamese, it was only from the late 1830s, barely a generation before colonial invasion of southern Vietnam.

It is well known that Rama I supported Nguyen Anh in his war against the Tay Son, but much more with troops and material than with ships. If Rama I gave Nguyen Anh a few ships in the 1780s, by 1789 he was asking Nguyen Anh to provide ships to Siam in return for his support:

> If and when Ong Chiang Su [Nguyen Anh] asked for military help, the king would be willing to send an army to help. However, to travel overland would be too far, and in going by sea, there would be only 70 to 80 ships available at the capital . . . therefore whenever Ong Chiang Su was free from fighting, it was asked that he construct some 60 or 70 *kular* ships, along with a very fine *kular* ship for the king's use and sent these to the king.[33]

The *kular* ship mentioned here was most likely the *ghe tau*, a type of vessel very frequently mentioned in the Nguyen chronicles for the eighteenth century because, as the following entry from 1789 shows, this was the type of ship Nguyen Anh made for Siam. The main construction sites were along the Gulf of Siam coast, as Nguyen Anh was exiled from Vietnam at the time. Indeed, this entry is most likely the very record of the Vietnamese ships being built at the Siamese king's request:

> Ordered that forty-plus big war ships and more than 100 *ghe tau* vessels be built. All the offices in Tran Bien [Bien Hoa area], Tran Dinh [Dinh Tuong] and Vinh Tran [Vinh Long] are to submit timber [for this purpose]. Every forty soldiers are to submit enough timber for building one ship. The number of ships submitted by Long Xuyen [the Bassac area] was ten, Kien Giang three, Tran Giang [modern Can Tho] five, and Phu Quoc eight.[34]

The four latter areas in the west of Nguyen Anh's territory, nearer Siam, shouldered the building of the bulk of the big ships. Obviously Nguyen Anh regarded the matter as urgent, so a quota was set for different administrative areas. By 1791 the ships were ready, and Nguyen Anh sent them to Siam. The following paragraph is particularly interesting in revealing the subtle Siamese–Viet relations over this issue and how Nguyen Anh sought to exchange the ships for arms:

> On the first day of the waxing moon of the 11th month, in that year of the Pig, the king of Annam sent a letter asking to purchase 1000 flintlock guns and 1000 *hap* in weight of iron for wharfs. With this came thirty Vietnamese hammocks to be presented to the king, and also the seventy warships that had been ordered constructed. The ships were taken and moored at the Bang-o Peninsula at the king's order, and on Thursday, the second day of the waning moon of the third month, the king ordered that 200 *hap* in weight of iron for wharfs and 200 guns be sent out as gifts to the king of Annam.[35]

Despite this 1790s Vietnamese contribution, the size of the Siamese navy remained low compared to the Vietnamese fleet. When Edmund Roberts visited Siam in 1832, he estimated that there were about 500 Siamese war-canoes and 50 or 60 vessels, the largest of which did not exceed a hundred tons and carried from three to eight brass guns.[36] This contrasts sharply with the formidable Nguyen navy as reported by Moor in 1823: "his naval force is not less extraordinary, as to the qualities of design, finish and extent . . . [It] may be estimated as follows: 50 schooners of 14 gun, 80 gun boats, 100 vessels, about 300 galleys, from 80 to 100 oars, 500 galleys of from 40 to 80. In the provinces 500 vessels from 20 to 100 oars, making about 1530 vessels."[37]

It is certainly erroneous to say that there were fewer ships and boats built in Siam than in Dang Trong in the early nineteenth century. There had long been a continuous and lively shipbuilding industry in Siam, but it seems to have been principally a Chinese business activity involving those engaged in the China trade.[38] The large shipbuilding industry under direct Siamese government control seems to have started in the late 1820s, and its immediate stimulus came from Siam's rivalry with Cochinchina. As Gutzlaff reported in 1827, "the king of Siam, who was rather intimidated [by an exchange with the Cochinchinese over the issue of the Lao prince Chao Anou], ordered his principal nobles and Chinese subjects to build some hundred war boats, after the model made by the governor of Ligore."[39] Yet, judging from Roberts' report mentioned above, Siamese naval forces were still considerably inferior to those of Cochinchina as late as 1832. Not long after Roberts' observation, in the conflict with Vietnam following the Le Van Khoi rebellion in southern Vietnam in 1834, the Siamese navy failed miserably against their superior opponents. This defeat seems to have greatly spurred Siamese official interest in shipbuilding, and within a few years Chantaburi became the main Siamese state dockyard.

Vietnamese, Chinese, and Shipbuilding in Chantaburi

Although some earlier travelers had mentioned Chantaburi, nothing had been said about a local shipbuilding industry for most of the eighteenth century.

When Hamilton visited the region he reported that "the coasts of Liant and Chantaburi are the territories of Siam, but for 50 leagues and more along the seashore there are no seaports, the country being almost a desert."[40] From a very early stage Chantaburi was occupied mainly by Cochinchinese, according to the report of a French missionary in 1703 that described Chantaburi as "almost full of Cochinchinese, of which there are approximately 100 Christians."[41] Khmers also lived there. Missionary letters reveal that in 1702 there was a revolt in Chantaburi "instigated by a Cambodian who had married a Cochinchinese."[42]

When Taksin attacked Chantaburi in 1767 he captured some boats there, but no information indicates that it had been a major shipbuilding center. In Chantaburi, Taksin ordered five ships to be built, which he successfully then used to attack the Burmese. Comparing this with the massive shipbuilding industry of the 1790s Dong Nai area shows that shipbuilding in Chantaburi was only at an early stage. It was probably not so different from the situation in Hatien and Ligor: both had their own dockyards but only with limited capacity for shipbuilding.[43] In this context it is worth noting that the late eighteenth century saw a boom in shipbuilding, not only involving the Mekong and Menam Delta areas but also in the Malay Peninsula. In 1771, for example, the Dato of Jeram (or Yiring in Siamese) wrote to Sultan Mansur of Terengganu asking for his aid to attack Pattani. Sultan Mansur responded by leading an army of several thousand on eighty vessels.[44] Even so, it is unlikely that these centers—Hatien, Ligor, Chantaburi, and Terengganu—even though they built their own ships, could be compared with the shipbuilding industry in Bien Hoa before the Tay Son, and still less from the Nguyen Anh period.

But in 1835 Chantaburi became a dramatically different place. When Bradley visited it that year he stayed in a house at the dockyard not far from the mouth of the Chantaburi River where a few hundred people resided. He reported no fewer than fifty vessels on the stocks, two ships of 300–400 tons burden, thirty or forty war boats, and a number of smaller craft. Between the dockyard and Chantaburi the visitors found the house of *Chaophraya* Phrakhlang,[45] Rama III's treasurer and acting minister of war and of the southern province. This official was the mastermind behind the shipbuilding industry here. So important did he regard his task of setting Siamese naval forces on a new footing that he actually lived in Chantaburi to oversee the shipbuilding operation.

By 1839 when Rama III attacked Kedah the Siamese possessed a truly remarkable naval force. Even more remarkable is the number and size of ships that were built in Chantaburi after 1834.[46] *The Klaeo Klang Samut* (Ocean Warrior) for example, built at Chantaburi in 1835, was "the first European style vessel of any size to be constructed under Siamese supervision."[47] A much larger ship, the *Withayakhom* (Sorcerer), built here in 1836–1837 was estimated as between 800 and 1400 tons. Not only did the Chantaburi dockyards build Western-style ships, they also adapted Vietnamese-built Western ships to their own uses. There were at least two types of vessels involved in this. One style, the *Reua Pom Yang Yuan* (Vietnamese model gunboat), was a gunboat adapted by *Chaophraya* Phrakhlang in 1834–1835 "as a result of his appreciation of the effectiveness of the gunboats used against him by the Annamese in the 1833–34 campaign." Another type, called *Reua Sisa Yuan* (vessel with Vietnamese bows), was presumably a Vietnamese junk, perhaps with higher or squarer bows than Chinese junks.[48] This type of smaller junk might well have been what the Chinese called the "big head sampan of Annam," mentioned at the beginning of this chapter. Its bow was about 0.66 meter higher than the stern, and it carried about thirty crewmen.

What happened between 1832, when Roberts visited Siam and saw an inferior navy, and 1835, when Bradley reported a truly impressive one? As far as I can see, only one significant event took place during those few years that profoundly affected the shape of the Siamese naval forces, and that event happened in Cochinchina. It was the Le Van Khoi rebellion that swept the six provinces in 1833 and continued around Saigon until early 1835. By 1832, the conflict of interest between local southern elements, especially in the Saigon area, and the centralizing Nguyen court based in far-off Hue, was so intense that some form of armed conflict was unavoidable. After two years of struggle the rebellion failed, and more than 1500 people in Saigon citadel, many of them Chinese and Catholic Vietnamese, were massacred and the citadel pulled down to the ground.

Interestingly, one of the triggers for the Le Van Khoi rebellion was the very issue of logging and shipbuilding in the Mekong Delta. The Nguyen chronicles accused Le Van Khoi of illegal logging in the Saigon area. "Le Van Khoi often relied on the power of [his adoptive father, the influential Gia Dinh governor, Le Van] Duyet to send soldiers to log the forest without the permission [of the emperor]. Sometimes they sold planks to the Chinese and sometimes built their own ships."[49] One of Le Van Duyet's crimes, also according to the Nguyen chronicle, was that he possessed larger and better ships than the court.[50] From this it seems obvious that logging and shipbuilding had by this time become central to the power struggles both within and without the Nguyen territory.

It is no surprise to discover that the main participants in the thriving shipbuilding industry in Chantaburi were Cochinchinese and Chinese who had escaped from Minh Mang's repression and anti-Christian persecution. In 1835, there were five or six thousand people in Chantaburi, the majority being newly arrived Cochinchinese. According to the report of a local French missionary, "only very few of these represent the ancient refugees, for the ancient Christian Cochinchinese have returned, quite a few years ago, to their own country."[51] There were hardly any Siamese to be found in Chantaburi when Bradley strolled along its riverbanks. He observed that most local people were "Cochinchinese and Chinese, with only here and there a Siamese."[52] Among the Cochinchinese were skilled carpenters,[53] and some of the Cochinchinese Christians in Chantaburi were blacksmiths,[54] although most blacksmiths, an occupation indispensable for shipbuilding, were Chinese.[55]

Like the Mekong Delta, Chantaburi was rich in timber. Many travelers remarked on the gigantic trees they passed on the Chantaburi River.[56] The relatively late development of a shipbuilding industry here in itself, by the 1830s, indicated that it was an unexploited area for logging. More importantly, Chantaburi was located between the two major shipbuilding areas of the late eighteenth century, the Chaophraya Delta and the Mekong Delta. It was perfectly positioned to absorb both traditions and techniques from both deltas, to become the major mainland Southeast Asia shipbuilding site for several decades in the nineteenth century. This process was accelerated, if not in fact initiated, by the Cochinchinese and Chinese refugees, as is suggested by the speed with which Chantaburi became the major Siamese state shipbuilding yard almost immediately after the Le Van Khoi rebellion in 1834.

What I am suggesting here is that the shipbuilding industry in Chantaburi, the main shipyard involved in developing the new Siamese navy of the mid-1830s, relied on the technical knowledge and manpower supplied by Cochinchinese, Chinese, and Cham shipbuilders, who had migrated from the Nguyen territory. In other words, the very shipbuilding industry that helped to found the modern Siamese state was built by a decidedly foreign workforce. Modern Thais might be as surprised by this as by other historical realities of the early nineteenth century, as Baas Terweil has remarked in a different context: "For [contemporary] Thais . . . it may be hard to believe that in the 1840s . . . the inland areas of the southeast had vast tracts where the Thais did not rule, and that there was sufficient space for the monkey, the tiger and the rhinoceros."[57]

Some evidence goes even further to show the active involvement of Cochinchinese in the same Siamese naval forces that their compatriots were helping to build. By 1839 some of these Cochinchinese had become important naval officers, doubtless because of their maritime knowledge, and were mentioned in official documents. For example, in 1839 Phrakhlang, the aforesaid Siamese treasurer and acting minister of war and southern province who lived in Chantaburi, sent "Khun Ritthironakrai, the Lieutenant of the Annamese unit, up to the capital in a pirate-chaser vessel with a letter containing instructions to speed up the departure of the remaining vessels."[58] Interestingly, Cochinchinese and Chinese messengers were the ones who carried Siamese official letters concerning the plans and instructions of its expedition to Kedah, traveling between Chantaburi, Bangkok, and the Malay coast.[59]

Virtually all the big Siamese ships of the 1830s were built in Chantaburi, as the following excerpt in the Chinese Repository of 1837 suggests:

> *The Singapore Free Press* of 27th of July notices the arrival at that port of his Siamese majesty's frigate "Conqueror", a vessel of 600 tons, just launched from the docks at Chantibun. She is armed with forty guns, of what calibre is not said; but, notwithstanding her warlike equipment and name, she is at present to be employed only as a peaceful carrier of the goods of his golden-footed majesty's subjects. Another vessel of 1000 tons has been laid down, and is to be similarly equipped and employed.[60]

Ships built in Chantaburi in the 1830s by Cochinchinese and Chinese were the main force in the Siamese attack on Kedah in 1839. Rather ironically, they were also the backbone of the forces used in the Siamese conflicts with Vietnam in

1841–1842, as well as in transporting supplies and patrolling the coast off Hatien.[61]

Conclusion

The foregoing discussion suggests certain conclusions. First is that the most distinctive development of Cochinchinese marine technology of this period was perhaps in a few types of warships, galleys, and ships. What most distinguishes these vessels from those of other Asian countries at the time was the Cochinchinese adaptation, from the final decades of the eighteenth century, of Western-style shipbuilding techniques. This characteristic only began to be shared by the Siamese in the 1830s after the influx of Cochinchinese refugees fleeing the repression of the Le Van Khoi revolt in far southern Vietnam.

Second, the late-eighteenth and early-nineteenth century was certainly a period of high pressure that saw direct and intensive supervision of shipbuilding by the courts of Cochinchina and Siam.[62] This direct involvement in shipbuilding at the highest official level undoubtedly accelerated the industry's development, while shipbuilding offered the courts of both countries a way to exert their power over their populations in such an effective and concrete way that it accelerated the pace of the state building in turn. Of all the economic activities undertaken in nineteenth-century Vietnam and Siam, there was nothing more conducive to the foundation and development of new states than shipbuilding.

Going hand in hand with shipbuilding and state building was competition over controlling waterways in the region. The immediate victim of this struggle was Cambodia. In 1795 for example, the Khmer king asked Nguyen Anh to let foreign ships trading to Nam Vang (Phnom Penh) pass by Bassac, and Nguyen Anh agreed.[63] But the situation did not last. Losing control of its major waterway put Cambodia constantly at the mercy of the Vietnamese, as the Bangkok chronicle recognized: "But later, it turned out that those towns that Vietnam promised to return to Cambodia were never returned. . . . Cambodia wanted to build ships, put masts on them and sail them, in order to trade with other countries, but Vietnam would not permit Cambodia to sail in and out."[64] This shows more clearly than ever Cambodia's eagerness for an effective maritime outlet, its desire for the capacity to build its own ships, and its desperation to stand on its own feet. To Khmers the first two were the necessary conditions for the last. Ships were not only the symbol but also the embodiment of national strength.

What happened to the once proud Nguyen navy at the hands of the French is well known. Even the memory of this once powerful navy was lost. What reduced Vietnam from the master of those powerful warships, galleys, brigs, and schooners to a powerless, colonized country? Was it simply because "one generation abandons the enterprises of another like stranded vessels," as Henry Thoreau said in *Walden*, or was the brilliant but short-lived experience lost with the departure of most of the population that had made the shipbuilding industry so unusual?

Christopher Goscha was certainly right when he argued that "in the eighteenth century, the regional and political economics of war, perhaps more than anything else, were the driving force behind a new level of mainland contacts."[65] But conversely, does this mean that it would be more insightful to start from these regional contact points, in this case southern China, Cochinchina, and Siam, to trace the political economies of individual countries? Such an approach might help avoid the mistake of studying "each culture as if it were a discrete text, not a changing part of a regional picture," to borrow Richard O'Connor's point. The shipbuilding industry that this chapter has considered seems to confirm that regional analysis using more general and less concrete boundaries is not only possible but also necessary.

Notes

My gratitude goes to Professor Pierre-Yves Manguin for his extremely helpful comments on this chapter.

1. Wang Zhong Yang, "Yuenan zhanchuan shuo" [On the Warships of Annam] in *Hai guo tu zhi* [Illustrated Gazetteer of the Countries Overseas], ed. Wei Yuan, first printed 1842 (Taipei: Chengwen Press, 1967) vol. 53, 3091–3095. For Lin Zexu's biography and activities from 1840-1842, see Yang Guozhen, *Lin Zexu zhuan* [A Biography of Lin Zexu] (Beijing: People's Press, 1981), 478–79.

2. J. B. Pietri, *Les Voiliers d'Indochine* (Saigon: 1949), quoted in the *Blue Book of Coastal Vessels of South Vietnam* (Columbus, Ohio: Battele Memorial Institute Columbus Laboratories, 1967), 14.

3. John White, *A Voyage to Cochin China* (London: Longman, 1824), 265.

4. *Singapore Chronicle*, no. 157 (25 March 1830): 1.

5. "Relations between the US and Cochinchina," *Chinese Repository* 5 (April 1837): 157.

6. *Dai Nam Thuc Luc Chinh Bien, De Nhi Ky* [Primary Compilation of the Veritable Records of Imperial Vietnam, the Second Reign] [hereafter *DNTL*]. (Tokyo: Keio Institute of Cultural and Linguistic Studies, 1974), vol. 71

7. Zhou Kai, *Xiamen Zhi* [Xiamen Gazette] (Taipei: Taiwan yinhang, 1961), Taiwan Wenxian Congkan no. 95, 253.

8. Zhou Kai, *Xiamen zhi*, 191.

9. Dian Murray, *Pirates of the South China Coast, 1790–1810* (Stanford, Calif.: Stanford University Press, 1987), 49.

10. *DNTL*, vol. 1, 25. John White described a ship belonging to Le Van Duyet which might have been a variation on the ship mentioned above: "Between the mast and the stern, and occupying about one quarter of the length of the galley, and the whole of her breadth, excepting a passage-way inside each gunwale, was a neat wooden house . . . at the after-extremity of the vessel, which was considerably elevated above all other parts." White, *Voyage to Cochin China*, 327–28.

11. For praise from Western visitors, see Frédéric Mantienne, "Military Technology Transfers from Europe to Lower Mainland Southeast Asia, c. 16–19th centuries" (paper presented at the Association of Asian Studies conference 2002, Washington), 3–5.

12. *DNTL I*, vol. 5, 80.

13. Trinh Hoai Duc, *Gia Dinh thong chi: thanh tri chi*, in *Lingnan zhi guai deng shi liao san zhong* [Three Primary Sources of *Linh Nam trich quai, Gia dinh thong chi*, and *Hatien tran dipe tran Mac thi gia pha*], ed. Dai Kelai and Yang Baoyun (Zhengzhou: Zhongzhou Guji Press, 1991), 21.

14. *DNTL I*, vol. 5, 83.

15. Trinh Hoai Duc, *Gia Dinh thong chi*, 84; Son Nam, *Ben Nghe Xua* (Saigon's Yesteryears] (HCM City: Van Nghe, 1992), 40–41.

16. Nguyen Dinh Dau, "Dia ly lich su Thanh pho Ho Chi Minh" [Historical Geography of Ho Chi Minh City] in *Dia chi van hoa thanh pho Ho Chi Minh*, ed. Tran Van Giau et al [Cultural Gazette of Ho Chi Minh City] (Ho Chi Minh City: NXB Ho Chi Minh City, 1987), 182.

17. Nguyen Dinh Dau, "Dia ly lich su," 80.

18. Ng Chin-keong, *Trade and Society: The Amoy Network on the China Coast, 1683–1735* (Singapore: Singapore University Press, 1983), 60.

19. Chen Xiyu, *Zhongguo fan chuan yu hai wai mao yi* [Chinese Junks and Overseas Trade] (Xiamen: Xiamen University Press, 1991), 117.

20. "Bowyear's Narrative," in *The Mandarin Road to Old Hue: Narratives of Anglo–Vietnamese Diplomacy from the Seventeenth Century to the Eve of the French Conquest*, ed. Alastair Lamb (Hamden, Conn.: Archon Books, 1970), 55.

21. White, *Voyage to Cochin China*, 235.

22. Le Quy Don, *Phu bien tap luc* [Miscellaneous Border Records (seized in 1775–1776)] in *Le Quy Don Toan Tap* [Complete Works of Le Quy Don] (Hanoi: Khoa Hoc Xa Hoi, 1977), 104.

23. *Secret Palace Memorials of the Qianlong Period: Q'ing Documents at the National Palace Museum* (Taipei: National Palace Museum, 1983), no. 15 (Aug. 1756–Dec. 1756), 485–86.

24. *Phu Bien*, vol. 4, 41. The boats levied per region were: Trieu Phong, 40; Quang Binh 10; Nam Bo Chinh, 10; Quang Nam, 60; Quy Nhon, 93; Phu Xuan, 44; Dien Khanh, 32; Binh Thuan, 45; and Gia Dinh, 7.

25. Chen Xiyu, *Zhongguo fanchuan*, 121.

26. *The Dynastic Chronicles Bangkok Era, the First Reign*, trans. Thadeus and Chanin Flood (Tokyo: Centre for East Asian Cultural Studies, 1978), vol. 1, 303–04.

27. Edmund Roberts, *Embassy to the Eastern Courts of Cochin-China, Siam and Muscat during the Years 1832–34* (New York: Harper and Brothers, 1837), 311. "The entire junk was built in Siam and subsequently sold in China." G. R. C. Worcester, "Six Craft of Kwangtung," *The Mariner's Mirror* 45 (1959): 134, quoted in Jennifer Cushman, *Fields from the Sea* (Ithaca: Southeast Asia Program, Cornell University Press, 1993), 50, fn. 28.

28. *Colleccao de Documentos Sincos do Ian/TT Referentes a Macau durante a dinastia Qing* [A Collection of Qing Archives on Macao, Held in Torre do Tombo, Portugal] (Macau: Macau Foundation, 1999), vol. 1, 247.

29. *Colleccao de Documentos*, 452.

30. *Colleccao de Documentos*, 460.

31. Huynh Minh, *Gia dinh xua va nay* [Gia Dinh in Former Times and Today] (Saigon: Loai sach than khao, 1973), 97.

32. Cholthira Satyawadhna, "Ban Khrua Community: Ethnohistory, Struggle, Resistance, and Social Movement," *Tai Culture* 5, no. 2 (Dec. 2000): 198–99.

33. *Bangkok Era, the First Reign*, 167.

34. *DNTL I*, vol. 4, 64.

35. *Bangkok Era, the First Reign*, 174–75.

36. Roberts, *Embassy to the Eastern Courts of Cochin-China*, 311.

37. J. H. Moor, *Notices of the Indian Archipelago* [Singapore 1837], reprint (London: Cass, 1968) 232–33. First published in *Calcutta Journal*, 2 February 1823.

38. See Sarasin Viraphol, *Tribute and Profit: Sino–Siamese Trade, 1652–1853*, (Cambridge, Mass.: Council on East Asian Studies, Harvard University, 1977), 180.

39. Charles Gutzlaff, *Journal of Three Voyages along the Coast of China in 1831, 1832 & 1833* (London: Thomas Ward and Co., n.d.), 77.

40. Alexander Hamilton, "A New Account of the East Indies," in John Pinkerton, *A General Collection of the Best and Most Interesting Voyages and Travels in All Parts of the World* (London: n.p., 1811), vol. 8, 185.

41. B. J. Terwiel, "Towards a History of Chantaburi, 1700–1860: The French Sources," *Proceedings of International Conference on Thai Studies*, August 22–24, 1984 (Bangkok: Chulalongkorn University, n.d.), 3.

42. Terwiel, "Chantaburi," 4.

43. Trinh Hoai Duc, *Gia Dinh thong chi: thanh tri chi*, annotated by Chen Chingho, *Nanyang Xue bao* 12, no. 24 (1956): 30.

44. Hsu Yun-tsiao, *Bei da nien shi* [A History of Pattani] (Singapore: Nan Yang Press, 1946), 76–77;

45. B. J. Terwiel, *Through Travellers' Eyes: An Approach to Early 19th Century Thai History* (Bangkok: Editions Duang Kamol, 1989), 188.

46. The following information on Siamese vessels is from *Rama III and the Siamese Expedition to Kedah in 1839: The Dispatches of Luang Udosombat*, trans. Syril Skinner, ed. Justin Corfield (Clayton: Centre of Southeast Asian Studies, Monash University, 1993), 317–18.

47. *Rama III and the Siamese Expedition*, 317.

48. *Rama III and the Siamese Expedition*, 316. The Siamese had apparently learned some Vietnamese techniques before 1834, in particular the use of the double rudder introduced by Do Thanh Nhan in 1780. This had added a round rudder more suitable for river navigation to ships also fitted with the long rudder better suited to maritime navigation. The Siamese appear to have used double-ruddered ships in their 1792 war against the Burmese. Interestingly this happened right after Nguyen Anh sent ships to Rama I in 1791. For Do Thanh Nhan's invention, see Trinh Hoai Duc, *Gia Dinh thong chi* in *Lingnan zhi guai deng shi liao san zhong*, 195. For its use by the Siamese, see *Bangkok Era, the First Reign*, 198. But Anthony Reid in *The Age of Commerce* (New Haven and London: Yale University Press, 1993), vol. 2, 38–39, says that such double rudders were traditional in Southeast Asian junks. Could it be that the Vietnamese and Siamese here had readapted the double rudder?

49. *Dai Nam Chinh Bien Liet Truyen de Nhi Tap* [Second Collection of the Primary Compilation of Biographies of Imperial Vietnam] (Tokyo: Keio Institute of Linguistic Studies, 1962), vol. 45, 8110.

50. M. Regereau, copy, letter of 1 March 1834. Archives of the Missions-Etrangères de Paris, Cochinchine vol. 748, 262. My thanks go to Jacob Ramsay for this information.

51. Terwiel, "Chantaburi," 8–9.

52. Terwiel, *Through Travellers' Eyes*, 186. As late as 1965, nearly half the population of Chantaburi was ethnic Vietnamese. Peter Poole, *The Vietnamese in Thailand* (Ithaca: Cornell University Press, 1970), 30.

53. Poole, *Vietnamese in Thailand*, 28.

54. Terweil, "Chantaburi," 11.

55. Terweil, *Through Travellers' Eyes*, 200.

56. Terweil, *Through Travellers' Eyes*, 201.

57. Terweil, *Through Travellers' Eyes*, 201.

58. *Rama III and the Siamese Expedition,* 118.

59. *Rama III and the Siamese Expedition,* 163, and many more.

60. "Journal of Occurrences," *The Chinese Repository* 6, no. 5 (1837): 256.

61. *The Klaeo Klang Samut* (Ocean Warrior). "She had a displacement of about 150 tons and mounted six guns . . . she saw action again in the Annamese campaign of 1841–42 as the flagship, cleared with the duty of transporting supplies to Chao Phaya Bodin Thradecha's forces and patrolling the coast off Banteay Mas (Hatien)." *Rama III and the Siamese Expedition,* 316–317.

62. This seems to contrast with late-seventeenth-century island Southeast Asia. See Pierre-Yves Manguin, "The Vanishing Jong: Insular Southeast Asian Fleets in Trade and War (15th to 17th Centuries)," in *Southeast Asia in the Early Modern Era*, ed. Anthony Reid (Ithaca and London: Cornell University Press, 1993), 197–213.

63. *DNTL* I, vol. 7, p.411.

64. *Bangkok Era, the Fourth Reign*, 170–71.

65. Christopher Goscha, *Thailand and the Southeast Asian Networks of the Vietnamese Revolution, 1885–1954* (Richmond: Curzon Press, 1999), 5–6.

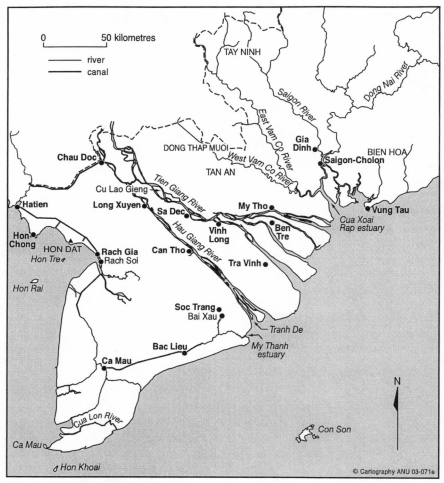

Map 5: The Mekong Delta

III

BEYOND THE WATER FRONTIER

9

Water World: Chinese and Vietnamese on the Riverine Water Frontier, from Ca Mau to Tonle Sap (c. 1850–1884)

Nola Cooke

> Nomadic people par excellence, carrying everything with them in their boats, they are made to live on the water.
>
> —H. Buchard (1880)[1]

The Mid-Nineteenth-Century Transbassac Region as a Water Frontier

When the French took western Cochinchina (the Transbassac) in 1867 it was a multiethnic region of considerable complexity, in border areas especially, where nominal Vietnamese control in some places had not precluded villages from paying taxes to both Cambodian and Vietnamese kings as late as the early 1850s.[2] Elsewhere, the absence of private land ownership suggested both a continuing influence of Khmer customary law and the uncertain nature of many existing Vietnamese settlements.[3] Non-Vietnamese locals, like the Malayo-Cham settled near Chau Doc and many Khmer villages, had often been indirectly ruled by Hue, whose mandarins had done little more than collect taxes and approve local men to run local affairs.[4] Even in the mid-1830s, at the height of Minh Mang's assimilationist "Vietnamization" of Khmers, when the first southern village land registers were being compiled during the repression of the Le

Van Khoi rebellion, the largely Khmer (and Chinese) region of Ba Thac (Bassac, now Soc Trang) was not included.[5]

The mid-nineteenth-century greater Transbassac area thus exhibited one characteristic feature of the earlier maritime Water Frontier, that is, it eluded the normal degree of central government control exercised elsewhere at the local level. Its unusual population mix was also similar. From Tra Vinh (Preah Trapeang) on the eastern Bassac shore south to the Ca Mau (Tuk Khmau) peninsular, and west to Chau Doc and beyond, with some notable exceptions like the Viet-dominated rice granary of Can Tho (Umor), Vietnamese often formed only a plurality and in places still a minority at the start of the 1850s.

Even by the early 1880s, official Cochinchinese population statistics still revealed a decidedly frontier mixture. Figures from 1884 showed ethnic Viets formed almost 90 percent of the general Cochinchinese population, with an estimated 105,333 Khmers comprising a tiny 6.5 percent and the 50,526 declared Chinese an even smaller 3 percent. However, in Chau Doc, Soc Trang, and Rach Gia, plus Tra Vinh on the eastern Bassac shore, things were different. These four areas contained fewer than 16 percent of the total declared local population, but in a ratio of 58 percent Vietnamese, 35.5 percent Khmer and 4 percent Chinese. Comparing these provinces to the rest of Cochinchina highlights their exceptional nature. In the early 1880s, they contained ten percent of the declared adult male Vietnamese in the French colony, but 86 percent of Khmer and 20 percent of Chinese. Soc Trang reported the second highest Chinese concentration outside the urban *arrondissement* containing over half the declared Chinese residents.[6] In nearby Kien Giang and Ca Mau (Rach Gia *arrondissement*), Chinese formed 9 percent of the declared taxable male population (1,585),[7] no doubt mostly in two Fujianese congregations as the two local Hainanese groups were highly mobile small traders keen to elude official notice.[8]

By this time the French counted local descendants of Chinese immigrants as "natives," so many Sino-Vietnamese (Minh Huong) and Sino-Khmer were undoubtedly hidden in the wider total. Early figures, at best indicative, suggest several thousand men of Chinese ancestry in the west. The 1868 inspection of Rach Gia district had found 868 adult males of mixed descent and 289 Chinese among a total male population of 16,341 (or 7 percent).[9] To the southwest, the 1868 inspection of Soc Trang improbably recorded no Sino-Vietnamese despite discovering at least 5,426 adult Chinese men. Two generations later, however, in adjacent Bac Lieu Province the colonial administrator in 1902 reported about four thousand declared Chinese but estimated that Minh Huong formed one-third of the population, adding that almost all natives of the province also spoke "Chinese."[10] This blend of Vietnamese and Chinese (or part-Chinese) living among an indigenous farming population is also typical of the earlier maritime Water Frontier. Table 9.1 gives the approximate population in the four selected provinces in 1883.

Also typical of the earlier Water Frontier, contemporary accounts reveal that many mid-century Vietnamese and Chinese immigrants here made their

Table 9.1: Approximate Population in Four Selected Provinces, c. 1883

Province	Viets	Khmer	Chinese	Total
Chau Doc	63,837 [71%]	18,849 [21%]	1,614 [2%]	90,181
Soc Trang	28,026 [44%]	29,835 [47%]	5,946 [9%]	63,854
Tra Vinh	38,793 [52%]	33,871 [45%]	1,337 [2%]	74,432
Rach Gia	16,695 [64%]	8,200 [31.5%]	1,150 [4%]	26,054
Total	147,351 [58%]	90,765 [35.5%]	10,047 [4%]	254,523

Source: Annuaire de la Cochinchine française, 1884, cited in Bouinais et Paulus, *L'Indo-Chine française contemporaine*, 224.

livings mainly outside the subsistence agricultural sector, particularly as fishermen. A substantial proportion of these people existed in a market-driven symbiotic relationship with the junk trade, especially with the seasonal comings and goings of a myriad of small craft that purchased their products and provided many of their daily necessities in return. Such economic interactions are reported from the Ca Mau peninsula to the great lake of Tonle Sap. Taken together, it all suggests that another Water Frontier flourished in the mid-nineteenth century along many of the waterways of the Transbassac and eastern Cambodia. As with the earlier era, trade and commerce on this riverine Water Frontier benefited from a mid-century period of relatively loose state control at the local level. With ethnic rebellions crushed in southern Vietnam by the early 1840s and peace largely restored to Cambodia at the end of that decade, the years between 1850 and the early 1880s formed a comparatively peaceful hiatus between widespread war and Nguyen military repression, on one hand, and the 1884 administrative, then military, tightening of French control in Cambodia, on the other. This relatively less troubled interim was a real time of opportunity. From the economic perspective of this floating world of junk traders, smugglers, boatmen, itinerant workers, fishing families, pirates, and hopeful wanderers on the western waterways, from Tonle Sap to the Mekong Delta, these decades might have seemed like the replacement of two competitive, but comparatively ineffectual, indigenous powers with a novice foreign regime very much starting from scratch and often as stretched by the difficulties of policing the area and its inhabitants as had been its indigenous predecessors.

The rest of this chapter surveys some of what contemporary published sources reveal of the economic life of Chinese and Vietnamese on this riverine Water Frontier from about 1850 to 1884. Though connected by junk trade routes and the itineraries of its floating denizens, geographically and politically this water world formed two basic regions. The first was the low-lying marshes, canals, and arroyos of old Kampuchea Krom, now western French Cochinchina, while the second was the upper Bassac and its connecting waterways in eastern Cambodia.

The Water World of Soc Trang, Bac Lieu, Ca Mau, and Rach Gia

This immense area, well over a million hectares, was very lightly populated and its agricultural potential barely touched at this time. Around 1880, the cultivated area declared for tax purposes barely topped 30,000 hectares, with nearly 27,500 hectares of them in Soc Trang.[11] Even so, this was an insignificant portion of the whole. If some early colonial officials had feared the immense swampy forests and flooded marshes of Ca Mau and, to a lesser extent, Kien Giang districts (Rach Gia Province) concealed vast stretches of illicit rice fields, later explorations revealed instead a veritable water world whose tiny hamlets were scattered at great distances and where all transport and communication was waterborne. If fertile land existed in the southeast, elsewhere small parcels of poor quality soil had to be constantly wrestled from encroaching melaleuca (*tram*) forests.[12] South of the flooded inland depression of central Ca Mau, brackish tidal water made cultivation impossible. Indeed, the districtwide lack of potable water created a market opportunity for junk traders. Large southern fishing villages and the wealthy in Ca Mau town relied on small Hainanese junks that imported drinking water from the offshore Poulo Obi islands; while the poor had to accept less palatable alternatives shipped from Rach Gia or the Ganh Hao River.[13] Unable to grow cereals, dependent on junk traders for daily necessities including water, the fishing villages of mid-nineteenth-century south Ca Mau were among the most market-related primary producers in Southeast Asia at the time.

Despite its apparent desolation, Chinese had been coming to this wild area in considerable numbers from at least the early eighteenth century, thanks to its maze of interconnecting waterways. These watercourses enabled small junk traders to penetrate the vast hinterland, right through to the Bassac and beyond, as well as giving safe passage to boats of all sizes not intending to round the peninsular via Poulo Obi. Small traders sailing east during the southwest monsoon especially favored its river systems, since strong winds neutralized the ebb tide current in the gulf and made sailing dangerous for small craft there. In the wet season (July to October), they could go from Rach Gia port up the Cai Lon River and via connecting waterways to Ca Mau town. From there an all-season arroyo went to the Bac Lieu-Soc Trang area, or the Ganh Hao River flowed straight to the favorable winds of the China Sea. Small Hainanese traders especially preferred this latter route, but it was hardly the only choice. Many other junks, including large seagoing ones, preferred a year-round route beginning in the Ong Doc River one hundred kilometers south of Rach Gia. Trading vessels rode the tides up to its confluence with the Ganh Hao, and thence to the China Sea via Ca Mau. By 1880 this was the standard route for cargo junks between

Hainan and Singapore. Seagoing junks of low tonnage even made commercial trips to Cambodia from Ca Mau.[14]

An example from the 1820s gazetteer of the six southern provinces, *Gia Dinh Thanh Thong Chi*, by the senior official Trinh Hoai Duc, himself a Minh Huong of Fujianese descent, illustrates how these western waterways interwove the whole Transbassac area. The starting thread is the Ba Thac River, which began 117 *dam*[15] south of the An Giang provincial seat and ran south for 36 *dam* to join the sea via the Ba That mouth of the Bassac River. Sixty *dam* from the river mouth to the west was Tau Truong ["ship wharf"], a "place where western merchant ships come to trade" and where there were "plenty of Vietnamese, Chinese and Khmers living mixed in together, with streets and markets and shops in a prolonged succession."[16]

> At a distance of 65 *dam* [from here the Ba Thac forms] a three way junction with the Nguyet Giang (commonly called the Soc Trang): the northern course runs 23 *dam* to Phu Dao (commonly called Bua-thao, "phu dau" in Chinese meaning Bua Thao [Axe]), going upstream to the northwest for 165.5 *dam*, it passes Ba Dinh, Tam Vu, Cai Tau, Cai Cao and Sai Quang and then reaches the great port of Kien Giang [Rach Gia].[17] The branch going west (Soc Trang) runs for 8.5 *dam* to the market of Bai Xao, where there are shops and inns almost touching each other, [and where] mixed in together there live Viet people and aboriginal [Khmer] people who make their living from the business of producing red salt. After a further distance of 25.5 *dam* [from here] comes the three way junction of Co Co . . . the southern branch runs 17.5 *dam* to the sea at the My Thanh estuary; the western branch runs 211.5 *dam* to Tra No and Cai Cham and then to the fort of Long Xuyen district [Ca Mau].

Though several names are unrecognizable today, this one extensive system obviously wove together the commercial centers of Rach Gia, Soc Trang (Bassac or Ba Thac),[18] the important nearby market town of Bai Xau, the China Sea at My Thanh estuary, the Bac Lieu area, and Ca Mau town. Of Kien Giang Trinh Hoai Duc wrote: "its streets and markets are densely populated, and crowds of trading vessels converged on it."[19] Of Ca Mau town (Long Xuyen fort) his text reported "many big fish in the sea, and many crocodiles in the rivers . . . the streets and a market . . . Viets, Chinese and Khmer gather, and Siamese ships come to trade," adding "only the Chinese work diligently, in terms of catching fish in the sea or from the rivers, or doing business in town or with the outside."[20]

From the early to mid-nineteenth century, it was the economic opportunities provided by this established junk trade that, in my view, most attracted Vietnamese and Chinese newcomers to the west. One example is the lucrative beeswax industry exploiting the immense inland *cai gia* forests of Rach Gia and, to a much lesser extent, Ca Mau. So much wax was found floating in the flooded forests of Kien Giang district that the Khmer had called it "wax land," and the settlement that later became Rach Gia, Kramwm Sa, or White Wax Market.[21] It was not Khmer who exploited this lucrative resource, however, but immigrant

Chinese and Vietnamese. Under Nguyen rule, the principal beneficiaries had been the fifty Chinese members of the "Wax Taxpayers' Association" (*Ho Sap*) of these two districts. For an annual payment of 2,000 *quan* (1,000 in tax and 20 per head for membership), these men had enjoyed exclusive and highly profitable rights to exploit the forests. When the French abolished this arrangement in 1867, Vietnamese and Chinese adventurers moved in to exploit the new opportunities that opened up. So lucrative were profits that violent disputes over competing interests could split settlements with the losers establishing new hamlets, irrespective of official permission, where faction leaders lived "as real kings."[22] In the 1870s, exploiting an average forest parcel required practically no capital investment. In a good year, Brière calculated, it yielded about 120 kilos of wax in the three-month honey-gathering season (mid-September to mid-December), with each hive supplying one to four wax loaves. The wax was sold in 750 gram lots (two loaves), each worth one piaster. In good conditions, gross profits per section could exceed 1,000 French francs before tax (10 percent).[23]

If the local junk trade made wax processing much more profitable than it would otherwise have been, the most important local industry by contrast owed its entire existence to the junk trade. This was the nineteenth-century growth industry in live or processed fish and seafood located in the Ca Mau peninsular.

While cadastral registers show that most agricultural land was communal in precolonial Ca Mau, nonagricultural resources were private property. Settlement founders and their descendants were allowed private ownership of their hamlet's natural resources in return for an annual tax payment, often in kind. Where inland fisheries and estuary prawning operations were concerned, no officially recognized monopolist farm like the Wax Taxpayers' Association intervened to draw off profits. As a result, the splitting of villages over economic disputes occurred here under the Nguyen rather than the French (who had immediately vested fisheries in the state in 1867 and leased them back to the villages). One extreme example was Phu My commune, founded in 1848, whose thirty-three registered taxpayers were spread among eleven effectively independent hamlets by the 1870s.[24]

Freshwater fish were caught in virtually every Ca Mau village territory during the season (October to January). After they had bred in the flooded inland plains, the drying waters naturally channeled huge quantities of fish into the local arroyos or specially dug ditches where they were mechanically trapped and sold by 14 kilo loads, each worth 15 *quan*, to junk operators coming from as far away as Cholon. Using "fish-tank" junks designed so the fresh water in their holds could be changed daily, these operators transported their live cargo for up to ten days from Ca Mau to distant markets in Saigon, Cholon, and Bien Hoa. Considerable profits could be made, but at some capital investment for such a seasonal undertaking. When salty water contaminated the Bac Lieu arroyo in late January, the Ca Mau season ended. No doubt these fish-tank junks then turned up the Mekong to service the Cambodian live fish trade that, according to official customs records in 1873, was moving more than 1.5 million live fish each year downriver to Phnom Penh and French Cochinchina.[25]

By 1880, a favorite location for the far southern fisheries was the arroyo linking Ca Mau and Bac Lieu, possibly because proximity to Bac Lieu enabled smaller local junks to supply its thriving market, perhaps several times a season. But whatever their ultimate destination, the number of boats involved by 1880 was substantial for such a sparsely populated area: in that year 216 junks carried 4,500 piculs (270 tonnes) of live fish to other parts of Cochinchina.[26]

In the far south, other fishing villages equally relied on a close relationship with the junk trade to market their catch. Some specialized in particular types of dried fish, no doubt including some of the eleven hamlets of Phu My (mentioned above) whose people lived near the rich waters of Dam Cung lagoon. This place contained three highly prized fish species that were sold to Hainanese junks that came for them between September and June. Oysters from the same lagoon were also processed into sauce. In December and January, large Hainanese cargo junks came to Ca Mau's southern estuaries for the best-quality local prawns, also especially reserved for them by the producers, as well as for dried fish and fish oil.[27] Dried salted fish was one of Ca Mau's principal exports by 1880 with most taken by Hainanese junks to sell on the Singapore market. The terms of trade at the time strongly favored Ca Mau. In that year, its market attracted 45 coastal junks with a carrying capacity of 800 tonnes. Singapore's most valuable export here was 1,700 piasters' worth of cotton cloth, but Ca Mau sent back 7,400 piasters' worth of dried fish.[28]

Crucial to this developing export trade was ready access to salt for processing, in this case supplied by Chinese operators in nearby Soc Trang and Bac Lieu.

Salt was being produced commercially here in Trinh Hoai Duc's time. Indeed, Bassac (Soc Trang) was famous for its special "red" salt whose purity and mild flavor were greatly desired. Although highly valued in the production of fish sauce, it was equally used to salt fish. In the early nineteenth century, these Chinese salt makers mainly exported to Cambodia in packages designed for transport by buffalo cart after leaving the cargo junks. Profits were extremely high.[29] Unfortunately, because the 1836 cadastral survey lacks Ba Xuyen prefecture, the location of most of the salt marshes, the extent of its mid-1830s productive area is unknown. However, in adjoining Long Thuy canton of Long Xuyen district (in later Bac Lieu Province), three privately owned salt marshes totaling over twenty hectares[30] were recorded in 1836, with one ten hectares in size and another nearly nine hectares.[31] As red salt production was complicated, the capital needed to operate such holdings argues for Chinese involvement here too.

If fields of this size were replicated in larger number in Ba Xuyen, the industry would have been quite big in the 1830s but surely nothing like the two hundred hectares of salt marshes discovered there by the French in 1868. This acreage undoubtedly represented an expansion over the previous half-century, perhaps to double the earlier size.[32] Indeed, it may be that over half the twenty hectares registered in 1836 in Long Thuy canton had only been recently developed, since Trinh Hoai Duc's text recorded only one of the two salt producing villages there.[33] As population increase was negligible before colonialism, any such expansion must have responded to increasing demand for Soc Trang salt by the growing fish and seafood processing industry whose participants by the late 1860s stretched from Ca Mau up the Mekong to Tonle Sap in Cambodia.

Setting aside these examples of interdependent economic activities, the pattern of Transbassac Vietnamese settlement itself provides an even more striking example of the centrality of the junk trade to life here. As Viet people arrived in the western provinces (and Cambodia), they always settled first on the estuaries of navigable rivers and along their banks, pushing local Khmer onto raised sandy banks (*giong*) suitable for agriculture, where in many parts of the Transbassac they still remained when the French arrived.[34] While this pattern indicates most immigrants arrived by boat, it also demonstrates they saw a real advantage in settling on existing (or potential) junk routes. Thus most settlements were founded either with an eye to local commodity production for sale to junk traders, as discussed above, or in places that could service passing boats.

The eighteenth-century estuarine village of My Thanh, mentioned above by Trinh Hoai Duc, is one example. Located a day by sea or two by river from the Chinese market at Bassac, its people grew herbs and vegetables to sell to junk crews.[35] Even more illustrative of this symbiosis with the junk trade was the settlement pattern in southeast Kien Giang district before and after its Vietnamese governor, Nguyen Ngoc Thoai, dredged a canal in 1817 to create a more direct link between Rach Gia and the Bassac River. Before this, the trip took eight to ten days, and hamlets were regularly spaced along the route to trade with the crews. "This circumstance explains the numerous villages southeast of Rach-gia . . . and the advanced state of cultivation in Tra-nieng and Rach-soi," Benoist noted. When the new route displaced the previous commercial traffic, "new villages, colonies of Van-tap," sprang up along the canal banks to service the junks. So keen were Nguyen rulers to maintain this commercial traffic that the Rach Gia canal was cleared of vegetation by each of the following three kings. As with the other commercial canals redredged and extended by the Nguyen,[36] the early colonial regime failed to maintain the canal. By the end of the 1870s, it was only eight to ten meters wide and almost impassable by the end of the dry season.[37]

Chinese and Vietnamese on the Riverine Water Frontier in Eastern Cambodia

Chinese had been trading with and sojourning in Cambodia for centuries before they began to form a settled community there from the later fifteenth century after Phnom Penh first became the capital. Portuguese who arrived in the early sixteenth century found Chinese weights and measures in use and a commercial decimal system whose numbers closely resembled those in Cantonese dialect. By 1606, Iberian sources reported three thousand Chinese living in the capital.[38] Perhaps less well-known than this Chinese presence near the early-seventeenth-century Khmer court was that of 600 to 1,000 Vietnamese similarly relocated less than two decades later as attendants to the Nguyen bride of the Khmer king's oldest son and successor.[39] Protected by this influential royal personage, Vietnamese merchants and others later followed, in numbers rivaling the Chinese if the contemporary European report of the massacre of 1,000 Vietnamese émigrés by a small freebooting Chinese army in 1666 is accurate.[40] The reigning king immediately took advantage of the fighting to close the Cochinchinese border and break off commercial contacts with Nguyen Cochinchina. In 1667, the ruler, Hien Vuong, retaliated by sacking the Khmer capital. Thus began a two-century ebb and flow of slow infiltration or organized violence by Viets, interspersed with hasty retreats, followed by persistent returns after massacre or defeat that became a slow but inexorable tide of Vietnamese acquisition of Cambodian lands and waterways.[41] This unrelenting expansionary pressure culminated in the 1830s and 1840s with an ill-conceived Vietnamese attempt to occupy and then assimilate its Cambodian tributary. By this time, Viets had spread as far inland as Battambang, northwest of Tonle Sap, and many died yet again as the inevitable Siamese invasion and popular anti-Vietnamese revolts provoked a wave of massacres across the country.[42] Defeated, Hue finally accepted a peaceful settlement in 1847.

Chinese had always been welcome in Cambodia. From at least the seventeenth century, they had been eligible for certain royal posts, in particular those involved with harbors and gambling, and enjoyed considerable freedom in the absence of compulsory dialect associations. If they adopted Cambodian ways, Sino-Khmer offspring were treated as normal subjects in the second generation.[43] Many Chinese migrated here either during the late-seventeenth-century Ming loyalist exodus or after the Qing eighteenth-century relaxation of official restrictions on overseas residence. The most famous example was Hatien under the émigré Cantonese Mac family, but other ports, right up to Chileang on the northern Mekong near Laos, became mainly Chinese during the eighteenth century.[44] In this era, farmers formed an important element among the migrants. If many specialized in commodities like cotton, rice, or pepper, many others were simple market gardeners. By the mid-nineteenth century, the combined Chinese and first-generation Sino-Khmer population probably exceeded 50,000 and growing. Indeed, in 1874, the protectorate head Etienne Aymonier estimated from Cambodian records that over 100,000 Chinese lived among 750,000 Khmer.[45] While both numbers are indicative at best, if Aymonier's figure included first-generation Sino-Khmer among the Chinese, as it probably did, then it may not have been entirely unreasonable, even though long-established Chinese and Sino-Khmer communities in the southern provinces (Peam, Kampot, Banteay Meas) had been hit hard by piracy and rebellion following Norodom's succession in the early 1860s.

Undeterred by the bloody convulsions of earlier decades, Vietnamese were also visibly returning to eastern Cambodia by 1850. Their presence was reported by Charles-Emile Bouillevaux, a missionary seeking asylum from Cochinchina, who had arrived in 1850 and spent several years in Cambodia during which he traveled extensively. His book *Voyage dans l'Indochine, 1848-1856* is the earliest and best-informed European account available for the precolonial decade. His main observations were later confirmed by Henri Mouhot, who traveled in Cambodia in 1858–1859, as well as by others in the 1860s. That certain specific features Bouillevaux reported about the Vietnamese presence in the early 1850s were confirmed in the late 1850s and mid-1860s suggests these elements predated colonialism in the area. Bouillevaux' observations therefore question the conventional view that attributes the Vietnamese population in Cambodia essentially to French colonialism.[46]

First, it is clear from Bouillevaux and confirmed by Mouhot that Phnom Penh was a largely Sino-Vietnamese town in the 1850s. Already a major commercial center, Phnom Penh, "composed in the great part of Chinese and Annamites, increases every day," Bouillevaux wrote.[47] If this largely Sino-Vietnamese market town was visibly growing in the early 1850s, it seems reasonable to assume that increased Cambodian trade after the 1847 peace settlement was attracting Chinese and Vietnamese to Phnom Penh, "the great bazaar of Cambodia" as Mouhot called it, to profit from it. In 1858, Mouhot put Phnom Penh's population at "about 10,000, almost all Chinese," but he added its boat-dwelling population of Cochinchinese and Cambodians was "more than double that number." There was also a floating suburb at its southern edge comprising at least five hundred boats, mostly large, on which many merchants lived and stored their goods and money, ready to flee at the first alarm. Given that historically Vietnamese had most to fear in Cambodia, it seems likely that a considerable proportion of these nervous traders would have been Viets. In a town whose seasonal population might thus have exceeded 35,000, from Mouhot's account at least 10,000, and probably more, were Vietnamese, since the seasonal influx he described largely comprised "a crowd of small merchants" come to buy the cotton crop, most of which went to Cochinchina, and fishermen from Tonle Sap, many of them Viets, come to sell their excess catch.[48] The presence of a substantial number of Vietnamese in preprotectorate Phnom Penh was also confirmed in 1860 by an English traveler, D. O. King, who recalled encountering "crowds of Cochin Chinese in its streets."[49]

Second is the role of Vietnamese in the Cambodian commercial economy. While discussing economic activity at the time, Bouillevaux noted that commerce was entirely in foreign hands. There was "quite a considerable colony of Malays" and "the Chinese [were] also very numerous." But he continued:[50]

Much more active, much more scheming than the Cambodians, *the Annamites are invading this kingdom little by little: all petty commerce is in their hands.* The Chinese and the Malays principally carry out external commerce; they are those who buy the cargoes that come from Canton or from Singapore,[51] and who resupply the ships with all the provisions necessary for their return.

As Cambodia was a missionary haven at the time, some of Bouillevaux' general comments probably reflected wider views than simply his own observations. On balance, missionaries probably knew more about Vietnamese numbers on Cambodian territory than anyone else, including Cambodian officials: a proportion of them would have been Christians fleeing persecution; while the presence of pagan Vietnamese always interested missionaries as prospects for conversion. Bouillevaux' observation that Vietnamese infiltration was visibly recurring by the early 1850s should therefore, in my view, be taken as a reflection of social reality in eastern Cambodia.

Equally intriguing is Bouillevaux' remark about the role of Viet small traders in the local distribution system in the 1850s. One might have assumed a preference by large Chinese importers for credit-worthy fellow dialect speakers to distribute their goods at the local level. If Vietnamese filled this niche, these small-scale peddlers and their families might have numbered into the thousands, mostly hidden from officialdom by their mobility within Cambodia and between Cambodia and Cochinchina. Further research is needed to uncover whether the sort of commercial partnership implied in Bouillevaux' comment did exist between large Chinese business houses and small Vietnamese traders here. But if Viets had played this role in the local distribution system from the 1850s, it helps explain Doudart de Lagrée's 1866 report of a great number of small Vietnamese shopkeepers in Phnom Penh.[52]

Finally, Bouillevaux mentioned one other significant group of Vietnamese in 1850s eastern Cambodia—waterborne woodcutters. Cambodian timber was almost a free good at the time. To cut timber required only that the local governor be informed before starting and a 10 percent tax be paid on the product.[53] The result was the wholesale pillaging of Cambodian forests by Vietnamese and Chinese. Their destructive methods, that had reached the Cambodian upper Mekong by 1880,[54] were well known in the 1850s. Praising the magnificent trees of superior quality that grew in dryland forests, Bouillevaux added: "every year, at the time of high waters, the Annamites come up to these fine forests and set about devastating them. They are happy to pay one-tenth at the customs, one tree in ten."[55]

Fifteen years later, Louis de Carné, a member of the Mekong Exploration Commission of 1866–1868, reported similarly profligate methods among waterborne Vietnamese bamboo cutters. These men took advantage of the high waters to travel upriver to Cambodia and fell large amounts of bamboo, which they made into rafts and floated down to sell in Phnom Penh. The ensuing glut on the market cut prices so dramatically that at some point it was common practice to "burn up a fourth of the stock" to raise its value.[56] Such behavior was unknown in the Vietnamese Transbassac, where wood gathering and timber cutting were important off-season activities. In Rach Gia and Ca Mau, however, natural resources were locally owned, so none could plunder at will, and the economic imperative of maximizing profits during the short high-water season was absent. In Cambodia, by contrast, Khmers rarely lived near the vast forests[57] and had no rights in them, as forests were royal domain. With the administration only interested in customs dues from lumber, conservation of even the most precious woods was effectively nobody's business, a situation ransacking Vietnamese and Chinese ruthlessly exploited to their own profit.

If many tens of thousands of Chinese and Vietnamese already lived in or made their living from Cambodia before the 1860s, when colonial power was established in southern Vietnam and French protection extended to Cambodia, the new regime soon introduced a number of liberalizing reforms that favored Vietnamese economic immigrants especially. In 1868 the protectorate abolished the local levy of one *quan* per man on Vietnamese boat crews employed in transportation or fishing, a valuable reform since Doudart had reported that all the boatmen in Phnom Penh who trafficked between Cochinchina and Cambodia were Vietnamese. In 1870 a border convention with Siam, as suzerain of Battambang and Angkor Provinces, freed Vietnamese from any local imposts when fishing on Tonle Sap.[58] If protectorate officials did allow a royal ordinance in 1877 to deprive Vietnamese living over a year in Cambodia of their status as French subjects, the Cochinchinese French governor forced its withdrawal in early 1881. Instead Vietnamese sojourners paid a capitation tax of ten francs per Christian and twenty per Buddhist.[59]

The 1881 decision on French subject status for resident Viets generated a flood of Vietnamese immigration into Cambodia, something encouraged by the French. Takeo, about forty kilometers from the Cochinchina border and long an important cattle-exporting center, is one example. It went from a largely Cantonese, Hainanese, and Hakka population, with perhaps twenty Viet inhabitants in 1880, to a town in 1882 in which Vietnamese occupied three streets to the Chinese four. The seasonal Viet presence in Takeo added a further 1,200 temporary huts and hundreds of junks to the local waterways. If these transients mostly came to fish, others settled permanently in the area in villages like Kabal Po, where they set up an illicit cattle-stealing operation. Cattle and buffalo were smuggled into Cochinchina, and some stolen animals were even sold directly to the agents of Chinese naval suppliers in the colony who came to Kabal Po expressly for that purpose. Good profits could be made in this trade: before the conquest, twenty animals fetched the same as three now did on the legitimate market in 1880s Cochinchina, ensuring a boom in stolen beasts from Cambodia.[60]

Finally, it is impossible to conclude without discussing the most valuable of Vietnamese enterprises in Cambodia in these years, the immense Tonle Sap fisheries. Bouillevaux never mentioned the Great Lake fisheries at all, possibly because he visited Battambang out of season in 1851 or more likely because few Viets had yet ventured as far north of Phnom Penh so soon after the peace settlement.[61] By the end of the 1850s, however, they had clearly reached Tonle Sap since Mouhot noted that "a number of enterprising Cochin-Chinese" took "literally miraculous" catches there each year.[62] By the mid-1860s these "numbers" had multiplied into "some thousands" of Vietnamese boats on the lake itself and in the arm that connected it to the Mekong, according to de Carné. He also observed that profits were so high that these Viet fishermen would pay 100 percent interest, no doubt from Chinese moneylenders, for advances to buy salt to preserve the catch,[63] something that supports Willmott's view of the fish trade then being "primarily in the hands of the Chinese who resided in Phnom-Penh and Kompong-Chhnang."[64]

The real escalation in numbers undoubtedly followed the 1870 Franco–Siamese border convention that replaced former royal fishing rights on Tonle Sap with a simple customs duty on the catch. By 1880, Vietnamese had virtually taken possession of the lake, and its fishing industry was essentially a Sino–Vietnamese enterprise. Chinese capital still played a financial role, but almost all the large fisheries that might return up to 15,000 francs annually were in Vietnamese hands, employing thousands of Viet families whose needs were supplied for several months by hundreds of itinerant Chinese junk traders.[65] When Buchard reported in detail on the industry in 1880, he estimated there were "about 30,000" participants, including Cambodians, Siamese, Malays, Chinese, and Vietnamese, with the latter "in greater number than the others. Some come from [French] Lower Cochinchina," he noted, "but the greatest contingent is supplied by the Bassac and Cambodia,"[66] that is, by the floating Vietnamese denizens of the east Cambodian riverine Water Frontier.

On Tonle Sap, which required heavier equipment and larger numbers to maneuver the nets, Vietnamese operators usually hired twenty-five men and twelve women for six months; while the Thais and Cambodians normally fished the arroyos where lighter nets required half the number of hands. Some Chinese and Cambodians also used debt-slaves, or slaves purchased for the work in Siam, to reduce labor overhead.[67] Waterborne Viet families arrived in early December, bringing supplies to last at least until the first junks appeared seeking dried fish in January. They busied themselves preparing traps, building drying racks, and erecting temporary villages, some of which were so large that Cambodian and Siamese authorities appointed headmen from among the inhabitants. Women not hired on the lake worked in December and January at rendering oil from fish caught on the Mekong arms. So many fishing boats crammed the river at this time that they almost blocked the passage for other vessels. When the season ended, the temporary villages were dismantled and the occupants moved on, some to Phnom Penh and others to crowd into existing Vietnamese villages on Thai or Cambodian territory around the lakeshore.[68]

Yields were colossal. In 1873, Cambodian customs records showed 128,628 piculs (7,718 tonnes) of dried or salted fish and 233 piculs (14 tonnes) of fish oil passed through Phnom Penh, when the largest transport option was cargo junks carrying 48–60 tonnes each.[69] In the early 1880s, when steam transport became available to Phnom Penh and to Saigon-Cholon, the average amount of dried and salted fish exported south from Tonle Sap reached 200,000 piculs (12,000 tonnes), worth 4 piasters per picul (yielding an 800,000 piasters annual turnover for processed fish alone), with the lion's share of profits in Vietnamese and Chinese hands.[70] Despite high freight costs on the Chinese-run steam launch to Phnom Penh and its *Messageries fluviale de Cochinchine* competitor based in Saigon, this new mode of transport quickly became attractive as it avoided the risk of whole junks laden with fish being stolen by Chinese and Vietnamese pirates on Tonle Sap.[71]

Conclusion

From the 1850s to the 1880s, Chinese and Vietnamese spread along the Trans-bassac waterways of western Cochinchina and up the watercourses of eastern Cambodia. Although some became agriculturalists, more were motivated by the desire to profit from contacts with the existing, mainly Chinese, junk trade. A symbiotic relationship developed between junk traders and commodity producers and suppliers here that was exemplified by the large and expanding industry in fresh and processed seafood for local and export Chinese markets. Although assisted by the economic liberalism of the early colonial regime, this industry predated French colonialism. It drew its strength from being part of a well-established regional trade network woven together by the seasonal itineraries of a myriad of riverine, coastal, and seagoing junk traders, a network that stretched north to southern China and south to Singapore, where colonial British rule and Chinese laborers alike benefited from the ready supply of cheap food transported from distant Vietnamese and Cambodian fisheries.

Notes

1. Referring to Viet fishermen who, he added, had made Tonle Sap their own by 1880. H. Buchard, "Rapport à M. le Gouverneur sur la mission du Grand-Lac," *Cochinchine française: Excursions et Reconnaissances* 4 (1880): 279 [hereafter *ER*].

2. Pierre-Lucien Lamont, "La frontière entre le Cambodge et le Vietnam du milieu du XIXe siècle à nos jours," in *Les frontières du Viêtnam*, Centre d'Histoire et Civilisation de la Péninsule Indochinoise (Paris: L'Harmattan, 1989), 157; and Mak Phoeun, "La frontière entre le Cambodge et le Viêtnam du XVIIe siècle à l'instauration du protectorat française presentée à travers les chronicles royals khmères," 146–55.

3. Even in the 1870s, private land ownership did not exist "everywhere" here, while in parts of Soc Trang and Tra Vinh it "did not exist at all." A. Labussière, "Étude sur la propriété foncière rurale en Cochinchine, et particulièrement dans l'inspection de Soc-trang," *ER* 3 (1880): 331–32.

4. They had been paid Vietnamese auxiliaries earlier in the nineteenth century. A. Labussière, "Rapport sur les chams et les malais de l'arrondissement de Chaudoc," *ER* 6 (1880): 373–380. For similar arrangements with Khmer, see Labussière, "Étude sur la propriété foncière rurale:" 333, 338.

5. Nguyen Dinh Dau, *Nghien Cuu Dia Ba Trieu Nguyen, An Giang* [Cadastral Registers' Study of Nguyen Dynasty, An Giang Province] (Ho Chi Minh City: NXB Thanh Pho HCM, 1994), 81.

6. The figures predate Bac Lieu's becoming a province in 1883. My calculations from data in the *Annuaire de la Cochinchine française*, 1884, cited in A. Bouinais et A. Paulus, *L'Indo-Chine française contemporaine. Cochinchine–Cambodge* (Paris: Challamel, 1885), 224. Pierre Brocheux's 1886 figures are different but the Khmer–Viet-

Chinese ratios in Soc Trang and Rach Gia are similar. *The Mekong Delta: Ecology, Economy, and Revolution, 1860–1960* (Madison: Centre for Southeast Asian Studies, 1995), 24–25.

7. My calculations from data in Benoist, "Note complémentaire sur le Kien-giang (Rach-gia)," *ER* 1 (1879): 51. There were 105 in Kien Giang and 165 in Ca Mau.

8. Local Fujianese were market gardeners. The congregations in Ca Mau were Lac-phuoc (Fujian) and Lac-giuc (Hainan); and in Kien Giang Lac-lai (Fujian) plus an unnamed Hainanese one. Ca Mau also had two Minh Huong congregations containing "the richest" in the district, one with thirty-seven members and the other twenty-two. Benoist, "Note sur la population de Rach-gia et du huyen de Ca-mau, par M. Benoist," *ER* 1 (1879): 33–34.

9. For the figures for adult males collected for these four areas in 1868, see Philippe Langlet and Quach Thanh Tam, *Atlas historique des six provinces du sud du Vietnam du milieu du XIXe au début du XXe siècle* (Paris: Les Indes Savantes, 2001), 233, 238, 242, 246.

10. Presumably Teochiu dialect, as they predominated here. Brocheux, *Mekong Delta*, 99. Chinese and their offspring had lived here since the mid-eighteenth century. Huynh Minh, *Bac Lieu Xua va Nay* [Bac Lieu in Former Times and Today], reprint (n.p., Calif.: Bach Viet, 1994), 11–12.

11. Labussière, "Étude sur la propriété foncière rurale," 342. For Ca Mau, the declared area was 905 hectares and Kien Giang 1,948 hectares. E. Brière, "Rapport sur la circonscription de Ca-mau," *ER* 1 (1879): 5; and Benoist, "Note complémentaire sur le Kien-giang:" 51.

12. Brière, "Rapport sur Ca-mau," 18–19. A fine description of this watery wasteland in 1871 appears in "Exploration par M. Benoist de la partie déserte comprise entre les inspections de Rach-gia, Can-tho et Long-xuyen," *ER* 1 (1879): 44–50. See also Brocheux, *Mekong Delta*, 2–10.

13. The poor also collected rainwater. Brière, "Rapport sur Ca-mau," 16.

14. All details from Brière, "Rapport sur Ca-mau," 6–7, 10, 16; and Paul Moreau, "Rapport sur les cours d'eau de la presqu'île de Camau," *ER* 9 (1881): 440–41.

15. A traditional Vietnamese *dam* measured about 600 meters. See the note on measurements in appendix A.

16. Trinh Hoai Duc, *Gia Dinh Thanh Thung Chi*, 3 vols., trans. Nguyen Tao (Saigon: Nha Van Hoa, 1972), vol. 1, 94.

17. The Nguyet Giang thus became the Cai Lon at some point.

18. In 1768 a French missionary described Bassac as "for the most part Chinese, all merchants or boatmen. . . . A great many Chinese junks put in here . . . there are so many now . . . that I cannot count them. It seems to me that the number is closer to 100 than 50; they come seeking rice and sugar." Journal de M. Levavasseur, 22 Avril 1768. Archives des Missions-Étrangères de Paris [AMEP], Cochinchine vol. 744, 907–8. This document appears in *Histoire de la Mission de la Cochinchine. Documents historiques. II 1728–1771*, ed. Adrien Launay, reprint (Paris: Les Indes Savantes, 2000), 387–88, where it is dated to March.

19. Trinh Hoai Duc, *Gia Dinh Thanh Thong Chi*, vol. 1, 116.

20. There are at least three published versions available: a French one largely reorganized by Gabriel Aubaret in the early 1860s; a Vietnamese one from 1972; and a Chinese edition. The quote is from the Chinese text, kindly supplied by Li Tana, in Chen Chingho, "Annotations on the Chapter of "The Towns" in Gia Dinh Thong Chi, by Trinh Hoai Duc," *Nanyang xue bao* [Journal of the South Seas Society] 24, 12 (1956): 30. The passage illustrates the differences between the versions. The Vietnamese text only noted

"many big fish and many crocodiles," [*Gia Dinh Thanh Thong Chi*, vol. 3, 130] while Aubaret wrote: "One sees in this fortification [Long Xuyen *dao*] a great number of inns [*auberges*] of all sorts, around which are grouped seagoing junks and boats." Trinh Hoai Duc, *Gia Dinh Thung Chi. Histoire et Description de la Basse Cochinchine*, trans. G. Aubaret, reprint (Westmead, Hants.: Gregg International Publishers, 1969), 285. Local scholars probably amended the text when transcribing it.

21. Malleret, *Archéologie*, vol. I, 20.

22. Benoist, "Note sur la population de Rach-gia et de Ca-mau," 33.

23. Brière, "Rapport sur Ca-mau:" 20–21. The tax on honey and wax in Rach Gia in 1880 raised 21,030 francs. Benoist, "Note complémentaire sur le Kien-giang:" 52.

24. Brière, "Rapport sur Ca-mau," 12.

25. The precise figure was 1,559,800. A. Bouinais and A. Paulus, *L'Indo-Chine française contemporaine, Cochinchine–Cambodge* (Paris: Challamel, 1885), 549.

26. All details Moreau, "Les cours d'eau de Ca-mau:" 442; and Brière, "Rapport sur Ca-mau:" 19–20.

27. Benoist, "Note de M. Benoist, ancien inspecteur de Rach-gia, au sujet de l'exploitation d'une pêcherie de crevettes à Ca-mau," *ER* 1 (1879): 27–29.

28. Moreau, "Les cours d'eau de Ca-mau:" 441–42.

29. Trinh Hoai Duc, *La Basse Cochinchine*, 303–4; *Gia Dinh Thanh Thong Chi*, vol. 3, 40.

30. Or two *mau* per hectare.

31. These are very large holdings in a district where all other private land totaled 40 hectares, and the area under cultivation was less that 970 hectares. Nguyen Dinh Dau, *Nghien Cuu Dia Ba Trieu Nguyen, Hatien* [Cadastral Registers, Hatien Province] (Ho Chi Minh City: NXB Thanh Pho HCM, 1994), 257, 263, 274.

32. The 1836 cadastral survey found Bien Hoa, the other local salt-producing area, had only 13.2 hectares of salt marshes, giving a Cochinchinese total of 33 hectares plus Soc Trang. By 1868, the total area was 576 hectares, with former Bien Hoa accounting for 371.4 hectares (or 44 times the 1836 figure). This expansion may have partly predated colonialism, due to population growth in the eastern provinces. But far more important would have been the post-1858 disruption of the former supply of cheap salt from adjacent Binh Thuan Province, which had previously limited Bien Hoa's production. [Trinh Hoai Duc, *Gia Dinh Thanh Thong Chi*, vol. 3, 40.] Neither factor pertained in the west, yet it held one–third of the productive salt marshes (205 hectares) in 1868. From this one can calculate notionally that if Soc Trang had four times the area of salt marshes as the contiguous canton in Long Xuyen in 1836 (20 h + 80 h = 100 h), the area under production would have doubled from 1836 to 1868. Data from Langlet and Quach, *Atlas historique*, 202, 214, 242.

33. Compare *Gia Dinh Thanh Thong Chi*, vol. 3, 109–10 with Dau, *Dia Ba Hatien*, 263, 272.

34. Labussière, "Étude sur la propriété foncière rurale," 337–38.

35. Levavasseur described My Thanh in 1768 as a Chinese and Cochinchinese market gardening hamlet in good contact by river with all other important local settlements. Trinh Hoai Duc in the 1820s said it "was inhabited by a great number of Vietnamese, Chinese and Khmer" and that as well as market gardening, its people dried prawns." Journal de M. Levavasseur, 22 juillet 1768. AMEP Cochinchine,vol. 744, 939–40 and Trinh Hoai Duc, *La Basse Cochinchine*, 259, *Gia Dinh Thanh Thong Chi*, vol. 1, 96.

36. Malleret showed that none of the four commercial canals Hue chronicles claimed were dug on Gia Long's orders were new, but rather that the Vietnamese had cleared and extended former canals. *Archéologie*, I, 27–31, 78–79, 93–94, 106–07.

37. Benoist, "Note complémentaire sur le Kien-giang," 54, 56.

38. W. E. Willmott, "History and Sociology of the Chinese in Cambodia Prior to the French Protectorate," *Journal of Southeast Asian History* 7, no. 1 (1966): 24.

39. Mak Phœun, *Histoire du Cambodge de la fin du XVIe siècle au début du XVIIIe* (Paris: Ecole française d'extrême orient, 1995), 148–53.

40. This figure for deaths could be exaggerated but may reflect the size of the community. If all survivors fled, the missionary might have believed them all dead. Mak Phœun, *Histoire du Cambodge*, 323–26.

41. This checkered process was not the simple one-way movement Vietnamese historical documents assert, as Mac Phœun has shown in "La frontière entre le Cambodge et le Vietnam," 136–55.

42. In Siem Reap, Thai general Bodin in 1839 had ordered "the general massacre of all those numerous [Viets] already established" in Battambang Province, though some surviving families had finally escaped to Laos where they settled along the Mekong. A. Pavie, "Excursion dans le Cambodge et le Royaume de Siam," *ER* 7, no. 18 (1884): 405. Another early account confirms that the massacre was countrywide. Charles-Emile Bouillevaux, *Voyage dans l'Indochine, 1848–1856* (Paris: Victor Palmé, 1858), 180.

43. Willmott, "Chinese in Cambodia," 29–32.

44. Letter from M. Faulet, 3 juin 1775, quoted in Bouillevaux, *Voyage dans l'Indochine,* 227, described its people as Cantonese dressed as Ming loyalists.

45. Cited in Bouinais and Paulus, *L'Indo-Chine française contemporaine*, 499–500. However, if Aymonier's figure (106,764) was based on capitation taxes, the real number might have been quite different. Cambodian officials decided the tax rate during the triennial census according to an individual's wealth, in a range from the equivalent of ten to thirty Vietnamese *quan*. For the capitation tax see Bouinais and Paulus, *L'Indo-Chine française contemporaine*, 477.

46. For example, David P. Chandler, *A History of Cambodia*, 2nd edition (Sydney: Allen and Unwin, 1993), 100.

47. Bouillevaux, *Voyage dans l'Indochine*, 161.

48. All quotes from Henri Mouhot, *Travels in Siam, Cambodia, Laos and Annam,* unattributed reprint (Bangkok: White Lotus Press, 2000), quotes 171–73; also see 128, 262–63.

49. Cited in Willmott, "Chinese in Cambodia:" 28. Willmott thought King "mistook the large Chinese population for 'Cochin Chinese,' no doubt through unfamiliarity and perhaps because many of the Chinese had in fact migrated from Cholon." This seems unlikely: Minh Huong from Cho Lon would have looked different from other Chinese, and for my purpose here would effectively count as Vietnamese.

50. My emphasis. Bouillevaux, *Voyage dans l'Indochine*, 199–200.

51. Under Ang Duong, Cambodia had a small maritime port at Kampot. Populated by Chinese, Vietnamese, Sino-Khmer, and Cambodian women, Kampot each year attracted several European ships plus a number of small coastal traders and large Chinese junks. Mouhot, *Travels in Cambodia,* 128; Pavie, "Excursion dans le Cambodge," 470; and Bouillevaux, *Voyage dans l'Indochine*, 256.

52. Cited in Bouinais and Paulus, *L'Indo-Chine française contemporaine*, 496.

53. Bouinais and Paulus, *L'Indo-Chine française contemporaine*, 547.

54. Even as far north as Stung Treng, past Chileang, wasteful Vietnamese timber-getters typically felled all precious trees, even low-value immature specimens. A. Bonnaud, "Rapport sur une voyage de reconnaissance dans le Haut-Mekong," *ER* 9 (1881): 451.

55. Bouillevaux, *Voyage dans l'Indochine*, 199.

56. Louis de Carné, *Travels on the Mekong: Cambodia, Laos and Yunnan* (Bangkok: White Lotus, 1995), 39. The same attitude occurred among Chinese woodcutters. When precious *trac* wood was found in the Pursat Mountains in the early 1880s, so much was felled for sale in Tonkin, Canton, and Hong Kong that the price collapsed within two years. E. Prud'homme, "Excursion au Cambodia," *ER* 13 (1882): 69

57. Auguste Pavie, *Pavie Mission Exploration Work: Laos, Cambodia, Siam, Yunnan, and Vietnam*, vol. 1, trans. Walter E. J. Tipps (Bangkok: White Lotus Press, 1999), 104, 113.

58. Bouinais and Paulus, *L'Indo-Chine française contemporaine*, 496, 548, 571.

59. Bouinais and Paulus, *L'Indo-Chine française contemporaine*, 482.

60. Prud'homme, "Excursion au Cambodia:" 62–63. The problem of Chinese official suppliers dealing in stolen cattle had been noted as early as 1868. Lamant, "La frontière entre le Cambodge et le Viêtnam," 164, 170.

61. Few Viets had returned to Battambang by 1856, when the rowers of a European traveler were mistaken for an invading party and attacked at Siem Reap. A. Pavie, "Excursion dans le Cambodge et le Royaume de Siam," *ER* 7, no. 18 (1884): 405.

62. Mouhot, *Travels in Siam, Cambodia*, 262.

63. De Carné, *Travels on the Mekong*, 38.

64. Willmott, "Chinese in Cambodia," 28.

65. All details from Buchard, "Rapport sur le Grand-Lac," 250–281.

66. Buchard, "Rapport sur le Grand-Lac," 278.

67. A male employee cost 100 francs in wages and 102 francs to outfit (with a women roughly half), totaling nearly 4,300 francs to set up a fishery with hired labor, while debt slaves were very common in Cambodia at the time or others could be bought for 500–600 francs in Siam. Buchard, "Rapport sur le Grand-Lac," 251–52.

68. In 1884 Pavie found several such Viet villages in Battambang Province. Pavie, "Excursion dans le Royaume de Siam," 396.

69. There were also twelve piculs of fish fins and eighty-three piculs of fish bladders sent to China for industrial processing that year. Bouinais and Paulus, *L'Indo-Chine française contemporaine*, 549.

70. M. Badens, "Rapport sur la situation économique du Cambodge," *ER* 11, no. 26 (1886): 168.

71. In 1884 fear of these pirates actually deterred some big cargo junks from venturing onto the lake, largely because the French administrative shake-up of that year had transferred weapons' control in Phnom Penh to the Cochinchinese *régie* for indirect taxes, which had confiscated the crews' firearms en route. M. Brien, "Aperçu sur la province de Battambang," *ER* 9, no. 25 (1886): 33–34.

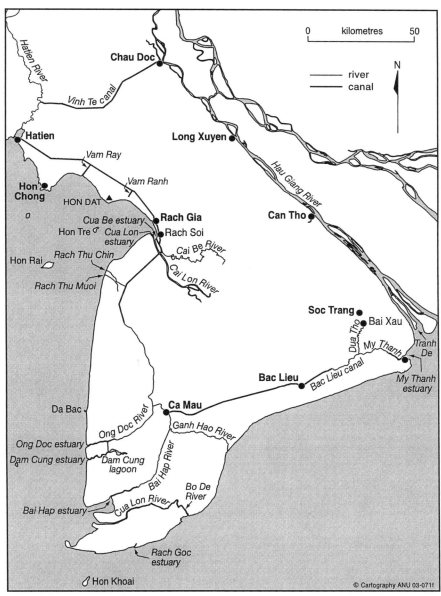

Map 6: The Bassac Area

10

The Internationalization of Chinese Revenue Farming Networks

Carl A. Trocki

A study of Chinese revenue farming networks in the late nineteenth century may not seem immediately relevant to the Water Frontier discussed by most contributors to this book. By the time the events analyzed here took place the old eighteenth-century centers of Hatien, My Tho, and Chantaburi had all become backwaters. Political and economic activities had come to focus in the large colonial cities of Singapore, Saigon, and Hong Kong or in major national capitals like Bangkok. The Water Frontier itself had been largely forgotten and Chinese economic life had, it was long thought, been thoroughly subordinated to the aims and initiatives of Europeans.

The events discussed in this chapter suggest something different was happening. On the one hand, they show the resilience of deep-seated Chinese business networks constructed across Southeast Asia and southern China while, on the other, they expose some of the fundamental strategic weaknesses of the Chinese economic position in colonial Asia. As such, this story tells us something about the long-term impact of the Water Frontier and its role in molding Asian economic life. It also tells us something about why the specific centers and personalities of the Water Frontier did not survive, and why they systematically fell victim to the inroads and pressures of expanding nation-states and colonial imperatives.

The extensive syndicate cobbled together by the protagonists of my story seems a truly bold and adventurous scheme, carried out with extraordinary skill and alacrity. Within a period of a few months a small group of fairly wealthy capitalists, all of them Fujianese Chinese of well-established Straits Chinese families, put together a business enterprise that sought to control the flows of both opium and Chinese coolie labor to and from southern China, Southeast Asia, Australia, Hawaii, and the western shores of North and South America. The fact that it all ended up in a Hong Kong law court is evidence that the grand scheme ultimately came unstuck, partly because of excessive greed and ambition among the various partners to the enterprise. It seems an appropriate concluding parable on the manner in which Chinese economic actors have dealt with the risks and opportunities of Asian economic life.

Basically, this chapter examines a lawsuit that was filed in Hong Kong's supreme court in 1880.[1] The testimony reveals a tale of ambition and enterprise among a group of Southeast Asian Chinese who, it seems, were attempting to create a monopoly over the global opium traffic. At the same time, it shows the colonial governments of Southeast Asia at a moment of major change as they sought ways to meet a threat from Chinese merchant cliques. The threat, as they saw it, grew out of Chinese control of the revenue farming concessions that were an important institution in every colony. Of these, the opium farming concessions were the most lucrative and thus, the most problematic.

While it is well established that every city in Southeast Asia and the colonial areas of India and China drew significant proportions of their taxes from opium revenue farms, it is also clear that fairly similar systems of operation seemed to exist in all of these places.[2] Whether in Penang or Singapore under the British, Batavia or Medan under the Dutch, Saigon under the French, Bangkok under the Chakkri kings, Manila under the Spanish, or even Hong Kong under yet another British colonial government, by the 1870s, virtually all of the opium farms of colonial Asia were operated in quite the same fashion. Most were auctioned off at regular intervals, usually every three years. Most gave the right to manufacture smokable opium (*chandu*) from raw opium to a group of Chinese capitalists who also controlled a distribution system and a security force. These Chinese, of course, mobilized the requisite financial resources to support the enterprise. They formally contracted with the local government to pay a monthly rental for the privilege of running the farm. Perhaps this regional uniformity is not so extraordinary, but given the well-known differences in indigenous cultures, governments, languages, and economies, not to mention differences between European colonial systems, the question of such similarity does call for investigation.

The incident under study here brings the revenue farms of Southeast Asia and China into sharp focus for one historical moment. It allows us to see the contours of the system and makes it possible to get a snapshot of some significant aspects of Southeast Asia's colonial society as of 1880. Although the events reported in these documents occurred in Hong Kong, their relevance to Vietnam as well as other parts of Southeast Asia is quite important.

One clear factor is that many of the opium farmers in Southeast Asia were not only acquainted with each other, but also did business among themselves. Trading relations between Chinese in Singapore, Penang, Bangkok, Saigon, and Hong Kong appear to have been well established during the earlier years of the nineteenth century. This may help to explain why opium farming was a more or less unified, Chinese-dominated system of interlocked networks that stretched from Burma to Shanghai and Sydney. The second circumstance is that by 1880, a group of these wealthy and powerful Chinese merchants, or *taukeh* as they were often called, attempted to combine their enterprises in an effort to monopolize a major share of the opium trade in Southeast Asia, China, and even the Pacific Ocean.

A series of articles in the Hong Kong newspaper, the *Daily Press*, reproduces the testimony given in a case before the colony's supreme court in December 1880 that go some way toward showing the contours of a truly extraordinary combination of interests. Near the end of 1880 a dispute arose among the members to the Hong Kong opium farm, and a number of the principal shareholders led by one Ko Leong Yuen filed suit against one Ban Hap and others. Ban Hap was the principal shareholder and the manager of the Man Wo Fung Company, which had recently taken over the Hong Kong opium farms. The suit was a rather complicated affair and most of the details are not necessary for this discussion, but some of them do give us a look at the contemporary status of the farms, not only in Hong Kong but elsewhere in the region.

The Man Wo Fung Company took over the Hong Kong farms at the beginning of 1879. An article in the *China Mail* announced, with some fanfare, the establishment of the new farming syndicate.[3] Governor John Pope Hennessy was praised for his skill in outwitting the Chinese:

> There is one thing in which the Chinese have discovered the Governor to be their match—in diplomacy; and when this quality is exercised in the true interests of the Colony, it gives us pleasure to note His Excellency's success . . . it has been reserved for the present Governor to secure a higher price for the Opium Farm in Hong Kong than has ever yet been obtained for that monopoly.

The article further lauded the governor's accomplishment at getting this high price ($205,000 annually) for the farm, by unrolling the usual litany of stereotypes of Chinese business behavior.

> If half be true that we have heard on the subject, the sea of intrigue, falsehood, overreachings, and finesse that has been successfully waded through by the head of the Government on this occasion has been wide and deep. As we have previously stated, this was to have been expected. When Chinese have a famous opportunity of making money, or when they are likely to lose hold of a favorable means of doing so, all the powers of cunning and chicanery of which the Celestial nature is capable are called into the most active operation.[4]

Hennessey was no doubt happy to take credit for having bested the Chinese at their own game, and thus reinforcing his credibility as the colonial executive. Unfortunately, by the end of the following year after only one year of operation, the syndicate that had taken the farms had collapsed and its various principals were before the supreme court.

The Rise of the Man Wo Fung Company

The filing of the suit in December 1880 and the testimony that arose out of it give a somewhat different picture of Hennessy's great success. They also expose a vision of "Celestial cunning" that is at once far more subtle and yet far less acute, than had been imagined by the *China Mail*. Despite everyone's cleverness, the testimony that was recorded in successive editions of the *Daily Press* between 30 November 1880 and 8 December 1880 shows that some serious blunders had been made both by the Chinese and the British.[5] As a result, the farm had encountered serious financial difficulties and had been losing money throughout the first year of its operation. According to the plaintiffs, the continued losses were part of the reason for their suit. Although the full rationale for their action was somewhat difficult to fathom, they were certainly trying to dissolve the Man Wo Fung.

The individual who headed the Man Wo Fung was not a Hong Kong Chinese; in fact, he was not even a Cantonese. Rather, he was the head of a syndicate that apparently was made up partly of a group of Fujianese that had controlled the opium farms for Cochinchina for over a decade and a group of Straits-born Chinese from Penang and Singapore. The former had recently added the monopoly for opium sales in Cambodia to its list of Indochinese franchises. The latter group seems to have been involved in a well-established syndicate from Penang that had recently taken over the Singapore farms. It was clear that the Man Wo Fung Company's managers were in control of the Saigon opium farms, the farms of Singapore, and possibly those of Penang. Ban Hap had created the Cochinchinese farming syndicate and he also dominated the Hong Kong company. Another key individual was one Tan King Sing, a Singapore Chinese. Whether or not the same incorporated body controlled all these revenue farms, or whether there was simply a series of interlocking partnerships, is not at all clear. The *Daily Press*, however, lists Tan as involved in all of the various groups. At the Hong Kong trial, Tan was the major witness for the Ban Hap group, and Ban Hap himself never testified.[6]

In Hong Kong this collaborative effort ran into considerable difficulty, and it was not long before the Singapore and Saigon companies also came unstuck as well. In his testimony, Tan King Sing claimed that in Hong Kong they had lost money because the previous farming syndicate had sabotaged their operations. The losing syndicate had sought to undermine their enemies by adopting two strategies. First, they prepared an excess of *chandu* and dumped it on the market at fairly low prices in the last few weeks prior to the handover of the farms in 1879. Secondly, the former Hong Kong syndicate, a company known as the Sun Yee Company, had acquired the farming rights for the nearby Portuguese settlement of Macao where they could legally manufacture smokable opium and sell it to smugglers who could bring it to Hong Kong. Finally, since the Sun Yee Company had been the previous farmers, they still controlled three well-known trademarks or *chaps* for different brands of *chandu*. These had a great deal of popularity in the Hong Kong market and made it much easier for the smuggled product to outsell the legal opium of the farm.[7]

In his testimony, Tan King Sing claimed that as an outsider, he was ignorant of local conditions. The smuggling from Macao surprised him because he had never heard that there was another farm in Macao. His comment seems somewhat disingenuous since dumping and smuggling from nearby territories were standard ploys that opposing opium farming syndicates used against one another. The Singapore farmer was regularly pressured when his competitors gained control of the nearby Johor or Riau farms.[8] James Rush has shown that similar tactics were common in Java.[9] It is hard to believe that someone like Tan, who had been a member of the Singapore group, did not understand the facts of geography and their implications for the security of the farm. It was the business of opium farmers to know these things. It is more probable that the Ban Hap syndicate had somehow miscalculated their ability to manage smugglers and to take control of the three trademarks in question. Certainly, much of the succeeding testimony turned on control of the trademarks.[10]

The importance of brand names and trademarks is a matter that is rarely mentioned in most of the other sources on the nineteenth-century opium trade. Nonetheless, China was a highly developed consumer economy well before the nineteenth century, and brand names had been in use since as early as the eleventh century. By the Ming period, brand names were widely used throughout China's consumer economy.[11] It should not come as a surprise that a commodity such as opium should be differentiated by its brand, particularly since there were so many general varieties of raw opium and many different tastes and qualities of the smokable product. Such an identifying characteristic would have been an important consideration when capitalists calculated their prospects in markets where they might not have a monopoly.

When he realized the farm was in trouble Ban Hap tried to reach some sort of agreement with the Cantonese owners of the Sun Yee Company Ban Hap sent one of his Cantonese partners to negotiate with them, but initially they could reach no agreement. Sun Yee was in an advantageous position and could sabotage the efforts of the Saigon/Singapore interlopers with impunity. Moreover, they had discovered a loophole in the Hong Kong laws that enabled them to ship their opium directly to Hong Kong on French vessels. Despite these difficulties, ultimately Ban Hap was able to reach an accommodation with some of his rivals. As it turned out, Sun Yee Company was composed of two other companies: the Yan Wo and the Chap Sing. By the end of 1879, these two groups had fallen into dispute among themselves for reasons that are not clear. As a result, Ban Hap was able to step in and make a separate deal with Yan Wo and brought them into partnership with the Man Wo Fung. As it happened, Yan Wo also controlled the three desirable *chaps* that they brought with them into the deal. This move made the Man Wo Fung much stronger and now enabled them to expand their operations even further, which may have been their reason for venturing into the Hong Kong farms in the first place.[12]

If we look at relative values, the Hong Kong opium farm was really small potatoes, worth only $205,000 per year. In 1879, the Singapore farm had been auctioned to Koh Seang Tat of Penang (apparently Tan King Sing's partner) for $600,000 per year,[13] and the farms of Cochinchina had been acquired by Ban Hap for over $2 million.[14] Despite its relatively low value, the Hong Kong franchise held yet another advantage. Hong Kong was the major port of departure for Chinese emigrants to the "Gold Mountain," or the gold mines of California. In addition to the United States, it was also the jumping off point for migrants bound for Hawaii and Australia.

In these distant markets Yan Wo's famous three *chaps* had also established a reputation, and the company was, it seems, exporting large quantities of prepared opium. We should probably assume that gaining access to this vast and growing market as well as to the *chaps* was one of the aims of the Man Wo Fung Company in the first place. Control of the Hong Kong farms would give control over the prepared opium exported from Hong Kong. This would also give privileged access to the China market itself. Successful control of the Hong Kong nexus could have made Ban Hap and his group one of the largest business enterprises in Asia with near monopoly control over all the opium moving between Singapore, San Francisco, Sydney, and perhaps even Shanghai. The lawsuit, however, was not the only problem for Ban Hap and his friends, their empire was already coming under increasing pressure from other quarters, and in fact, it collapsed the very next year in 1881. The big syndicate never happened, but it seems that some Southeast Asian Chinese had at least already come to see how it could be done.

The Consolidation of Revenue Farming Syndicates

The history of Ban Hap and his syndicate seems to have been similar to that of other opium farming groups in Southeast Asia. A process had been under way in the region for several decades that saw the creation of constellations of revenue farming syndicates around the various capital cities. Normally, these were based on concurrent control of one or several of the local economies. For instance, in Singapore the farming syndicates had grown up around the pepper and gambier industry. By the 1840s, two mercantile factions in Singapore had established control of both the pepper and gambier economy and the opium and spirit farming system which fed off of it. This was a natural combination. The pepper and gambier industry produced marketable commodities and employed large numbers of Chinese laborers. The laborers, in turn, consumed provisions, clothing and tools, as well as opium, spirits, and other taxable products. They were also users of pawnbroking, gambling, and prostitution farms, all of which were controlled by the same group of merchants who financed and exported their products. Beginning in the 1840s, this economic system had spread out from its original bases in Bentan Island and Singapore into Johor, Melacca, and the other islands of the Riau Archipelago. Since each of these areas represented a separate political or administrative jurisdiction, it meant that there were always offshore bases from which rival syndicates could launch smuggling operations in order to sabotage the farms of Singapore. Each administrative district had its own revenue farms that were let separately. In the long run, it was necessary for one group to control all of them, and thus unify all the local revenue farms, if they were to preempt the threat of smuggling and sabotage.

In Singapore, this process of consolidation led to the creation of the so-called Great Opium Syndicate in 1870 under a trio of powerful *taukehs*. They set up a combination that controlled all of the areas of the pepper and gambier industry: Singapore, Riau, Johor, and Melaka. They combined the interests of the largest mercantile factions, not only in Singapore, but also in the adjacent areas and simultaneously collected taxes for the British, the Dutch, and the maharaja of Johor.[15] The pattern of association between revenue farming and the pepper and gambier industry in and around Singapore was reflected throughout Southeast Asia.

A process of consolidation of revenue farming systems around capital cities had been in progress throughout the decades of the 1860s and 1870s. In Saigon, Ban Hap and his clique of Fujian merchants had created a similar cluster of adjoining jurisdictions, extending itself into Cambodia[16] and, one must assume, into neighboring regions still controlled from Hue. Ban Hap had, in fact, already been in business in Saigon before the French even arrived and the Nguyen archives report dealings between him and the court as early as 1865.[17] The connections between this center and the Siamese territories is less clear, but it would not be surprising to learn that at least some of the farms of towns around the Gulf of Thailand were financed from Saigon.

The major difference between the Singapore farms and those of Cochinchina was in the nature of the local economy. Whereas Singapore's system was built largely on Chinese labor and the pepper and gambier economy, that of Cochinchina was somewhat more diverse including both Chinese and indigenous consumers with interests in a variety of endeavors including rice, salt, sugar, indigo, pepper, and other commodities produced by Vietnamese and Cambodian peasants. In this respect, the farms of Cochinchina more closely resembled those of Batavia and Bangkok, where as James Rush[18] and Constance Wilson[19] have shown, similar processes of expansion and consolidation had been at work during the 1870s. In each area, opium had come to make up 20 to 30 percent of the entire revenue.

A final area in need of attention is the Straits Settlement of Penang. Here the general configuration was somewhat similar to the situation in Singapore, however the farms of Penang itself were less important than those of the surrounding territories. In the neighboring states of what was to become British Malaya, in the Dutch-controlled plantation zone of eastern Sumatra, and in the provinces of southern Siam large populations of Chinese laborers were at work in tin mines and plantations. The expanding activities of Penang's merchants brought them into all of these areas.

Penang, however, seems to have been unique in that it was both a center from which capital and opium radiated as well as one to which other powerful Chinese gravitated. Some Chinese mercantile groups first took control of the island's revenue farms and then moved out of Penang into the tin-mining areas of Perak, Selangor, and the Siamese states. Others established themselves first in a hinterland and then formed a base in the British port. Jennifer Cushman[20] has written of the activities of the Khaw syndicate of Penang and Ranong, which although always maintaining a base in Penang, really built their fortunes in Siam before asserting their influence in Penang. Michael Godley has described the career of Thio Thiau Siat (Chang Pi Shih), who began his career in Sumatra and later moved to Penang and Singapore.[21] The activities of these groups was more apparent however in the 1890s than in the 1870s. Penang, however, was already an important center by the 1870s. It appears that the rapid expansion of the tin industry had left the Chinese entrepreneurs of that city with an excess of capital and this circumstance seems to have had a rather sudden and unsettling impact throughout Southeast Asia.

The Internationalization of Chinese Capital

So far as one can tell, the international expansion of Chinese capital, from one major colonial port city to another, occurred rather rapidly around the end of the 1870s for an apparent variety of reasons. The situation prior to this time appeared rather stable. In each of the major centers of Southeast Asia, a cluster of opium-farming syndicates had been more or less unified by one major company, which often represented a coalition of the major Chinese merchants of that city. The region could be seen as a collection of discrete systems which, while they may have overridden local political and administrative boundaries, were focused on the Chinese mercantile clique or cliques of that city: e.g., Singapore, Penang, Batavia, Bangkok, Saigon, Hong Kong, etc.

While it would be naive to suggest that these were not already interconnected in some ways, it seems that the various cliques in each colonial city already had relationships with members of cliques in other cities. Some of these links would have been of long standing, others perhaps were more tenuous, but clearly there were prior connections before 1879 that would have facilitated more extensive collaborations such as those now under study. Whatever these connections were before 1879, they did not override the influence of the local cliques.

Each opium-farming system was focused on its own local base. In each area, it appears that a kind of partnership had grown up between the leaders of the Chinese community and the colonial governments. The Chinese collected taxes, controlled most of the migrant groups of Chinese laborers, and developed the local economy. Colonial authorities provided protection for the Chinese magnates and afforded them an environment in which to grow wealthy. In the meantime, they were content to allow the Chinese to generally manage their own affairs. These arrangements had developed in the laissez-faire days of the early nineteenth century and had come, for many, to represent the established order of things.

The situation however did not provide the same level of satisfaction for all concerned. Colonial governments, in particular, were growing impatient with the system. In the first place, the fact that Chinese cliques had reached certain agreements among themselves, while it generally assured a level of social peace, meant that competition for the opium farms had been substantially reduced. In Singapore, for instance, the annual income from the opium farms during the 1870s had only increased by about $40,000: from $360,000 in 1867 to an average of $400,000 in 1877–1879. In Saigon, the value of the farms had actually begun to decline toward the end of the 1870s. In Hong Kong too, the annual rent for the opium farm had stood at just above $100,000 before the arrival of Ban Hap and Tan King Sing. There they nearly doubled the value of the monopoly. The same thing had also happened in the same year in Singapore, when Koh Saeng Tat came from Penang and took over the opium farm of Singapore for $600,000.[22]

What had happened in these places? In both places not only had the rent nearly doubled, but new farming syndicates had appeared from out of town. This was a phenomenon that seems to have had no precedent in the region. Significant increases in the opium farm rental had taken place in the past, but these rises were usually the result of local competition. This was the first time in which the competitors were newcomers to the local economy. If the writer in the *China Mail* was correct, some of the credit for the new state of affairs should go to the colonial governors of Hong Kong and the Straits Settlements. It appears that they went shopping.

Realizing that all of the local competition had either been absorbed or eliminated while the value of the farms had attained levels that prohibited another local group from arising, they had to find competition on the outside. Governor Archibald Anson of the Straits Settlements had spent an earlier tour of duty as the lieutenant governor of Penang in 1865–1877 and he certainly must have become well acquainted with Koh Saeng Tat during that period. Possibly Governor Hennessy of Hong Kong established communications with Ban Hap or Tan King Sing, when he was administering the British settlement of Labuan in the early 1870s, prior to his stint in the Bahamas.[23] He may also have worked through some of the Hong Kong merchants who later became partners in the Man Wo Fung Company

More was at stake in these maneuverings than simple revenue. It was clear that these Chinese cliques had gained a great deal of power, not only over the local economy but, by extension, over the local populations. At a time when colonial governments were coming under more direct control from the metropoles and when there was an increasing insistence on rationalization and more direct control, the continuation of independent, informal power networks run by Chinese cliques seemed an uncomfortable, if not intolerable situation. The aim of the new generation of colonial administrators was to seize back, or more correctly to acquire from the Chinese (since the Europeans had never actually had it), control over the local populations. They realized that the local Chinese mercantile cliques had gained significant social and political power through opium addiction, indebtedness, and the influence of their security forces, not to mention their power over the colony's tax base. It seems that the appearance of these new competitors had much to do with the new administrative agenda of the colonial governments. It should be noted, however, that there is little direct evidence in British sources to document such a strategy by the colonial governments.[24] Nonetheless, the French, at least, did record their misgivings about the power of Chinese revenue farmers in their colonial possessions.[25]

On the other hand, it seems that at least some Chinese had greater ambitions than the colonial authorities gave them credit for. It is possible that Governor Hennessy expected to have more control over Ban Hap and Tan King Sing, since they were outsiders and since they needed his influence more than the local Cantonese cliques in the Sun Yee Company. The problem was, however, that the Sun Yee Company still maintained its power base in Hong Kong, and it would be necessary for the outsiders to somehow defeat them on the streets that they already controlled. As it turned out, this was also a problem in Singapore, where the old "Great Syndicate" did not accept defeat easily. It would be even more surprising if Hennessey had been aware, prior to the suit, that the control of certain trademarks and access to the opium markets of the North American and Australian goldfields was a motivating force for the new opium syndicate.

The Chinese mercantile groups in the colonial port cities were well aware of the greater world around them and had already extended their networks into the global economy that was being created by European colonialism. Chinese merchants of Singapore had been dealing with the merchants of Saigon well before the arrival of the French, and these connections grew during the first two decades of colonial control, despite the perceived decline in British trade at the same time. One reason that Ban Hap never testified at the trial in Hong Kong was because he was always traveling. If he was not in Saigon, then he was in Xiamen or some other city on the China coast looking after his interests in those places.[26] Similar Chinese networks extended throughout the region, and the Chinese not only profited from colonial advances, they actually made many of them possible.

If the shifts in colonial policy toward the Chinese in Singapore and Hong Kong in 1879 provided the initiative for Chinese merchants to move their capital out of Penang and risk it in the unfamiliar circumstances of other colonies, the same may not be true of Saigon and Cochinchina. The writer of the *China Mail* makes an interesting comment. He seems to have been unaware of Ban Hap, but he was familiar with Tan King Sing, whom he said, "now farms the preparation of the drug in Singapore, and the Straits, in Saigon and in Hongkong."[27] If accurate, this indicates that Tan King Sing had been a partner of Koh Saeng Tat in taking over the farms of Singapore, but also must have held an interest in the farms of Penang, although the involvement of Koh in the Penang syndicate at that time is not entirely clear. Moreover, it must be assumed that Tan, and perhaps Koh, had already moved into a partnership with Ban Hap in Saigon. If that was the case, then it is possible that the tin-rich *taukehs* of Penang were already on the move, even without the blandishments of aggressive colonial governors.

It is doubtful that the French authorities in Saigon would have invited Tan King Sing to join Ban Hap, in fact one may wonder if they were even aware that such a partnership even existed.

This information thus suggests that the Chinese opium farmers of the Straits Settlements and Cochinchina were already seeking to consolidate a regionwide amalgamation of opium farms, covering not only Southeast Asia and the China coast, but also stretching across the Pacific and following the Chinese migration wherever it went. This is all the more extraordinary when we consider that most of the business of creating this combination seems to have taken place within the rather short space of two or three years, much of it actually in 1879 alone! It is probable that this joint venture was more plural than singular in nature and more segmented than unified. Even today, Chinese have a tendency to operate through relatively autonomous locally based establishments rather than through tightly organized and hierarchical structures. In each place there was a separate company, often managed by local partners, and international connections were limited to infusions of capital from outside and the involvement of external managers, at least enough so that they could protect their investments and repatriate their profits. As a result of this sort of organization, it is rather difficult to establish who was working with whom. Sometimes alliances in one place coexisted with competition in others.

One important partner in the Man Wo Fung in Hong Kong was Cheang Hong Lim of Singapore. He had been part of the trio that controlled the so-called Great Syndicate about which I have written elsewhere. Ironically, Koh Saeng Tat and his partners had pushed his syndicate out of Singapore. We should assume that Tan King Sing was one of them. During 1880, Cheang and his son-in-law together with others involved in the former Singapore syndicate were busy trying to sabotage the opium farm controlled by Koh and Tan. At the same time, however, they were part of the very same syndicate in the Hong Kong farms; of course, they were also partners in the Singapore farms as well.[28] It is no wonder that the colonial authorities were frequently mystified by Chinese business dealings.

This was apparently not the only attempt to gain monopoly control over the opium trade of the region. The following year, 1881, Li Hongzhang, the Chinese statesman, memorialized the throne proposing that a Chinese company be chartered with a capital of $20 million to buy up all opium to be exported to China.[29] The instigator of this scheme was a Cantonese, Ho Hsien-ch'ih. His name does not appear among those in the suit discussed here, but he may easily have been connected to one of the Hong Kong companies.[30] As Spence points out, these were very wealthy men and in each of the colonies they had come to appreciate the power that their wealth had created. Clearly, the time had come when some Chinese in the "fraternity" of international opium farmers that had come into existence by 1880, saw that an areawide monopoly of either the opium trade or the opium farms, or perhaps both, was a possibility.

The End of the Affair

It is not clear how the trial ended. Whether or not Ban Hap succeeded in maintaining the Man Wo Fung in Hong Kong, he ultimately fell victim to the rationalizing ambitions of the French colonial authorities. In 1881, the French conducted a series of hearings, which have been reported by Groeneveldt. His document formed the basis for studies by Dumarest and others on the opium farms of Cochinchina. Ultimately, the French decided to abolish the farming system and to create the first operable Southeast Asian government-run opium monopoly.[31] Testimony in the hearings commented on the "virtual stranglehold" which the Chinese merchants, in particular the opium farmers, held over the retail and wholesale trade of Vietnam. This included rice, opium, and even French commodities. Ban Hap, himself, was the object of considerable comment for the system that he had created. His distribution system was based on a central warehouse in each of the three provinces his company controlled. Extending out from this was a network of opium dealerships in each village and small market. The opium shops also offered credit to the local people, but on fairly exorbitant terms. Local Vietnamese officials were ready to vote against the Chinese opium farmers in an alliance with French officials and merchants.

While the French were concerned about Chinese power, they do not seem to have been overly concerned about the extent of the Chinese networks around them. In many respects, cities like Saigon and Bangkok were important complements to colonial port cities like Singapore and Hong Kong. The two former cities were major centers of large Southeast Asian states and each housed major rice-milling and rice-exporting businesses. Certainly many Singapore merchants owned rice mills in Saigon, and probably some had been there since before the French takeover of Cochinchina. Individuals such as Khoo Cheng Tiong of Singapore and his son Khoo Teck Saeng were known to own large rice mills in Saigon and to play a major role in the trade between Singapore and Saigon. Tan Kim Cheng, an important Singapore merchant, owned rice mills in both Saigon and Siam.

As a Fujian trader, Ban Hap most certainly had long-standing relations with other merchants from his part of China, such as those who dominated the trade of Singapore and Penang. It is instructive that the partners that can be identified in the syndicate involved here were all members of established Straits-born/Fujian families.[32] Cheang Hong Lim and his son-in-law Lim Kwee Eng were from old "baba" families in Singapore, and Koh Saeng Tat and his Penang partner Foo Tye Sin were likewise connected.[33] It is probable that Tan King Sing had similar connections, but it has been difficult to find additional information about him.

In 1883 the Cochinchinese Colonial Council abolished the opium farms and established the *Régie Directe*, a government-run monopoly. However, even before this occurred, Ban Hap lost the Saigon farms and was reduced to smuggling.[34] But the French move to establish a government monopoly was not as successful as they had hoped. It proved impossible for Frenchmen actually to manage the enterprise and, as Nankoe makes clear, they ended up hiring, or contracting with, many of the same individuals who had formerly run the opium farms. Chinese continued to manage the day-to-day affairs of the new monopoly and, despite these changes, or perhaps because of them, profits were generally quite modest and never lived up to expectations. Smuggling continued in Cochinchina and later it was even worse in Tonkin. Nevertheless, the process of colonial oversight in the opium business had been initiated.

As time passed, colonial authorities became more familiar with the operations of the opium production and distribution system and it became possible to create more reliable colonial police and customs forces to guard the monopoly. Within another decade, the Dutch adapted the French system to Java and established their own monopoly, which was, in fact, far more successful than that of the French. Early in the twentieth century, the British and Siamese too, eliminated their farms and created government monopolies and opium farming ceased to be a Chinese-controlled business. In the years between 1883 and 1909, however, Chinese capitalists continued to move their money at will around Southeast Asia, and despite attempts to control the Chinese economy, it expanded to both the concern and profit of the various colonial establishments. The move toward internationalization of Chinese capital was largely a successful one. Although the actual capitalists involved may not have achieved their grander ambitions of breaking away from or out of the restrictions of colonial rule, they were able to regularly transgress the increasing maze of colonial borders and administrative divisions.

Notes

1. I am grateful to Li Tana for bringing these documents to my attention and for providing me with copies of her research materials relating to this case.

2. *The Rise and Fall of Revenue Farming: Business Elites and the Emergence of the Modern State in Southeast Asia*, ed. John Butcher and Howard Dick (London: St. Martin's Press, 1993), vol. 1.

3. *China Mail*, 17 January 1879 [herafter *CM*].

4. *CM*, 17 January 1879.

5. *Daily Press*, 2 December, 1880 [hereafter *DP*].

6. It is quite difficult to establish the identity of members of most revenue farming companies. These groups often included as many as twenty or thirty individuals and perhaps two or three principle directors or partners. Different sources may therefore give different names. For instance, Singapore sources for this period indicate that Koh Saeng Tat of Penang held the Singapore farms between 1879 and 1882, and no Singapore sources mention Tan King. See Carl Trocki, *Opium and Empire: Chinese Society in Colonial Singapore 1800–1910* (Ithaca: New York, Cornell University Press, 1990); Carl Trocki, "The Collapse of Singapore's Great Syndicate," in *The Rise and Fall of Revenue Farming*, ed. John Butcher and Howard Dick (London: St. Martin's Press, 1993), vol. 1, 166–81. By contrast, reports in the Hong Kong *China Mail* and the *Daily Press* only name Tan King Sing as the head of the Singapore syndicate.

7. *DP*, 1 December 1880.

8. Carl Trocki, "The Rise of Singapore's Great Opium Syndicate, 1840–1886," *Journal of Southeast Asian Studies* 18 (1987): 58–80; Trocki, *Opium and Empire*.

9. James Rush, *Opium to Java: Revenue Farming and Chinese Enterprise in Colonial Indonesia* (Ithaca: Cornell University Press, 1990), 70–89.

10. It may seem odd, but this is the first mention I have found to indicate that *chandu* was being marketed under brand names in nineteenth century Asia. Perhaps in the other European colonies where opium was sold locally and was under the farmer's monopoly, brands may have been superfluous. In Hong Kong, however, where *chandu* was manufactured for more open and thus more competitive markets such as those in China, the United States, and Australia, brands were needed to attract and hold consumers.

11. Gary Hamilton and Chi-kong Lai 1989. "Consumerism without Capitalism: Consumption and Brand Names in Late Imperial China," in *The Social Economy of Consumption*, ed. Henry J. Rutz and Benjamin S. Orlove (New York and London: The University Press of America, 1989), 253–79.

12. *DP*, 1 December 1880

13. Trocki, "The Collapse of Singapore's Great Syndicate," 166–81.

14. Hakien Nankoe, Jean-Claude Gerlus; Martin J. Murray, "The Origins of the Opium Trade and the Opium Regies in Colonial Indochina," in *The Rise and Fall of Revenue Farming*, ed. John Butcher and Howard Dick (London: St. Martin's Press, 1993), vol. 1, 182–95.

15. Trocki, "The Collapse of Singapore's Great Syndicate," 166–81.

16. Nankoe et al., "Opium Regies in Colonial Indochina," 182–95.

17. Personal communication, Li Tana.

18. Rush, *Opium to Java*, 17–30.

19. Constance Wilson, "Revenue Farming, Economic Development and Government Policy during the Early Bangkok Period, 1830–1892," in *The Rise and Fall of Revenue Farming*, ed. John Butcher and Howard Dick (London: St. Martin's Press, 1993), vol. 1, 142–65.

20. Jennifer Cushman, *Family and State: The Formation of a Sino–Thai Tin-mining Dynasty, 1797–1932*, ed. Craig Reynolds (Singapore: Oxford University Press, 1991); Michael Godley, *Mandarin Capitalists from Nanyang: Overseas Chinese Enterprise in the Modernization of China, 1893–1911* (Cambridge: Cambridge University Press, 1981).

21. Michael Godley, "Thio Thiau Siat's Network," in *The Rise and Fall of Revenue Farming*, ed. John Butcher and Howard Dick (London: St. Martin's Press, 1993), vol. 1, 262–66. Jennifer Cushman and Michael Godley, "The Khaw Concern," in *The Rise and Fall of Revenue Farming*, ed. Butcher and Dick, Vol. 1, 267–71.

22. Trocki, "The Collapse of Singapore's Great Syndicate," 171–72.

23. Sir Archibald Anson, *About Myself and Others* (London: John Murray, 1920), 313.

24. Surprising as it seems, my extensive searches in the CO 273 series for Malaya and Singapore, and among other available sources from the nineteenth century, have uncovered no internal policy documents discussing such issues as government strategies for opium farming or anything similar. Apparently little or no administrative documentation exists concerning relations between British colonial governments and revenue farmers.

25. W. P. Groeneveldt, *Procès verbaux du Conseil Colonial* (Saigon: Conseil colonial de la Cochinchine, 1881), 50, 57–59.

26. *DP*, 1 December 1880.

27. *CM*, 17 October 1879.

28. *DP*, 30 November 1880.

29. Hosea Ballou Morse, *The International Relations of the Chinese Empire,* volume 3, *The Period of Submission* (London: Longmans, Green, and Company, 1918), 385.

30. Jonathan Spence, "Opium Smoking in Ch'ing China," in *Conflict and Control in Late Imperial China*, ed. Fredrick Wakeman Jr. and Carolyn Grant (Berkeley and Los Angeles: University of California Press, 1975), 165.

31. Chantal Descours-Gatin, *Quand l'opium finançait la colonisation en Indochine: L'elaboration de la régie générale de l'opium (1860–1914)*, vol. 1 (Paris: Editions l'Harmattan, 1992); Jacques Dumarest, "Les Monopoles de l'opium et du sel en Indochine," Doctorat en Droit, Université de Lyon, Faculté de Droit, 1938; Groeneveldt, *Procès verbaux du Conseil Colonial*; Nankoe et al., "The Origins of the Opium Trade," 182–95.

32. *Twentieth Century Impressions of British Malaya*, ed. Arnold Wright (London: Lloyds Greater Britain Publishing Company Ltd., 1907), 705.

33. Song Ong Siang, *Hundred Years History of the Chinese in Singapore*, reprint (Singapore: University of Malaya Press, 1967), 168–70.

34. Nankoe et al., "The Origins of the Opium Trade," 191–92.

Appendix A

A "Coastal Route" from the Lower Mekong Delta to Terengganu

Geoff Wade

The route partly translated here is one of six detailed in *Xiem-la-quoc Lo-Trinh Tap-luc* ("Collected Routes to the Country of Siam"). This text, dating from about 1810, is remarkable for two main reasons. First, unlike earlier Arab and Chinese routiers for Southeast Asia, this collection provides highly detailed directions and information about six different routes by land and sea that connected the ports, estuaries, islands, and settlements of mainland Southeast Asia. Second, and even more unusual, the text itself was compiled by Vietnamese court officials for the first Nguyen king, Gia Long (r. 1802–1819), who was a man of considerable personal knowledge of this same region from his years in Siamese exile during the 1780s. It is the earliest such Vietnamese text on record.

While the map that formed part of the original book of descriptions has unfortunately been lost, the text and accompanying memorial remained extant. They came to the attention of that fine pioneering scholar of traditional Vietnam, the late Professor Chen Chingho, in Hue in 1959. Immediately aware of the value of these itineraries, he later arranged for his annotated edition of them to be published by the New Asia Research Institute of the Chinese University of Hong Kong in 1966.[1] The abridged English translation that follows is based on this work, as is the suggested identification of some of the places mentioned within.

The coastal route described in this appendix comprises an estuary-by-estuary sailing guide for a route that began in the Mekong Delta and followed the coast to Cambodia and the Gulf of Thailand before turning east down the Malay

Peninsular and subsequently up its west coast to Phuket. It gives information necessary for safe navigation while also recording local products and economic activities. Interestingly, the compilers never located places within specific territorial jurisdictions, only noting the ethnicity of any resident officials. This surely suggests that the mariners who had provided the original information preferred to frequent smaller ports lacking the customs and imposts of large trading centers like Saigon or Bangkok. The extra detail about Hatien, a free port throughout the eighteenth century, supports this interpretation.

This translation is a new abridged version that gives place names, distances, and depth measures in modern equivalents wherever possible.[2] Some details, including certain small, unidentified places, have been excluded. The itinerary ceases at Terengganu in modern Malaysia.

A "Coastal Water Route" from the Lower Mekong Delta to Terengganu

The route proceeds from the Ba That mouth,[3] where the estuary is about two *lý* [1,200 m] wide and about eight *xích* [3.5 m] deep. On both sides are woods and marshes. Take a bearing of 240 degrees along a winding coastline for one watch [two hours] to reach the My Thanh estuary. It is about 25 *tam* [55 m] wide and four *xích* [1.8 m] deep. Both sides are covered in forests and marshes. Eastward to sea, about one *lý* [600 m] out, is a mud-bank about two *lý* in length and breadth. . . . At high tide, it is covered and cannot be seen. . . .

From My Thanh, take a bearing of 210 degrees along a forested and marshy coast. The land is saline and the people rely on fishing for a living. After traveling four watches one arrives at Ganh Hao. The estuary is about 30 *tam* [66 m] wide, and four *xích* [1.8 m] deep. Its sides are covered in woods, marshes and coconut palms.

From Ganh Hao, on a bearing of 210 degrees, go along a forested and marshy coastline for two watches to Bo De. The estuary is about 30 *tam* [66 m] wide and four *xích* [1.8 m] deep. Both sides are covered in forests, marshes, and coconut palms. From Bo De, take a bearing of 225 degrees. After one watch along a forested and marshy coastline comes Rach Goc. The estuary is 16 *tam* [35 m] wide and 4 *xích* [1.8 m] deep. Coconut palms are on both sides. The people produce dried prawns for a living.

From Rac Goc, on a bearing of 225 degrees, go to Pulo Obi [Hon Khoai Son] after two watches along a forested and marshy coastline. On the northern part of this island people produce charcoal, otter oil and timber for a living. There are layers of peaks covered with forests and jungles. There is also a stream and a rock well. Eastward in the ocean is . . . a further small islet shaped like a reclining elephant [Hon Go]. At this island, ships traveling to and from various foreign countries can anchor, draw water and take their bearings. . . .

From Pulo Obi, take a bearing of 315 degrees to the forested and marshy coast. After traveling for one and a half watches there come two estuaries named Bai Hap and Dam Cung Nhi. The main estuary is one *lý* [600 m] wide, and eight *xích* [3.5 m] deep. Its banks are forested and marshy. This estuary divides into two branches. The Dam Cung branch follows a bearing of 60 degrees to connect with Dam Cung. The other Bai Hap branch extends on a bearing of 330 degrees to connect with the district seat of Long Xuyen [modern Ca Mau].

From Dam Cung on a bearing of 345 degrees the coast is forested and marshy. After one watch comes Ong Doc. The estuary is 30 *tam* [66 m] wide and four *xích* [1.8 m] deep, with banks covered with coconut palms. Out to sea on a bearing of 240 degrees, after about one watch, there is a range of soaring peaks covered in dense vegetation and timber. Around about are smaller islands and many dangerous rocks. It is popularly called Hon Chuoi [or "'False Puolo Obi"]. The island is uninhabited and ships cannot anchor there. To the south . . . two *lý* [1,200 m] across the ocean is a belt of rocks [Hon Buong].

From Ong Doc, the coastline is forested and marshy. After one watch comes Da Bac Island, near the coast. . . . There is a small stream, [and people] cultivate fields here. There are many crocodiles and mosquitoes.

From Da Bac, go to Bai Nai Tuy then take a bearing of 360 degrees. After two watches along the forested and marshy coastline comes the joint estuary of the Thu Chin and Thu Muoi waterways. It is about five *tam* [11 m] wide and two *xích* [0.9 m] deep. Two watches westward out to sea is the [Nam Du archipelago], with many large and small islands around it. To the east . . . is an islet called Hon Mao, which produces much black-stone, useful for testing gold. Boats can anchor there. . . .

From Thu Muoi waterway, take a bearing of 30 degrees along a forested and marshy coast. After a day comes the joint estuary of the Cua Lon and Cua Be rivers.[4] The Cua Lon branch goes at a bearing of 90 degrees and is about 90 *tam* [198 m] wide and ten *xích* [4.5 m] deep. On both sides are coconut palms. . . . It connects to My Thanh estuary. The Cua Be branch goes at 30 degrees and is nearly 70 *tam* [154 m] wide and eight *xích* [3.5 m] deep. There are coconut palms on both sides. It connects with Lang Sen and then it joins the Greater Can Tho River.[5] . . .

From Cua Be estuary, on a bearing of 270 degrees, the coastline is covered with coconut palms, forests and marshes. After three hours comes Rach Soi. The estuary is about seven *tam* [15.5 m] wide and about one *xích* 5 *thon* [0.6 m] deep. Both sides are forested and marshy.

On a bearing of 255 degrees from Rach Soi estuary, follow the forested and marshy shore for one watch to Rach Gia port. Its estuary is about 20 *tam* [44 m] wide and three *xích* [1.3 m] deep. Both banks are wooded and swampy. There is much teak here. Outside the estuary, one watch south, is Hon Tre Island,[6] whose winding mountains are covered in forests and bamboo.

Take a bearing of 240 degrees from Rach Gia. After one watch along a forested and marshy coastline comes Vam Rang. The estuary is about 18 *tam* [39.5

m] wide and four *xich* [1.8 m] deep. Both sides are wooded and swampy. The people fish for a living and produce *thuy tran* ham[7] and beeswax. From [here], take a bearing of 225 degrees. After one watch along a forested and marshy coastline comes Hon Dat Mountain. [Here] the forests are dense. The people plant tobacco as well as producing otter oil, charcoal and honeycomb.

From Hon Dat, go along the coast on a bearing of 210 degrees. After half a watch at sea comes Son That Hon. This island has layers of soaring peaks covered with dense forests. Its many inhabitants produce otter oil, charcoal and bêche-de-mer. From Hon Than,[8] on a bearing of 120 degrees and after a sea voyage of half a watch, is Hon Tre.

Take a bearing of 300 degrees from Hon Than. After one watch along a forested and marshy coastline comes Vam Ray. The estuary is about ten *tam* [22 m] wide and three *xich* [1.3 m] deep. Both sides are wooded and swampy, and the inhabitants fish and gather honeycomb.

From Vam Ray, take a bearing of 270 degrees along a wooded and marshy coast. After one watch comes Hon Chong.[9] This mountain comprises jagged rocks, rough sandstone, and interlocking peaks. To its east are tangled forests and muddy streams. . . . There is a river, with the mountain to its west and forests and marshes on the east. The river is about eight *tam* [17.5 m] wide and four *xich* [1.8 m] deep. Many people live on both sides of the river and engage in agriculture. To the southwest, out in the ocean, are a number of islands [the Balua archipelago]. . . .

From Hon Chong, the coastline twists and turns [with] serpentine peaks and dense vegetation. After one watch comes Bai Ot [where] Chinese people reside who tend fields and orchards.

From Bai Ot, the coastline forms serpentine peaks and dense forests. After one watch comes Rach Hau. On both sides of the river are mountains of rugged rocks and dense vegetation. The river is about eight *tam* [17.5 m] wide and two *xich* [0.9 m] deep. Many Chinese people live here and tend fields and gardens.

From Rach Hau, heading north, the coastline comprises interlocking peaks. After half a watch comes Hatien port. Its estuary is about two *lý* [1,200 m] wide and to the left and right are large and small mountains. . . . The estuary divides into three river branches. One branch flows from the sea toward the West Bank [past where it] connects with Hatien. Another branch of the river runs southwest from the sea as the central channel connecting with Hatien. The sides of the channel are [close to two mountains]. . . . The river is about 40 *tam* [88 m] wide and five *xich* [2.2 m] deep. Ships often come and go along it. The other branch of the river proceeds from the sea at the southeast . . . [before it enters Hatien town]. This river is about 70 *tam* [154 m] wide and has shallow water. Ships cannot pass along it. Within the estuary, the three branches join and flow into the Great River Lake of Hatien. The lake . . . is surrounded by the West Bank, on which stands the market town of Hatien. There are many houses and markets, and all sorts of people congregate here, [including] Chinese trading ships. . . . On the east bank of the lake, across from the town, are great twisting peaks covered with dense forests. The bank of the river is forested and marshy. This place is popularly called To Chau. Here Chinese and Jawa people[10] have their houses and markets, and it is also where the Hoa-Nuong[11] live. Water can be obtained from three or four wells. Behind the town to the southwest the coastline consists of twisting mountain ranges and dense forests.[12] Southwards at sea, beyond the estuary, lies a group of islands [Hai Tac archipelago, or Îles des Pirates in colonial maps]. . . They are covered in dense forests and much bamboo can be had there.

From the town of Hatien go west to Mui Nai. The forested coastline is full of twists and turns and the mountain peaks are dense with vegetation. After two watches comes Mount Kep. The forests are thick. Resident Chinese plant tobacco here. Out to sea there is an island surrounded by smaller ones. . . .

From Mount Kep take a bearing of 240 degrees, along a forested and mountainous coast. . . . After [more than] two watches comes Kampot. East of its estuary is a mountain, to the west are forests, sand, and islets. The estuary is nearly 15 *tam* [33 m] wide and three *xich* [1.3 m] deep. There are local[13] officials and Khmer residents.

From Kampot estuary, take a bearing of 210 degrees. The coastline forms winding peaks covered with dense forests. After one watch there comes a large mountain, extremely high, lofty, and precipitous, with layer after layer of soaring peaks covered in dense vegetation. In the surrounding sea to the south is an estuary . . . about seven *tam* [8.8 m] wide and three *xich* [1.3 m] deep. It is full of twists and turns. Here there is a local administrative office and military officers. This island is popularly known as Phu Quoc, but is also called Hon Doc. There are many wild cattle here. The population is dense and people produce lodestone, gharu-wood, honeycomb, bêche-de-mer, and [three types of] rattan, as well as fish and fish paste. To the west is a high peak shaped like a steel spear. . .

From [that peak] take a bearing of 300 degrees along a densely forested coastline. After one watch is Xa Hot Lake. It is about eight *lý* [5 km] wide and contains a river-mouth . . . about 20 *tam* [44 m] wide and three *xich* [1.3 m] deep. Both sides are covered with forests and marshes. The natives[14] engage in agriculture and produce gamboge and [two types of] rattan. . . .

From Xa Hot go south along a mountainous, forested coast . . . [to] Huc Kha Ba. The estuary is about 20 *tam* [44 m] wide and eight *xich* [3.5 m] deep. On either side are layered peaks and dense forests. Siamese officials guard this place. The inhabitants produce sawn timber, otter oil, charcoal, and [two types of] rattan. To the south, in the sea beyond the estuary, are three bands of islands separated by three ocean channels. . . . The islands in the outside channel are curved and on the islets there is a stream. Trading boats passing here can anchor and obtain fresh water and firewood.

From [here] take a bearing of 285 degrees along a coastline of rugged peaks and thick vegetation. After two watches comes Chhak Ream. Out to sea are islands facing each other,[15] with densely forested twisting peaks. . . .

From [here], take a bearing of 255 degrees along a coastline marked by repeated peaks, twists and turns, and dense vegetation. After three watches comes a long island. . . . From [here], proceed along a coastline of multiple soaring peaks and dense forests. After two watches comes Vinh Thom Lake[16] and then Sa Hao Lake. The lake is one watch across. Khmer people who live here engage in cultivation and produce gamboge, bastard cardamom, and cardamom. West of the bank is a mountain. . . . From the coast of this mountain, twisting peaks circle around a bay that is 30 *lý* [18 km] across [possibly Chhak Som]. . . . Siamese officials guard this place with about 300 troops. The people seek a livelihood from forest products. In the seas beyond are three bands of islands, whose [thickly forested] peaks twist up to the skies. . . . Turtle-shell and bêche-de-mer are produced here. . . .

From Vinh Thom, after three watches on a bearing of 240 degrees, along a coastline of twisting peaks and dense forests, comes Hon Ham. . . . On shore, close to the ocean and to the northwest, are dense mountain forests. Much rattan and *ham* wood is produced here.

From Hon Ham, take a bearing of 240 degrees along a twisting mountainous shore covered with dense forests, until three small islands [appear]. . . . Between them are two sea channels, with many dangerous rocks.

From [here], take a bearing of 210 degrees along a coastline of twisting peaks and dense vegetation. After one watch comes Kas Kong Lake. On its northeast shore are dense forests and marshes. The river that flows into the lake is about 15 *tam* [33 m] wide and three *xích* [1.3 m] deep. Its banks are covered in woods and swamps. . . . It is densely populated here and the people produce dressed timber. Beyond the entrance is a small island. The lake itself twists and turns and is about one *lý* [600 m] across and two *xích* [0.9 m] deep. When boats come and go, they can pass close to the island where the water is about four *xích* [1.8 m] deep. Beyond are twisting peaks and thick forests. The forested and marshy shore to the northwest [has] an estuary about 12 *tam* [26.5 m] wide and four *xích* [1.8 m] deep. To the southeast is a small market town with much willow wood. There is also an old temple, known as Hoat Nhien Mieu. They produce ships, honeycomb, turtle-shell, and birds-nests. All of the ships conduct sacrifices at the temple.[17]

From the Hoat Nhien Temple at Kas Kong Lake, take a bearing of 300 degrees and go along a forested and swampy coastline for two watches to Lai Mon. The estuary is about 60 *tam* [132 m] wide and two *xích* [0.9 m] deep. Both sides are covered in thick forests and swamps.

From Lai Mon take a bearing of 270 degrees along a forested and swampy coast. After one watch comes La Khong.[18] The estuary is about 60 *tam* [132 m] wide and eight *xích* [3.5 m] deep. To the west is a mountain and to the east are forests and swamps. Southward, out to sea, is a large place covered with twisting peaks and dense forests [Ko Kut]. Turtle-shell is produced here. An island group comprising four peaks is to the west. . . . On the inner seaward side, there are two picturesque peaks. . . . Around them are islets, large and small, high and low, and dangerous rocks abound. Ships are unable to anchor around this area.[19]

From La Khong, take a bearing of 270 degrees along a mountainous, densely forested coastline. After a day's travel comes Dong Lan. The estuary is one *lý* [600 m] wide and seven *xích* [3 m] deep. Its sides are wooded and swampy. . . . Southwards, at sea, is a high, majestic island [Ko Chang], with peak lying upon peak and dense forests. Many people live here and engage in agriculture as well as producing charcoal and otter oil. . . . Fronting the island is a band of three small isles . . . beyond [which] are many dangerous rocks. Ships need to be very careful.

From Dong Lan, go in a southerly direction along a winding coastline with twisting peaks and dense forests. After two watches comes the sea outside Duong Kham Khem Mon.[20]

From [here], take a bearing of 300 degrees along a heavily forested, twisting, and mountainous coastline. After three watches comes the Wen River estuary. It is about 170 *tam* [375 m] wide and eight *xích* [3.5 m] deep. Both sides are forested and swampy. Southwards in the ocean are three small islands. . . .

From [these islands], go west along a forested shore. After four watches, there are three small islands just off the coast. From [here], take a bearing of 255 degrees along a densely forested coastline. After one watch comes the Chantaburi River. Its estuary is about 70 *tam* [155 m] wide and three *xích* [1.3 m] deep. To the west lies a mountain . . . [while] to the east the area is forested and marshy. Siamese officials guard this place. There is a small island [Ko Chula] outside the estuary [and one] within it. . . .

From the Chantaburi estuary, take a bearing of 240 degrees along a wooded and marshy coastline. After two watches comes the Khem Nu estuary. It is about 20 *tam* [44 m] wide and three *xích* [1.3 m] deep. There are mountains covered with forests both inside and outside the estuary [and] within the estuary are many dangerous rocks.

From [here] follow the mountainous and wooded coast for two watches to Khung Kraben bay. It is two *lý* [1,200 m] wide and five *xích* [2.2 m] deep. To the east are mountain peaks, with a well at their base. In the ocean . . . are small islands and many dangerous rocks.

From [here], take a bearing of 240 degrees along a woody coastline. After one watch comes the Prasae River estuary, about 14 *tam* [30 m] wide and two *xích* five *thon* [1 m] deep. On both sides are rocks and islets.

From [here] take a bearing of 225 degrees along a forested and marshy coastline. After one watch comes Ba Si. The estuary is about 40 *tam* [88 m] wide and six *xích* [2.5 m] deep. On both sides are many willow trees. In the seas beyond are three islands, Ko Man Nok, Ko Man Khlang, and Ko Man Nai. Bêche-de-mer is produced here.

From Ba Si, take a bearing of 210 degrees along a mountainous and forested shore for half a watch until three small islands appear near the coast [the Ko Thalu group]. . . . Many dangerous rocks surround them for about two *lý* [1,200 m] in length and breadth. Ships cannot approach them. Southward, further out to sea, there lies a small island . . . [with] a band of rough and dangerous rocks. . . .

From [here] on a bearing of 210 degrees, go past twisting peaks and dense forests for half a watch to reach Ban Tram.[21] The estuary is about 15 *tam* [33 m] wide and three *xích* [1.3 m] deep. It has densely wooded mountains on both sides. From [here] follow the twisting peaks and thick forests along the coast for half a watch to reach Ko Samet. [The Samet Channel runs] between it and the coast. . . . The channel is one *lý* [600 m] wide and 32 *xích* [14 m] deep. [On the heavily forested coastal mountain opposite] there is a stream and ships passing by can anchor here to obtain fresh water and firewood. In the sea in front of the mountain are many dangerous rocks. . . . Boats coming and going through here must be careful.

From the Samet Channel, take a bearing of 300 degrees along a mountainous and densely wooded coastline. After two watches comes the Rayong River estuary. It is 14 *tam* [30 m] wide and 2 *xích* [0.9 m] deep. On both sides are forests and rocks.

From [here] take a bearing of 240 degrees then veer to 210 degrees. . . . After three watches [along a woody shore] comes the Thot Not Channel.[22] It is 200 *tam* [440 m] wide and 12 *xích* [5.3 m] deep. On both sides are forested mountains. Dangerous rocks are widespread and on the coast to the northeast is a large rock with two peaks. At sea there are three bands of [heavily wooded] islands[23] [that] produce birds-nests and turtle-shells. Among them are four channels, and this is where the routes diverge. One channel leads to the Southern Sea, one to the Southwestern Sea, one to the Eastern Sea, and one to the Northwestern Sea. On both sides are rocks and islets. No one lives here. Eastward at sea lies an island with a mountainous shore. Gatherers of bêche-de-mer often congregate here.

From Thot Not Channel, take a bearing of 270 degrees to reach a twisting shore. Then switch to a bearing of 300 degrees and go along a coast of twisting peaks and dense forests. After half a watch comes Khao Kratha Khwam.[24] Its peaks rise back from the coast like a slanting peck measure. [They contain] a pointed rock extending upwards . . . called Hau Phu Son.

From Hau Phu Son take a bearing of 330 degrees along a coast of twisting peaks. After half a watch comes the Liet Dia area. This place has many islands and diverse peaks covered with dense forests. The sea here divides into a hundred channels, and some form lakes. . . . Some people live here, engaging in forest industries.

From Liet Dia, take a bearing of 345 degrees along a coast of twisting peaks covered with dense forests. After one watch comes the bay at Tay. Westward to sea about three *lý* [1,800 m] is a large piece of land [Ko Khram]. The mountain has layer upon layer of peaks and surrounding the island are many dangerous rocks, large and small. . . . Ships dare not anchor near it. About 30 *lý* [18 km] northwest of [Khram] out to sea, there is an island [Ko Luam] with layers of peaks covered with dense forests. . . .

From Tay Bay, take a bearing of 300 degrees along a twisting coast covered with thick forest. After one watch comes Nam Yeu hamlet. The people here engage in forest industries. At sea to the west, about 40 *lý* [24 km] away, is an island with layers of peaks, many surrounding smaller islands, and covered with dense forests [Ko Lan] . . . . Turtle-shell is produced here. From Nam Yeu, take a bearing of 330 degrees along a twisting, densely forested shore. After one watch comes Khao Pho Bai [where] people engage in forest industries.

From [here], take a bearing of 360 degrees along a heavily forested coast. After one watch comes the bay of Bang Mong [where] people engage in forest industries.

From Bang Mong, take a bearing of 240 degrees along a coast of forested mountains. After one watch comes Mount Samuk. This steep mountain is densely forested. . . . The inhabitants engage in agriculture and forest industries.

Out to sea, about 42 *lý* [25 km] to the west of Samuk, there lies an island [Ko Si Chang] comprising layers of twisting peaks covered with dense vegetation. There are also many smaller islands around it. . . . On the island there is a stream [which flows during the rainy season] but in winter and spring, and when it is extremely hot, the stream dries up. Then, to provision a ship, water can only be drawn from a stone well.

From Samuk, take a bearing of 30 degrees along a scrubby, marshy coast. After one watch comes the bay of Bang Hien [where] people fish for their living. From Bang Hien, take a bearing of 330 degrees along a forested, marshy coast. After one watch comes the estuary of Chonburi [or Bang Plasoi]. Its residents practice fishing and engage in commerce for a living.

From [here], take a bearing of 300 degrees along a forested and marshy coastline. After two watches comes Paetriu, which is also called the Bang Pakong River estuary. It is about 60 *tam* [132 m] wide and four *xích* [1.8 m] deep. Its sides are forested and marshy. There is an administrative office here, and the people who live here collect coconut-palm leaves for a living. From Paetriu, take a bearing of 270 degrees along a forested and marshy coast. After two watches comes the port of Paknam [at the Chao Phraya River mouth]. Its estuary is one *lý* [600 m] wide and both sides are covered with forests and marshes.

From Paknam, take a bearing of 240 degrees along a forested and marshy coast. After two watches comes Tha Chin River estuary. It is about 60 *tam* [132 m] wide and four *xích* [1.8 m] deep. The main channel flows directly to the east beyond a bar and on both sides of the estuary are forests and marshes. There is an administrative office here and the people fish for a living.

From [here], take a bearing of 225 degrees along a forested and marshy coast. After three watches comes the Mae Klong estuary. It is approximately 60 *tam* [132 m] wide and four *xích* [1.8 m] deep. The channel curves then flows east beyond a bar. The estuary's sides are wooded and swampy, and there is an administrative office here. The people fish for a living. There is fresh drinking water all year round here, and all the inhabitants between the estuary and the source rely on it.

From [here], take a bearing of 210 degrees along a forested and marshy coastline. After two watches comes Ban Laem estuary. It is about 14 *tam* [30 m] wide and one *xich* [0.4 m] deep. Both of its sides are forested and marshy.

From [here] take a bearing of 240 degrees along a forested and marshy coastline. After two watches comes Biet Kieu hamlet. Beside the village is a small stream that runs to Ban Bang Thalu. The people engage in agriculture and produce sugar and fish. At sea, there is a field of shoals [Ko Kolam] extending for half a kilometer in length and breadth. . . .

From Thalu, take a bearing of 210 degrees along a twisting coastline that has dense mountain forests. After one watch comes the small river of Muong Trang [Pran Buri?]. On its west bank stands a high mountain with layers of peaks covered with dense forests. At sea, two islands face it [Ko Sadao and Ko Khi Nok] . . . . Birds-nests are obtained there.

From the Pran Buri River, go south along a coast of forests, bamboo, and peninsulas. There are towering peaks and thick forests. After one watch comes Sam Roi Yot. On the western bank are layers of densely wooded peaks where mountain goats gather. Beside the mountain is a spring well. Out to sea, there are mountainous islands covered in dense forests. To the south along the ocean channel are reefs and islets extending to the coastal mountains. Ships passing must be cautious.

From this channel, go south along a coastline of twisting peaks covered in dense forests to Ban Kui . . . then advance to a stony mountain with multiple peaks [Khao Mong Lai]. Go along a mountainous and forested coast for two watches to reach Ta Nao Bay. Within the bay is a small stream whose source is in the densely wooded mountains. In the ocean beyond the bay is a small island, and south of the river are three mountains. . . . On the west bank is a mountain with a well at its side. There is much sappanwood in the forests here.

From Ta Nao, go east then steer south along a forested coastline. After one watch comes the Muong Mai estuary, [which is] about 20 *tam* [44 m] wide and two *xich* [0.9 m] deep. Both sides are forested. No one lives at the source of the river. To the east, about two *lý* [1,200 m] out to sea, are three small islands . . . [where] much birds-nest can be obtained.

In the ocean, about two *lý* east . . . is a craggy island covered with rocks and forests [Ko Chan]. . . . From Muong Mai, take a bearing of 135 degrees along a curving coastline of forested mountains. After three watches comes Mount Mae Ramphung. This mountain has layers of twisting peaks and is covered in dense forests. At its side is a small stream.

From [here], take a bearing of 225 degrees along a twisting coastline of wooded mountains. Half a watch brings the main estuary of the Bang Saphan River. It is about 50 *tam* [110 m] wide and one *xich* [0.4 m] deep. Both sides are forested. There is an administrative office here. . . . From [here] take a bearing of 120 degrees along a mountainous coastline covered with dense vegetation. After half a watch one reaches the Bang Saphan Noi estuary. It is about 30 *tam* [66 m] wide and four *xich* [1.8 m] deep.

From [here], take a bearing of 150 degrees along a forested coastline. After one watch comes Dat Do Tho Mountain. At the side of the densely wooded mountain there is a stream. Out at sea is an island [Ko Thalu] with two small islets nearby. . . . Much birds-nest is obtained here.

From Dat Do take a bearing of 240 degrees along a twisting mountainous coastline covered with dense vegetation. After one watch comes the small river of Khlong Pathiu. Forests and swamps occur on both sides of its estuary. Siamese officials guard this place. The people engage in agriculture. Out to sea is a craggy island [Ko Viang] covered with thick forests . . . [and] within the bay there are two small islands. . . . At sea about five *lý* [3 km] beyond Ko Viang, there is an island group of three peaks . . . [where] much birds-nest is obtained.

From the small river of Pathiu, take a bearing of 150 degrees along a forested shore. After one watch comes a mountain. It comprises layers of peaks covered with dense vegetation . . . . The ocean contains numerous dangerous shoals, while one *lý* [600 m] out to sea is an island [Swallow Island] . . . . At two watches' distance eastward out to sea from [this island] are two island peaks covered with dense forests [Ko Ngam Yai and Ko Ngam Noi]. . . . [From here], take a bearing of 240 degrees along a forested and marshy coast. After one watch comes the Chumphon estuary [at the mouth of the Tha Taphao]. It is 17 *tam* [37.5 m] wide and about three *xich* [1.3 m] deep. Both sides are forested. Beyond the estuary is an island. . . .

Eastward from [this island], about two *lý* [1,200 m] out to sea, there is a group of islands [Ko Samet] . . . [where] much birds-nest is obtained.

From Ko Samet port, take a bearing of 150 degrees along a twisting and forested coastline. After a voyage of one watch comes a mountain with craggy peaks and covered with dense forests. . . . From [this mountain] take a bearing of 225 degrees along a twisting coastline dense with forests. After one watch comes the small river of Ao Sawi. Its sides are wooded and swampy. The people engage in forest industries.

From Ao Sawi, take a bearing of 135 degrees along a twisting coastline with thick mountainous forests. After two watches comes Mount Pracham Hiang. . . . In the ocean off the mountain is a group of islands with three to five peaks of varying sizes. . . . These islands are covered with rough rocks and forests, and much birds-nest is obtained here.

From the Pracham Hiang peak, take a bearing of 240 degrees along a twisting mountainous coastline covered with dense forests. After one watch comes a group of large and small islands. . . . One island [Ko Phitak] has twisting peaks, dangerous rocks, and dense forests. Much birds-nest is obtained here.

From Phitak Island, take a bearing of 225 degrees along a coastline of thick mountain forests. After half a watch comes the small river of Lang Suan. Both banks are wooded and the people engage in forest industries. About two *lý* [1,200 m] out to sea from the estuary there are many dangerous rocks extending for an area of approximately three *lý* in circumference. . . .

From Lang Suan, take a bearing of 150 degrees along a twisting forested coastline. After four watches there is a mountain with layers of twisting peaks covered in dense forest. . . . There are rhinoceros, elephants, and wild tigers here.

From [here] take a bearing of 255 degrees along a twisting forested coastline. After one watch comes the Chaiya estuary. It is about 16 *tam* [35 m] wide and three *xich* [1.3 m] deep, with forested and marshy banks. People engage in agriculture around the estuary. Beyond it, about one day's voyage eastward to sea, there is a large island (Ko Pha Ngan) . . . [with] many surrounding islands, large and small. Siamese officials guard this place with approximately 500 troops. The people engage in agriculture. Much birds-nest is obtained here.

From Chaiya, take a bearing of 195 degrees along a forested and marshy coastline. After two watches comes the Khirirat estuary. It is about 40 *tam* [88 m] wide and three *xich* [1.3 m] deep. Both sides are forested and marshy. The inhabitants engage in agriculture. Beyond the estuary, about three *lý* [1,800 m] eastward, lies a small mountainous and wooded island [Ko Prap]. . . . Birds-nest is obtained here. In the ocean about three *lý* [1,800 m] north of Khirirat estuary are some sandy shoals half a kilometer long and wide. . . .

From the Khirirat estuary take a bearing of 150 degrees along a coastline of forested mountains. After one watch comes Ang Thong channel.[25] It is one *lý* [600 m] wide and 16 *xich* [7 m] deep. Beyond the channel is a large island [Ko Samui] . . . . Siamese officials in charge of about 500 troops guard this place. The people engage in agriculture and plant cotton. On the inner coastline, the dense population pursues agriculture and forest industries.

From the Ang Thong channel, take a bearing of 195 degrees along a twisting coastline of forested mountains. After two days comes Nakhon Si Thammarat.[26] The estuary is about 20 *tam* [44 m] wide and two *xich* [0.9 m] deep. Its sides are covered with forests and swamps and the people engage in agriculture.

From [here], go south along a forested and marshy coastline. After two watches comes Pak Phanang.[27] The estuary is about 20 *tam* [44 m] wide and two *xich* [0.9 m] deep. Its banks are covered with woods and swamps and the people engage in agriculture. The Pak Phanang River originates in Thale Luang in the Songkhla Lagoon.[28] Northward to sea are two small islands. . . .

From Pak Phanang take a bearing of 165 degrees along a forested and marshy coast. After a day, there is a shoal about two *lý* [1,200 m] in length and breadth, and about one *lý* [600 m] from the coast. . . . This shoal can be covered by the high tide . . . [so] boats passing here must be careful.

From [this shoal], go south along a twisting coastline of forested mountains. After three days comes Songkhla port. Its estuary is 50 *tam* [110 m] wide and six *xich* [2.6 m] deep. North of the estuary there are twisting peaks, while islets lie to its south. To sea eastward are two small islands close together [Ko Maeo and Ko Nu].

From Songkhla, go south on the sea along a coastline of beaches and forests. After two days comes Pattani Lake. It is about three *lý* wide [1,800 m] and 20 *xich* [8.8 m] deep. Southeast of the lake is a mountain covered with dense forest; to its northwest are forests and marshes. There are Jawa officials on guard here.

From Pattani, take a bearing of 135 degrees along a twisting coastline that is marked by curling peaks covered in dense forests. After two days comes the estuary of Kelantan. Out to sea there is an island where much birds-nest is obtained. Jawa officials guard this place.

From Kelantan, take a bearing of 165 degrees along a coastline of beaches and islets as well as dense forests. After a day and a half comes Terengganu estuary. At sea there are large and small islands in threes and fives. The forests here are dense. Malay officials guard this place. . . .

Notes on the Chinese Compass and the Measurements Used

Compass

Compass directions in the text are so accurate that they have only been surpassed by more modern European navigation manuals for the South China Sea. In the translation, the original compass directions have been converted from the 24 section, Sino-Vietnamese instrument, where a bearing is indicated by using one or two characters, into a western compass divided into 360 degrees.

Measurements

Measurements[29] of length and depth have been calculated from those in Huinh-Tinh Paulus Cua, *Dai Nam Quoc Am Tu Vi. Dictionnaire annamite* (Saigon: Rey, Curiol & Cie, 1895–1896). This source was privileged for its nineteenth-century Southern provenance, and also because it differentiates between Chinese, demotic Vietnamese (*nom*), and Chinese words with the same meaning in demotic Vietnamese. This point is stressed because following the definitions in Cua's dictionary has yielded a noticeably different length for a *ly* than that given in some modern Vietnamese dictionaries (444 m).

Cua says *ly* [Sino-Viet] and *dam* [*nom*] were interchangeable terms for a Vietnamese mile [vol. 1, 563]; and that one *dam* equaled 135 *truong*. One *truong* equaled 10 *thuoc* [vol. 1, 219] or 5 *tam* [vol. 2, 336]. Modern Vietnamese dictionaries give a *thuoc* [Sino-Viet *xich*] as 44 centimeters long. This agrees with Cua's definition of a "Western" meter (*thuoc tay*) as 2 *thuoc* 3 *tac* [vol. 2, 428], i.e., 44 + 44 + 12 = 100 cms. This gives the following table of equivalences used in the text:

1 *ly* = 600 m [4.44 x 135 = 599]
1 *truong* = 4.44 m
1 *tam* = 2.2 m
1 *thuoc/xich* = 0.44 m
1 *thon/tac* = 0.044 m

Notes

1. Tong Phuc Ngoan and Duong Van Chau, *Xiem-la-quoc Lo-trinh Tap-luc*, ed. Chen Chingho (Hong Kong: New Asia Research Institute Historical Material Series No. 2, Chinese University of Hong Kong, 1966).

2. A different and complete translation can be found in Geoff Wade, "A Maritime Route in the Vietnamese Text—*Xiem-La-Quoc Lo-Trinh Tap-Luc*," in *Commerce et Navigation en Asie du Sud-Est (XIVe-XIXe siècle)*, ed. Nguyen The Anh and Yoshiaki Ishizawa (Paris: L'Harmattan, 1999). My thanks go to Nola Cooke for her assistance in preparing the current version for publication.

3. Cua Ba That is the second mouth of the Hau Giang delta. See Auguste Pavie's 1902 map of Cochinchina in *Atlas of the Pavie Missions. Laos, Cambodia, Siam, Yunnan and Vietnam*, trans. Walter E. J. Tips (Bangkok: White Lotus, 1999), 132.

4. The Cai Lon and Cai Be Rivers.

5. This river then flows into the Bassac (Hau Giang).

6. An island seven miles southwest of Hon Dat mountain.

7. An unknown type of local fish or fish product.

8. From the directions this may be Hon Nghe island.

9. Literally Hon Chong "island," it is now part of the mainland and the site of Hon Chong town.

10. An inclusive term for all Malays, including Bugis.

11. A phonetic representation of "Frank," in Cantonese pronounced "Fa-liang." Professor Chen thought it referred to the site of the French Seminary of Saint Joseph, whose members had fled Hon Dat, 15 kilometers to the northwest, for Hatien in 1769. [*Xiem-la-quoc Lo-trinh Tap-luc*, 114].

12. Situated on the peninsula west of Hatien, near the current Vietnamese-Cambodian border.

13. The term translated as "local officials" here is "fen-shou" in Chinese or "phan-thu" in Vietnamese. It can be understood as a "local administrative office," where "local" contrasts with "central." At the time, this Khmer area was ruled from Hatien, so it seems likely that "local" here refers to Vietnamese officials rather than indigenous ones.

14. The text uses *Man*, a generic term for "uncivilized" people; but here it may refer to Khmers.

15. Kaoh Praeus, Kaoh Russei, Kaoh Chraloh, Kaoh Ta Kiev, and Kaoh Sra Maoch.

16. Professor Chen suggests Kompong Som.

17. These sentences are tentative translations of a possibly corrupted section of the text.

18. Possibly the estuary of the Kaoh Pao (Kaspor) River leading to Kaoh Kong town.

19. Apparently referring to the dangerous waters between Ko Kut and Ko Chang.

20. Possibly the bay between Laem Ngop and Laem Sok (Laem Nam) that lies opposite Ko Chang.

21. Probably Ao Phe.

22. Probably Pla Wai channel or Samae San channel, between Ko Samae San and the mainland.

23. Likely Ko Raet, Ko Samae San, and Ko Kham.

24. A tentative identification.

25. Chong Ang Thong, a channel lying between Ko Phaluai and Ko Ang.

26. Nakhon Si Thammarat, entered between Laem Talumphuk and a point near the entrance to the Pak Phaya River.

27. The Pak Phanang River estuary, connecting Songkhla Lagoon with Nakhon Si Thammarat.

28. Thale Luang, also known as Lampam Lake, the northern part of the Songkhla Lagoon.

29. This note was provided by Nola Cooke, who also calculated all the measurements in the text.

Appendix B

Glossary

General

baba	offspring of Hokkien-Malay intermarriage who became economically powerful in the early nineteenth century
bang	(Viet) Chinese dialect group congregation, cf. Chinese *bang*
bo zai	(Chinese) junk transportation
cai fu	(Viet) secretary who was in charge of finance of the junk
chandu	(Indian?) smokable opium
cong-hong	(Chinese) broker guild in Canton
cu lao	(Viet) islands, cf. Malay *Pulau*
dan chuan	(Chinese) egg-shaped junks from Zhejiang
Fu-chao Hong	(Chinese) guilds dealing with Hokkien and Teochiu merchants
hanh nhan ty	(Viet) office of traveling deputies or office of interpreters
hap	(Siamese measure) 60 kilos
Ho sap	(Viet) Association of Wax Taxpayers
hou zhang	(Chinese) boatswain
gian thuong	(Viet) "cunning merchants"
Kinh Luoc Cao Man	(Viet) royal delegate [controlling] Cambodia.
kwien or coyan	(Siamese measure) 25 piculs = 4.16 tons
lai or *cac lai*	(Viet) "merchant/s"
lek	(Siamese) "able-bodied men"

Minh Huong	originally Ming loyalist immigrants to southern Vietnam, but increasingly refers to offspring of Sino-Viet or Sino-Khmer intermarriage after the 1830s
Minh Huong Xa	government recognized organization in which Minh Huong males were registered
ngoen tra thai	(Siamese) silver Thai *baht* coins
ngoen naentu	(Siamese) Lao coins and coins other than of Siamese origin
Okna	(Khmer) governor
reua pom yang yuan	(Siamese) Vietnamese model gunboat
reua sisa yuan	(Siamese) vessel with Vietnamese-style bows
sala	(Siamese) shelters
sha chuan	sand junks, a special type of Suzhou flat-bottomed vessel designed for shallow waters
suai	(Siamese) head tax
sruk	(Khmer) place or province
taukeh	(Teochiu) powerful merchants
Thanh Nhan	(Viet) "Qing men," referring to Chinese who migrated in the Qing period
tong tran quan	(Viet) governor general
topes	(Singapore) Chinese/Viet junks
tua	(Chinese) maritime measure, about 2.5 meters
xe	(Khmer) a measure of about 100–120 kilos

Viet Ships, Junks, and Boats

chien thuyen	war boats
dai dich thuyen	government-hired rice junks transporting rice to the center and the north
gai bau	Cham-Malay style *prahu*
le thuyen	carved and decorated galleys
nhieu thuyen	government-levied boat
o thuyen	black galleys, often pirates
sai thuyen	bigger galleys
thanh thuyen dap khach	Chinese junks carrying passengers or immigrants
thuong thuyen	merchant junk
thuyen hanh thuong Tran Tay	boats trading to the "western protectorate," i.e., Cambodia
thuyen hanh thuong Luc Tinh	boats trading within the six southern provinces in the Mekong Delta

Viet Terms

can	600 grams, cf. Chinese *jin*
hoc	5 liters
phuong	38.5 liters
dong	1 cash
mach	60 cash
quan	600 cash
ly	600 meters
truong	4.44 meters
1 *tam*	2.2 meters
1 *thuoc/xich*	0.44 meters
1 *thon/tac*	0.044 meters

Index

Amoy. *See* Xiamen
Ayutthaya, 4, 8, 22, 24, 25

baba, 6–7, 170
Bac Lieu, 7, 140, 145
Bai Xau, 143
bamboo, 149
bang. See dialect associations
Bangkok, 1, 4, 9, 11, 23, 31; and 1820s
    coastal trading network, 74; and
    trans-Mekong trade, 101, 109
Bangkok dynasty, 31, 102, 106, 108,
    110. *See also* Chakkri dynasty
Ban Hap, 161, 162, 163, 164, 165, 167;
    and 1881 colonial enquiry in
    Cochinchina, 170
Banteay Meas, 40, 43, 62. *See also*
    Hatien
Bassac River, 9, 36, 38, 42, 140, 151;
    and trading routes, 142, 143, 146.
    See also Hau Giang
Batavia, 23, 31, 55, 76, 91
Ba Thac (Bassac), 11, 48, 131, 140,
    146, 151; in eighteenth century, 40,
    42, 143, 153n18
Battambang, 10, 11, 40, 105, 108, 110–
    14; and Franco-Siamese Conven-
    tion of 1870, 150
Ba Xuyen, 145
bêche-de-mer, 179, 180

beeswax, 111, 143–44
Ben Nghe, 9, 41, 90. *See also* Saigon
betel nuts, 80
Bien Hoa, 8, 11, 37, 39, 40, 41
birds-nest, 180, 184, 185, 186, 187

Bodin, *Chaophraya*, 108, 109, 110,
    113, 117n54, 155n42
Braudel, Fernand, 2
British, 3, 4, 26, 160

Cai Be, 41, 42, 80
Cai Lon River, 142
Ca Mau, 10, 38–39, 140, 142, 143,
    144–45
Cambodia, 2, 8, 46, 77, 78, 86; Chinese
    in, 94–95, 96–97, 146–47, 148,
    151; French economic reforms in,
    150; and Siamese warfare, 104,
    107–110; and trans-Mekong trade,
    102–3
Cambodians. *See* Khmer
Cancao, 9, 10. *See also* Hatien
Can Tho, 46, 140
Canton, 9, 22, 25, 26, 43, 55; as a
    trading port, 56–57, 62. *See also*
    Guangdong; Guangzhou
Cantonese, 4, 5, 6, 23, 24, 39; and
    Hatien, 62; and Southeast Asian
    opium farms, 163, 169

cardamom, 111–13, 180
cattle trade, 7, 8–9, 78, 81n54, 150
Chakkri dynasty, 4, 8, 12, 23, 28, 160. *See also* Bangkok dynasty
Champassak, 11, 105, 108, 109, 112, 113
Chams, 6, 7, 8, 32, 37, 42; as ship-builders in Siam, 125
Chantaburi (Chantabun), 5, 8, 11, 42, 43, 45; Cochinchinese in, 128, 129; as cardamom source, 112; and shipbuilding, 127–30; as a Water Frontier port, 103, 104
Chao Anu, 107
Chaochou. *See* Teochiu
Chaophraya Bodin. *See* Bodin
Chaophraya Phrakhlang. *See* Phrakhlang
Chaophraya River, 4, 8, 10, 28, 46, 105
charcoal, 176, 181
Chau Doc, 42, 43, 44, 45, 102, 106; late-nineteenth-century ethnic mix of, 140–41
Cheang Hong Lim, 169, 170
Chen Shangchuan, 39, 40–41, 44
Chileang, 147
Chinese, 2, 4, 5–6, 9, 10, 11; in Cambodia, 94–95, 96–97, 146–47, 148, 151; and economic expansion in eighteenth- and nineteenth-century Southeast Asia, 22–27, 31, 160, 165–66; as opium farmers in Southeast Asia, 160–71; as small traders in the Gulf of Siam, 74, 75–76. *See also* Cantonese; Chinese in southern Vietnam; Fujianese; Hainanese; Hakka; Hokkien-speakers; Ming Huong; Straits Chinese; Teochiu; Thanh Nhan
Chinese in southern Vietnam, 39–41, 43, 48, 85–86, 88–94, 125; in the Transbassac area, 140, 141, 143, 145
Cholon, 61–62, 80, 90, 96, 144
Cochinchina (Cochin-China), 8, 9, 23, 30–31, 56, 57; shipbuilding industry in, 120–27. *See also* Vietnam, southern; Gia Dinh
commerce. *See* trade
commercial networks, 5, 12, 36, 40, 41, 43; among Chinese merchants in Southeast Asia, 160–61, 166–68; in trans-Mekong region, 102–3
commodities, 9–10, 22, 31, 32, 61, 62; exported from Nguyen Vietnam, 74, 77, 78, 91, 144, 145; exported from trans-Mekong region, 102–3, 111, 112, 113; imported into Nguyen Vietnam, 63, 78, 88, 89; traded between the Mekong delta and Cambodia, 79–81; traded in Hatien, 62, 103. *See also* individual items
commodity production, 23, 24–28. *See also* rice; salt production
canoes, 80
copper, 24, 60
cotton, 27, 186
currencies, local, 61, 63, 114
customs duties, 3, 27, 61, 106, 114

Dang Trong. *See* Cochinchina
Dao Tri Phu (Dao Tri Kinh), 91–92
deerskin, 80
dialect associations, 86, 93, 94–95, 99n46, 153n8
dockyards, 122
don binh Xiem, 7, 47
Dong Nai, 36, 37, 40, 41, 56. 60
Dong Thap Muoi, 37, 38
dried fish. *See* fish, processed
Duong Ngan. *See* Yang Yandi
Dutch, 3, 6, 25, 26, 160

East India Company, 26, 54
elephants, 4, 10, 17n78
English. *See* British
ethnicity, ethnic mix, 5–8, 11, 125, 140–41

Faifo. *See* Hoi An
fish, processed, 126, 145, 151, 179
fisheries, 144–45, 150–52, 183, 184
fish oil, 145, 151
fish-tank junks, 144
forest products, 102–3, 105, 115, 182, 183, 185
French, 139, 140, 144, 150, 160, 168
fruit, dissemination of, 9
Fujian, 3, 23, 31, 54–55, 57, 59; and

Nguyen Vietnam, 78, 85, 90
Fujianese, 5, 54, 59, 140, 159, 162

gambier, 23, 26, 27, 164, 165
Ganh Hao River, 142, 176
Gia Dinh, 41, 62, 81, 86, 87–88, 89;
    Chinese in, 90–94, 95, 97. *See also*
    Vietnam, southern; Cochinchina
Gia Dinh Thanh Tong Tran (Gia Dinh
    administration), 86, 88, 92–94, 96
Gia Long, 10, 48, 72, 80, 86, 106
gold, 25
Guangdong, 3, 23, 25, 31, 54, 55; and
    Cochinchina, 61, 62, 89, 90, 94
Guangzhou, 56–57

Hainanese, 6, 56, 140, 142, 145, 150
Hainan Island, 54, 55, 56, 57, 78, 104,
    143
Hakkas, 6, 150
Hatien, 5, 7, 8, 11, 23, 24; under Minh
    Mang, 91; under Nguyen Anh, 84;
    and Siam, 44, 47–48, 102–3, 104,
    108, 115; and trade, 30, 51n49, 62–
    63; in *Xiem La Quoc Lo Trinh Tap
    Luc*, 178–79. *See also* Banteay
    Meas; Cancao; Mac Cuu; Mac
    Thien Tu
Hau Giang, 38–39, 44, 46, 72, 75, 90.
    See also Bassac River
Hoi An, 56, 57, 59, 60–61, 63, 78
Hokkien, 54, 55, 56, 57, 59
honey, 144, 178, 179, 180
Hong Kong opium farm, 160, 161, 162,
    163
Hue, 12, 27, 28, 56, 57, 59; as an
    emporium, 60
Hue court, 86, 87, 92, 95, 165

intermarriage, 5, 85, 94, 147
iron, 9, 10, 24, 60, 76, 86; Cochin-
    chinese demand for, 77–78

junk trade, 1, 3–4, 8–10, 22, 23, 28–33;
    between ports of South China and
    Nguyen Vietnam, 53–64; and small
    Chinese traders in Water Frontier
    region, 75–76; and southern Viet-
    namese rice transport, 87; on
    Transbassac waterways, 140, 142–

43, 144, 146. *See also* individual
    ports
junk types, 28, 32, 55, 59, 65n20, 79–
    80

Kampot, 38, 40, 43, 44, 46, 108; in
    nineteenth century, 147, 155n51,
    179
Khmers, 7, 9, 10, 11, 14n33, 37; anti-
    Vietnamese conflicts, 96–97; royal
    factional conflicts, 39–40; trade
    with Viets, 80–81, 108; in western
    Cochinchina, 139–40, 141, 143,
    146
Khorat, 40, 107, 108, 112
Kien Giang district. *See* Rach Gia
Koh Seang Tat, 164, 167, 168, 170
Koh Si Chang, 75
kongsi, 24, 25, 76

lai, 73–74, 75
Laos, 102, 107, 109, 112, 114
Laotians, 7, 102
lead, 10, 24, 86, 89
Le Van Duyet, 88, 89, 92–93, 95, 96,
    129
Le Van Khoi rebellion, 12, 79, 96, 107,
    127, 129; and Cochinchinese
    exodus to Chantaburi, 130, 131
live fish trade, 144, 145
Li Wenguang, 124
logging. *See* wood
Long Men corps, 39, 40, 41, 44
Long Xuyen, 44, 47, 48. *Also see* Ca
    Mau
Luu Tin, 92, 96
Luzon, 27, 28

Macao, 4, 10, 57–58, 106, 125, 162–63
Mac Cuu, 23, 35, 43–44, 62
Mac family, 5, 46, 47–48, 105
Mac Thien Tu, 5, 36, 42, 43–45 104
Malay Peninsula, 2, 3, 12, 24–25, 54,
    79
Malays, 2, 26, 30, 43, 45, 51n57, 148
Malay words in Vietnamese, 73
Man Wo Fung Company, 161, 162–64,
    169, 170
Mekong Delta,1, 4, 7, 8–9, 10, 12;
    early Sino-Viet settlement of, 40–

42, 63; geography of, 36, 37, 38; in the regional trade system, 27, 46, 63, 72–77, 78, 79–81; as a shipbuilding area, 74–75, 122, 123–24. *See also* Gia Dinh

Melaka, 3, 10, 28–30, 31, 165

Minh Huong, 6, 41, 85, 86, 89, 94; associations, 93, 95, 99n46; in 1902 Bac Lieu, 140; 1842 definition of, 93; graduates, 95; under French, 140

Minh loyalists. *See* Minh Huong

Minh Mang, 9, 12, 28, 32, 48, 79; and Chinese in Gia Dinh, 86–87, 93, 94–96; resumes state trading, 91

Mongkut, 6

"mountain king," 40

My Thanh, 143, 146, 154n35, 176, 177

My Tho, 11, 40, 42, 43, 47, 48; and betel nut production, 80; as a Chinese town, 51n40

Nam Bo Chinh, 74, 124

Nguyen Anh, 4, 5, 7, 9, 10, 11–12; Chinese and Siamese support for, 47–48, 86; in Gulf of Siam, 47, 72, 75; and shipbuilding, 121; and trade in strategic goods, 25, 75

Nguyen dynasty, 12, 23, 31–32, 85, 92–95, 104–5; and wax taxes, 144

Nguyen Huu Nghia, 92

Nguyen port charges, 61

Ningbo, 54, 59

Ong Doc River, 143, 177

opium, 3, 31, 32, 76, 77, 87; and rice smuggling in Gia Dinh, 88, 89, 91, 92; in Southeast Asia, 160, 169

opium brands, 162–63, 164, 168

opium revenue farming, 160, 161, 162–71

otter oil, 176, 178, 181

Penang, 3, 4, 10, 31, 72, 73, 165–66

pepper, 22, 23, 26, 27, 104, 164

Phnom Penh, 10, 11, 35, 36, 37, 39; and Mekong delta trade, 77, 78; as a Sino-Vietnamese market town, 148, 149, 151; as a trading centre, 102, 106, 108, 114, 144, 149, 150,
151; and Water Frontier politics, 40, 41, 42, 43, 107, 108

Phipit, *Phraya*, 45, 105

Phrakhlang, *Chaophraya,* 128, 130

Phuket, 23, 25, 72, 75, 76

Pigneaux, Pierre, 4, 75

piracy, 4, 30, 40, 41, 122, 152

Ponteamas. *See* Banteay Meas

port charges, Nguyen Vietnam, 61

Portuguese, 57–58, 61, 76, 124, 146

Portuguese National Archives, 58

prawns, 144, 145

Pursat, 105, 110, 112, 113, 156n56

Qianlong reign, 22

"Qing men." *See* Thanh Nhan

Rach Gia, 9, 39, 43, 44, 47, 140; and riverine Water Frontier 141, 142, 143, 146, 149

Rama I, 8, 10, 11, 47, 82, 105

Rama II, 107

Rama III, 8, 110, 111, 128

rattan, 179, 180

Reachea Setthi, *Okna*, 43, 48

revenue farming, 160, 164–65, 166, 169–70

rice, 1, 23, 26, 31, 32, 37; and link with opium trade, 88–89, 91, 92; and Mekong Delta, 46, 79, 80–81, 89; and connection with ship-building, 120, 123-25

rice mills, Cochinchina, 170

rice trade, 8–9, 10, 27–28, 48, 59, 62; of Cochinchina, 73–75, 76, 77, 86, 87–89

Sa Dec, 9, 42, 47

Saigon, 1, 3, 4, 6, 9, 11; early development of, 26, 27, 37, 40, 41, 46–47, 82; opium farm, 162, 165; in regional trade system, 23, 27, 28, 30, 31, 76–78, 80. *Also see* Ben Nghe; Cholon

Saigon, citadel, 4–5

salt, 31, 76, 80, 103, 143

salted fish. *See* fish, processed

salt production, 80, 145–46, 154n32

sappanwood, 9, 10, 103, 184

ships, 4, 28, 30, 76, 121

shipbuilding, 31, 74, 75, 79, 80; on the Water Frontier, 120, 121–31, 180

Siam, 3, 4, 6, 9, 10, 11; and Battambang, 110–14, 150; and local Chinese, 23, 26, 45; naval power of, 126–27, 128–31, 134n48; and Nguyen Vietnam, 105–7, 115, 126–27; and war in Cambodia, 107–110

Siam, Gulf of, 24, 32, 42–43, 45, 48, 72–73; and Chinese ship-building, 123, 124, 126; as trading region, 75–77, 78, 79, 103

Siam, trade, 22, 27, 28, 31, 32, 42; in regional system, 76, 77, 78, 81

Siamese people, 2, 6, 7, 78, 79, 129

silk, 8, 10, 32, 56, 59, 62; traded in Southeast Asia, 63, 77, 78, 86, 91

silver, 24

Singapore, 3, 4, 9, 26, 27, 28; opium revenue farming in, 160, 163, 164–65; in regional trade system, 30–32, 76, 78, 143, 152

Sino-Khmer, 6, 140, 147

smuggling, 10, 87, 88, 91, 92, 93–94; opium, 162–63, 164-65, 171

Soc Trang, 86, 140, 141, 142, 143, 145. *See also* Ba Thac

South China, 2, 3, 27, 53–54. *See also* individual ports or provinces

South China Sea, 1–2, 35, 46, 48, 142, 143

Southeast Asia, 1–2, 3, 5, 21–32, 35–36, 53; Chinese shipbuilding industry in, 104, 123; and colonial Chinese capital, 160–71

Straits Chinese, 159, 162, 170

suai (tax), 109, 110–13

sugar, 11, 22, 23, 31, 32, 61; trade in 1820 Gia Dinh, 90–91, 92

sulfur, 9, 10, 77, 86

Sun Yee Company, 162, 163, 168

Suzhou, 54, 59

Tan King Sing, 162, 163, 164, 167, 168, 169

Tau Truong, 143

Tay Son war, 4, 8, 12, 27, 46–47, 60; and commerce, 74, 105; and ships, 122

Takeo, 36, 38, 45, 81, 150

Taksin, 4, 5, 11, 24, 36, 45–46; and Water Frontier rivals, 103–5

taxes, 76, 77–78, 79, 80, 90, 93; on commodities, 106, 113, 114, 144, 149, 150

tea, 26, 32

Teochiu, 4, 5, 7, 23, 26, 45–46; Chaozhou port, 55, 57, 58–59

Terengganu, 3, 23, 121

Thai. *See* Siamese

Thailand. *See* Siam

Thanh Nhan, 86, 87, 88, 92, 93, 94–95; and anti-Nguyen revolts, 96

Thieu Tri, 95, 96

Tien Giang, 39, 44, 47, 48, 80

tin, 9, 10, 24–25, 32, 76, 166

tobacco, 9, 10, 77, 103, 178

Tonle Sap Lake, 36, 37, 38, 148, 150–52

Tourane, 60, 61, 78

trade, 2, 3, 4, 8–11, 22, 28–32; in drinking water, 142; Gia Dinh with Southeast Asia and China, 75–79, 86, 87–88, 89, 91–92; in Gulf of Siam, 73–75; trans-Mekong, 101–3, 109; South China ports with Nguyen Vietnam, 53–63. *See also* Siam, trade; rice trade

trade routes, 54, 63, 72–73, 103, 105, 108–9; on the Transbassac, 142–43; on the Water Frontier coast, 175–87

Tran Dai Dinh, 36, 41

Tran Lien, Tran Chieu Khoa. *See* Phipit, *Phraya*

Transbassac area, 139, 142–43, 149

Tran Thuong Xuyen. *See* Chen Shangchuan

Trat, 45, 102, 103

Tra Vinh, 38, 42, 47, 48, 86, 140

Trinh Hoai Duc, 73, 86, 93

turtle-shell, 180, 183

tutenague, 61, 62

Udong, 39, 40, 45, 46, 47

uplanders, 81, 102–3, 106, 107

Vam Co River, 37, 38, 40

Vientiane, 10, 105, 106, 107

Vietnam, 4, 11, 22, 24, 32, 77; and

trans-Mekong trade, 102, 103, 105, 107, 114
Vietnam, southern, 4, 25, 53,76, 81, 144. *See also* Chinese in southern Vietnam; Cochinchina; Gia Dinh; Mekong Delta
Viets (Vietnamese people), 6, 7, 11, 46, 73, 79; in Cambodia, 108, 147, 148–49, 150–51; and maritime skills, 74, 75, 76, 91, 119–21, 125
Vietnamese navy, 121–22, 127, 131
Vietnamese ship styles, 119–21, 126
Vinh Te canal, 108

warships, 119–20, 121–22, 135n61
Water Frontier, 1–12, 32, 35–39, 40–42, 43–46, 47–48; characteristic features of, 73, 79, 140, 141; mid-nineteenth-century Transbassac as another, 139–42; and shipbuilding, 120, 123, 124, 125
"water king," Cambodia, 40
wax. *See* beeswax
western weapons, 4, 10, 58,
wood, 74, 94, 106, 122, 124, 129; in Cambodia, 149, 150, 176

Xiamen, 31, 54–56, 57, 63, 121, 124

Yang Yandi, 39, 40

Zhanglin, 54, 55, 56, 58–59
Zhejiang, 54, 59

About the Contributors

James Kong Chin is a research officer at the Centre of Asian Studies at the University of Hong Kong. His research interests and publications focus on Chinese maritime history, Chinese emigration, and overseas Chinese diasporas. His most recent book is *Power and Identity in the Chinese World Order: Festschrift in Honour of Professor Wang Gungwu,* coedited with Billy So, John Fitzgerald, and Huang Jianli (2003).

Choi Byung Wook obtained a Ph.D. in Vietnamese history from the Australian National University. He currently works as a research professor in Vietnamese history at the Institute for Asian Studies, Seoul National University, South Korea. His works include *Southern Vietnam under the Reign of Minh Mang (1820—1841)* (2004), and several articles on nineteenth-century southern Vietnam under the Nguyen dynasty.

Nola Cooke gained her Ph.D. from the Australian National University where she is currently a research fellow. As part of an Australian Research Council funded project, she is further exploring issues arising from this book in nineteenth-century southern Vietnam and Cambodia. She was formerly an ARC Post-Doctoral Fellow in the Research School of Pacific and Asian Studies at ANU and has published on traditional Vietnam in several international journals.

Li Tana is a senior research fellow at the Research School of Pacific and Asian Studies, the Australian National University. She is the author of *Nguyen Cochinchina: Southern Vietnam in the Seventeenth and Eighteenth Centuries* (1998). Her major interest is the socioeconomic history of Vietnam, on which she has researched and published extensively, and the history of overseas Chinese in Southeast Asia.

Anthony Reid is now director of the Asia Research Institute of the National University of Singapore, but was previously professor of Southeast Asian history at the Australian National University (to 1999) and director of the Center for Southeast Asian Studies at UCLA (1999–2002). His books include *Southeast Asia in the Age of Commerce, 1450–1680*, 2 vols. (1988–1993) and (as editor) *The Last Stand of Asian Autonomies: Responses to Modernity in the Diverse States of Southeast Asia and Korea, 1750–1900* (1997).

Puangthong Rungswasdisab received a Ph.D. in history from the University of Wollongong in 1996 with a dissertation entitled *War and Trade: Siamese Interventions in Cambodia, 1782–1851*. Between May 1998 and July 1999 she was a research associate at the Cambodian Genocide Program, Yale University, where she wrote *Thailand's Response to the Cambodian Genocide* (working paper GS 12, 1999). She is currently an independent researcher.

Yumio Sakurai holds doctoral degrees in literature and in agricultural engineering. He is a professor in the Department of Asian History at the University of Tokyo. A noted Vietnam specialist, he has published widely in Japanese and English on issues of Vietnamese political economy and agrarian life from the fourteenth to the twentieth centuries, including recently on the history of Mac Hatien. His best known work is *The Formation of the Vietnamese Village* (1987), available in Japanese and Vietnamese translation.

Carl A. Trocki is the professor of Asian studies in the School of Humanities and Human Services at Queensland University of Technology. He has published on Singapore, Malaysia, Thailand, the Chinese diaspora, and the drug trade in Asia. His most recent book is *Opium, Empire, and the Global Political Economy: A Study of the Asian Opium Trade, 1750–1950* (1999).

Geoff Wade is a historian with interests in China–Southeast Asian historical interactions. After graduating in Southeast Asian studies from the Australian National University he undertook Chinese studies in Sydney, Beijing, and Nanjing before completing his Ph.D. at the University of Hong Kong in 1994. There he later coordinated the China–ASEAN Project at the Centre of Asian Studies during 1996–2002. He is currently a visiting senior research fellow at the Asia Research Institute, National University of Singapore.